The Insider's Guide to Golf Equipment

The Insider's Guide to Golf Equipment

The Fully Illustrated,
Comprehensive Directory
of Brand-Name Clubs
and Accessories

NICK MASTRONI

A Perigee Book

A Perigee Book
Published by The Berkley Publishing Group
200 Madison Avenue
New York, NY 10016

First edition: April 1997

Published simultaneously in Canada.

The Putnam Berkley World Wide Web site address is http://www.berkley.com/berkley

Library of Congress Cataloging-in-Publication Data

Mastroni, Nick.
    The insider's guide to golf equipment : the fully illustrated, comprehensive directory of brand-name clubs and accessories / Nick Mastroni. — 1st ed.
        p.   cm.
    "A Perigee book."
    ISBN 0-399-52277-8
    1. Golf—United States—Equipment and supplies.   2. Golf clubs (Sporting goods)—United States.   3. Golf equipment industry—United States.   I. Title.
    GV976.M376   1997
    796.352'028—dc20   96-30132
                                                                                                       CIP

Printed in the United States of America
10   9   8   7   6   5   4   3   2   1

Contents

The Insider's Guide to Golf Equipment

How This Book Will Help You

At last official report, the golf equipment industry had mushroomed to become a $6.25 billion industry. This is the amount, reported in a study by the National Golf Foundation (NGF), *Golf Consumer Spending in the U.S.* (August 1995), that the approximately 25 million Americans who play golf (avidly, occasionally, or sparingly) spent on their equipment alone in 1994. There can be little doubt that the amount spent on equipment in 1996 was substantially more than 1994's $6.25 billion (the studies are not done annually). Past trends toward annual increases in spending, in concert with the vast assortment of remarkably high-tech and, in some cases, remarkably high-priced equipment that hit the market with major fanfare during 1995 and 1996, virtually guarantee that that figure has been surpassed.

Marketing's Pervading Influence on the U.S. Golfer

Golfers in the United States have been convinced that it's possible to "buy" a better golf game through the latest in equipment. With the right information, it's certainly possible to accomplish this—to a degree. However, it's also evident to those in the golf industry, who are in a position to make an objective evaluation of the situation, that the U.S. golf consumer is being shamelessly led by the nose by many major manufacturers. We're taught to believe that if we just buy enough of the newest equipment, our games will magically turn around and we'll be the envy of not only our foursome but our entire club. In reality, this rarely occurs. In fact, you should know that an uninformed choice as to a change in your equipment, based on fad-following rather than an understanding of how you strike the golf ball, can just as quickly and easily put your game into a tailspin as it can lower your handicap.

The influence of the major manufacturers on us through television and print ads is enormous. One manufacturer boasted of its expenditure of over $1 million on its physical display alone at the 1996 PGA Merchandise show (who pays for this, ultimately?). Other companies routinely send out press releases telling the media of their multimillion-dollar annual product promotional budgets.

If you've watched enough TV ads during the various pro tournaments aired each season, you'll probably agree that many club manufacturers' messages are directed as much at our egos as they are toward helping us play our best golf. We see ads depicting golfers hitting a certain ball so far that they're breaking windows far beyond their intended targets (and presumably out of bounds!). Nearly every new driver offered is guaranteed to be "the longest-hitting club ever." As Barney Adams, president of Texas-based Adams Golf, says, "If you added up everybody's claims on the distance you're going to get with their drivers, then somehow picked out the one that was *really* the longest, you should reasonably expect to hit that driver about 560 yards!"

Why Haven't We Gotten Better, Then?

Recently I spoke with Dean Knuth, senior director of handicapping at the United States Golf Association, located in Far Hills, New Jersey. I asked Knuth what the trend was in the handicap level for the approximately 4 million U.S. golfers who carry an official handicap.

Knuth replied that in his sixteen years of involvement with handicapping for the USGA, *the average handicap for both males and females has not changed at all.* The average handicap for males has hovered steadily around 17, while the average handicap for females has stayed right around 31. When asked if there was any segment of the U.S. golfing population for which there had been specific improvement, Knuth replied, "In our national competitions, at the highest levels of women's amateur play we see improvement. The top women amateurs drive the ball about ten yards farther than they did fifteen years ago and are shooting better scores. That's a very small segment of the golfing population, though. Overall, in terms of average handicaps, there's no change."

As a nation, and given the presumed advances in equipment technology over the past decade or so, it's fair to say we are not putting on an extremely impressive performance.

This being the case, it seems likely that in terms of the equipment golfers select, despite (or perhaps, because of) the wide variety of choices available, we may be making *worse* choices regarding playing equipment than we have in the past. There's much more to obtaining the right set of equipment, and much more to playing the best game of golf you're capable of, than obtaining the "longest-hitting" driver or the "longest-hitting" irons. In fact, no such animal universally exists. What works best in terms of both distance and accuracy for you is *not* going to be exactly the same club as the one that delivers top performance to your best buddy in the Saturday foursome. The reason for this discrepancy is that your swing is not identical to anyone else's. The trick, really, is to gain a true understanding of how your full swing, as well as your short game, and putting strokes work; then to gain an understanding of which of the hundreds of clubs on the marketplace offer performance features that match your game; then to match *your* clubs to *your* game. And to no one else's.

My purpose in writing this book and supplying this information on equipment is not to simply urge you, along with the major manufacturers, to purchase more golf equipment. It's to assist you in making wise equipment choices that will improve your game, to help you to eventually write lower scores on your card. I hope this book will also help you to avoid unwise choices that will hurt your game and waste money.

Don't Forget to Invest in *You*

As a lifelong player of the game at a reasonable level of competency (as this book went to press I jealously nurtured a 3.7 handicap), as one who has competed extensively, and as a golf writer, I have observed golf at private and public courses all over the country. Having done so, I feel it's important to make this statement to members of the golfing public with a real desire to improve their games: It is more important that you invest in *yourself* than it is to invest in a full new set of clubs and then assume that by doing so you will automatically perform better.

Suppose your current set is getting old and/or you're not happy with how they (or you) have performed of late. Let's say you're aware of the cost of a full new set of top-of-the-line woods, irons, wedges, and a putter, and are willing to allocate $2,500 toward the purchase of the best equipment you can find.

Well, I suggest you heed the following advice. It comes not merely from me but from a great many manufacturers I have spoken with who bring an honest, well-rounded perspective to the industry: *Put part of your investment in improving your game into taking lessons.* Shop around in your region—find the instructor who has the best reputation for improving his or her students' swings and/or overall playing ability. Once you find that person, sign up for a series of lessons, not just one. This may draw $250 or $300 from your $2,500 equipment budget, but it will do several very important things for you:

1. It will identify the flaws in your swing mechanics and the changes you need to work on.
2. Assuming you give yourself a couple of months to incorporate these changes, you'll have a more technically efficient swing motion. This overrides anything any golf club by itself can ever do for you.
3. Once you've developed a more consistent and effective swing pattern, *you'll be able to define your swing much better, and you'll have a much better chance of making the right match between your equipment and your golf swing.*

Make sure you know your golf swing and your game *before* you make a major investment in equipment.

The Swing's Still the Main Thing

Not long ago, I spent a day with the noted sport psychologist Dr. Bob Rotella at his home and workplace in Charlottesville, Virginia. We spent the morning discussing my travails with the game. In the afternoon, we headed for a nearby golf course and, in a number of different ways, tried to blend the optimum mental approach with actual execution in various "real golf course" situations.

One of the areas we worked on the most was my personal bugaboo, driving accuracy. Bob was convinced that I had a slight case of the "yips" with the driver which caused me to tighten up, to not release the club completely, and subsequently to hit a lot of tee shots to the right. He emphasized the need to feel "soft" in the forearms and to let the arms whip the clubhead freely through impact, rather than trying to control the shot. Gradually, a nice little draw started to show up.

We came to a par-4 hole. Bob motioned me onto the tee and I grabbed my driver and stepped onto the tee. Then Bob laid two other drivers on the ground to the side of where I was getting ready to hit. He motioned me to go ahead and hit a couple of balls with my own club. That freer swing and the draw seemed to be in place. Next Bob said, "Hit some balls with that second driver, then the third one. Don't spend too much time thinking about anything. Just use the routine you've been using and hit them."

I remember picking up the second driver with a bit of trepidation, wondering, "I seem to be doing okay with my own driver now, but are these other clubs going to mess me up?" I dismissed the thought and went ahead as best I could. I can honestly report that the ball flew very similarly with all three clubs, down the right edge of the fairway with a slight draw.

Bob just grinned at me. He didn't need to verbalize anything. His point, of course, was that if we are swinging well and trusting that swing, *we have an innate ability to adjust to our equipment.* I can tell you what the specs were for my own driver, but I couldn't tell you what I was swinging in the other two. If I recall correctly, both had graphite shafts while my own had steel, and I believe one of the two clubs Bob laid down was longer than the other, or than my own. But I believe there is a great lesson here. *Keep your thoughts focused on making your own truest golf swing.* If you accomplish that, you can hit reasonably good golf shots with almost anything. Of course, having the best-fit clubs possible can only help you. Regarding your own equipment, though, you'll be better off if you keep everything in perspective. There's no such thing as a magic golf club.

Contents of This Book

Preaching aside, let me explain what you will learn from this book.

Quite possibly, Chapter 1, "What You Need to Know Before You Buy a Set of Clubs," is the book's most significant chapter. From it you will learn important points such as how to gain information on your own golf swing; how this information about your swing translates into characteristics of the clubs and balls you should buy; and what kind of specific information and feedback you should insist on getting from a golf club retailer before going ahead with a buying decision.

Chapter 2 will include information from top design people in the industry on the subject of golf shafts and their performance characteristics. The major club manufacturers offer each of their models with a variety of different shafts, which feature different materials, weights, and degrees of flexibility. You can't make a good club selection without choosing the right shaft for your game, whether you're talking about a driver, a middle iron, or a wedge. So, shafts will be discussed in depth here, and this discussion will apply to all clubs discussed in the ensuing chapters.

Chapter 3, "Choosing a Driver: Pick What's Right, Not What's 'Hot,' " covers all the key considerations about "the big stick," including clubhead design and material, static weight, correct clubface loft for your game, and length of clubshaft. You'll find a list of the driver offerings of many major manufacturers, including their important specs as well as their pricing, in the table that concludes this chapter. (Chapters 3 through 8 will each feature similar table information obtained from manufacturers in the various club and ball areas.)

In Chapter 4, "The Fairway Woods: A Growing Segment of the Savvy Player's Set," we'll examine the wealth of "metalwood" (an oxymoron if there ever was one!) offerings that range from a "fairway driver" all the way up to lofted or "utility" woods that do the same duty as some longer irons. You'll learn how many and which fairway woods you should carry, given your particular golf swing, along with the types of grasses and terrain on the courses you customarily play.

Perhaps the most fascinating chapter in the book will be Chapter 5, "The Iron Game: How Manufacturers' Aims May Steer Yours Off Course." There have been some remarkable changes in the design and specifications of irons over the past two decades, as well as of the materials used (and their cost). And it can be argued that many of these changes are *not* to every golfer's benefit. This chapter will describe the various design features available in irons, and also consider what appears to be their shrinking role within the fourteen-club set allowed by the Rules of Golf.

Building a better wedge arsenal is the subject of Chapter 6. Most golfers, particularly beginners, are lacking in tools that fall under the umbrella of "the wedges." As such, they are ill prepared to cope with the infinite variety of situations they may encounter anywhere from 110 yards in to the hole. The discussion of various wedge designs, as well as matching the type of wedge to the shots where it proves most useful, will be key information in helping the smart golfer shave strokes from his or her game.

Putters are the topic in Chapter 7. While there is definitely some science involved in finding the best putter for any individual, this is one area in which the scientific element takes a bow to art. Great putting is more an art than a science, and choosing the right putter is a very personal choice. Plenty of photos will help you select the right "mate."

The golf ball will be covered in detail in Chapter 8. You'll learn why most of the claims of companies to have the "longest ball" are, frankly, much baloney. More important, significant areas of design such as cover and core materials, dimple configurations, spin rates, and trajectories will be examined, to help you narrow the list of spheres that are suitable for contact based on the way you swing the golf club.

Chapter 9 will discuss the golf grip, an often-overlooked element of the club. In the very extensive Chapter 10, you will learn about the various "peripheral" items that can go a long way toward improving both your game and your enjoyment in playing it. This chapter will include reviews on shoes, gloves, bags, and golf rainwear that will combine to keep your footing solid, your grip secure, and you and your clubs dry in any conditions.

The final segment of this book is a directory of addresses and phone numbers of the major manufacturers of golf clubs, balls, and accessory items that appear in this book. Sincere attempts (in some cases repeated many times) were made through questionnaire and telephone/fax requests to obtain and list the current product lines of as many major manufacturers as possible, in all areas of golf equipment, and with as much detail as possible. While many manufacturers were very helpful in providing information, some opted not to do so, or did not divulge all of the design information that was requested. The listings in the directory provide addresses and telephone numbers for those companies that responded to the questionnaires.

I'd like to state that this book would not have been possible without the expertise and generous sharing of knowledge by several highly respected equipment designers: Tom Wishon, Vice-President/Chief Technical Officer, Golfsmith International, Austin, Texas; Don Wood, Vice-President of Research and Development, Zevo Golf, Vista, California; Barney Adams, President, Adams Golf, Richardson, Texas; and Terry Pocklington, President, Ram Tour, Pontotoc, Mississippi. I thank all of them profusely for their contributions and their interest in this project.

It's my sincere hope that in coming years, avid golfers will be able to use the information provided here to make better, more informed equipment choices. And perhaps we can all start making a dent in that national handicap average!

CHAPTER 1

What You Need to Know Before You Buy a Set of Clubs

You may be quite new to the game, having perhaps tried it out during the last year or so while using older, borrowed clubs. Now that you know you intend to play golf regularly, you need to learn all you can about equipment in order to help your game as much as possible, as well as to invest your money wisely.

On the other hand, you may have been playing golf religiously for ten, twenty, thirty, or more years. You may have already purchased several different sets of irons and woods over that span. But when your current clubs are getting a little tired-looking, advances in club technology have started to make them look a little outdated, and your golfing buddies have bought new drivers, irons, or wedges and claim to be "hitting it so much better," you may think, "It's time for me to get some new clubs, too."

Before you buy, keep in mind that even if you're an amateur golfer who's played for a number of years and used several different sets of clubs, chances are there's a tremendous amount for you to learn regarding the selection and fitting of the best set of clubs for you.

Why do I suggest you have so much to learn about buying clubs? Because in the past, you've probably been badly misinformed about clubs you've bought, or have had information withheld that prevented you from buying a certain set. In my discussions with some of the most knowledgeable people in the club-making industry, time and again they iterated the point that when the consumer goes into a golf retail outlet or even some on-course golf pro shops, where you have a right to expect expert guidance on what will work best for you, this service is usually sadly lacking.

Another difficulty in buying the right clubs is that very often, whether you realize it or not, *you are being strongly influenced by the marketing campaigns that the major companies create for their club lines.* It's well known that a high percentage of golfers buy their clubs based on the endorsements of PGA Tour stars. The buying public muses, "If Nick Faldo plays the Mizuno T-Zoid driver, it's got to be a great club, doesn't it? He won his third Masters with it in 1996." "If Corey Pavin plays those Cleveland VAS+ irons, they've certainly got to work, don't they? After all, he won the 1995 U.S. Open and a couple of million dollars that year." You begin to wonder if someday you'll pick up the newspaper on Monday and instead of seeing a list of players and how they finished in the just-completed PGA Tour event, you'll see a list of club, shaft, and ball manufacturers' names instead!

However, you should ask yourself, just what does it mean if a top player happens to endorse a certain brand of club? To you and your game's needs, it should mean *nothing*! Top players are paid hundreds of thousands of dollars annually, sometimes more, to recommend a certain brand or model of equipment. (You'd probably think a lot differently about the value of that endorsement if you were allowed to look in a top player's bag on any given day and see exactly which fourteen clubs he or she happened to be using.) And in many cases, these allegiances are short-lived. A higher bidder will always turn up on a player's doorstep with a big-bucks offer if that player has had an exceptional year.

In sum, do yourself a favor. Don't decide what clubs to buy based on player endorsements!

PGA Tour Clubseller's Classic Top 10 Finishers*

King Cobra II Irons	70-65-67-71-273	$360,000
Titleist Professional Ball	68-69-70-68-275	$216,000
Taylor Made Burner Bubble Driver	73-66-66-71-276	$136,000
Callaway Great Big Bertha Driver	65-71-71-70-277	$96,000
True Temper Rocket Shaft	67-69-72-70-278	$73,000
Odyssey Rossie II Putter	71-71-70-66-278	$73,000
Cleveland VAS+ Irons	70-68-68-72-278	$73,000
Wilson Staff Brass Insert Lob Wedge	67-73-70-69-279	$58,000
Lynx Black Cat Irons	74-64-71-70-279	$58,000
Top-Flite Strata Tour Ball	68-69-70-72-279	$58,000

* Fictitious event and results.

Don't get me wrong. There are many, many high-quality clubs on the market today. However, for any manufacturer's particular model, there is a tremendous variety of specifications to choose from. We'll discuss most of these club specs in this chapter, or they will be specifically explained in the chapters that follow on the various categories of clubs.

Granted, there's a lot to digest, but for many of you an initial understanding of these elements of both the club and its fitting is necessary to get you started in the right direction.

Clubfitting

Let's say you've decided that the irons you like the most are Titleist DCIs. Chances are that if you know enough about your game and your fitting needs, you can buy a set of Titleist DCIs that will serve you very well. If you know nothing about your own fitting needs and take whichever set of Titleist DCIs is available at the retail outlet you visit, you're rolling the dice. That particular set might not fit you at all.

It has generally been thought by many golfers (including myself!) that careful assessing and fitting of clubs is something that's really only necessary for the very fine player—the professional or the amateur player with a handicap near zero. Tom Wishon, vice-president and chief technical officer of Golfsmith International, the world's largest supplier of clubmaking components, sees it differently. "A lot of players think that the higher the handicap, the less there is to be gained from being custom-fit. That's like saying if you're fat, you shouldn't bother going to a tailor because he won't be able to do you any good.

"Believe me, most people involved in clubfitting would much rather see a high handicapper walk into their shop than a scratch golfer," Wishon continues. "Because a high handicapper will have flaws in the setup or swing which are easy for the clubfitter to address." Barney Adams, president of Adams Golf in Richardson, Texas, concurs. "The purpose of custom-fitting golf clubs is to minimize the mistakes caused by an improper fit of the club to the player," Adams says. "Actually, custom-fitting won't make your good shots any better, but if your clubs fit you well, when you hit a bad shot, the magnitude of the error will be minimized."

Adams adds the following significant point: "The top-notch player who owns a set, or certain clubs within a set, that do not fit him or her well will be able to adjust to that club or that set. That's why he or she is a good player! It's the average guy that is going to have more trouble adjusting to a club with specifications that aren't right.

"I'm not trying to tell you that if you take a 16-handicapper and outfit him with a perfect set of clubs, you can turn him into an 8-handicapper within a week," Adams concedes, "but I am saying that if you get that 16-handicapper into a good set of golf clubs, he's going to have a far better opportunity to improve than ever before."

Elements That Entail a Good Fit—and a Good Selection

Today, nearly all the major club manufacturers will tell you that they offer some form of "custom-fitting" to the buyer. That's fine as far as it goes, but the definition of "customization" of a golf club from one company to the next will vary. No matter where you buy your clubs or what brand and model you select, you need to make a determination on all of the following items. This list goes well beyond certain "static" specifications of the various clubs:

1. Your personal, accurately measured swing speed with a driver
2. Length of clubshaft that allows you to make optimum contact with a driver
3. Loft angle for the driver that provides maximum carry and roll distance, given your swing path
4. *Dynamic* lie of the clubshaft—that is, the correct angle between the club-head and the clubshaft at *impact* (rather than at address)
5. Clubshaft selection (to be discussed in Chapter 2):

   - Clubshaft material—steel, graphite, or other
   - Degree of flex in the clubshaft, as measured in cycles per minute (cpm—a term we'll describe later)
   - Degrees of torque (flex in a rotary direction) in the clubshaft when swung
   - Total weight of the clubshaft

6. Total weight of the entire, finished club (to be discussed in Chapter 3)
7. Shape of the clubhead and weight distribution within it (to be discussed in Chapters 3, 4, and 5)
8. Material used in the clubhead (to be discussed in Chapters 3 and 5)
9. Type of grip and grip size (to be discussed in Chapter 9)
10. Entire makeup of your fourteen-club set

Let's spend a few minutes discussing these aspects of clubfitting and selection, which apply equally well if you're purchasing woods or irons.

Know Your Swing Speed with the Driver

You need to find a retail outlet or pro shop that offers a device by which you can get an accurate reading of your swing speed, in miles per hour. There are many, but one of the best known of these swing-speed calculators is the Sportech Swing Analyzer.

It's important to know whether you swing the driver through impact at 78 mph, 91 mph, or 102 mph. Your swing speed will have a major effect on the club specs you select such as clubface loft on the driver (as well as clubs throughout the set), shaft flex, shaft torque, the total weight of the club, and possibly also the shape and weighting of the clubhead, along with the total configuration of your set.

Tom Wishon of Golfsmith notes, "A lot of golfers think they can sort of 'estimate' their swing speed at impact. They try to make a correlation of sorts—for example, they may have heard, correctly, that a swing speed for a strong Tour pro who averages 270 yards with a driver, is about 115 mph. So they figure, 'When I hit a good drive, it goes about 250, so I'd say my swing speed is about 105 mph.' Usually such estimates are inaccurate. It's well worth it to find a golf retail outlet where you can get a true swing-speed measurement."

When Gauging Swing Speed, Check Your Ego at the Door

When you find a retail store or teaching facility that has a swing-speed analyzer available, remember that your goal is to find out your *average* swing speed with the driver, so that you can make the most accurate judgments possible on all aspects of your club "fit."

When you swing at the ball while being measured by a swing-speed analyzer, imagine that you're playing a tee shot on a golf course, where you want to hit a solid shot in the fairway. *Then swing accordingly.* There's a natural tendency to want to go for a big number when you're getting your swing speed measured. When the Sportech Swing Analyzer was in its infancy in the 1980s (and I was quite a bit younger and less humble), I managed to ring up a swing speed of 117 mph by flying out of my shoes. I've also had readings as low as 98, but I now know that my average driver swing speed is currently in the 102–104 mph range.

The point is to get an accurate reading of your average swing speed. Anything else will cause you to make your clubmaking decisions based on false information.

Learn Your Optimum Clubshaft Length for the Driver

We will discuss clubshaft length in detail in Chapter 3—it is a major industry issue in that the length of drivers has tended to increase substantially during the 1990s, with disputable benefit, particularly to the average golfer. It is important that you determine the length of driver that allows you to hit the ball solidly the most consistently, and to stick with that length. Learning your optimum driver length will also help ensure that you choose the correct length for all your other clubs as well.

Determine the Right Driver Clubface Loft

Loft angle relates directly to your swing-speed measurement. Every golf club (even the putter!) has a certain amount of loft on the clubface. The loft angle is what allows you to get the ball airborne on your full shots. As a general rule, with less loft on the club, the ball will shoot out lower and travel a greater total distance. This is why a 7-iron sends the ball farther than a 9-iron, and a 5-iron sends the ball farther than a 7-iron (we'll discuss the lofts of these clubs specifically in Chapter 5).

Most golfers believe that the lower the loft on the driver, the farther the ball will automatically travel. This is often a major misconception that costs amateurs countless strokes—and golf balls, too.

In order to send the golf ball out on a long, soaring carry for optimum distance, the driver clubhead must be delivered to the ball at a considerable speed. The lower the loft of the driver clubhead, the faster it must be delivered. If a player with a relatively low swing speed (for example, 75 mph) tries to hit a low-lofted driver (which is to say, 8 or 9 degrees of loft), even if he or she makes good contact, the ball will "nose-dive" into the ground quickly, so the player will lose distance. Not only that, but, as Barney Adams points out, in this situation most golfers will end up trying to compensate for the low loft by "lifting" the ball during the swing. "If players could learn to hit 'down' with a higher-lofted driver, they will hit it farther and better than if they try to hit 'up' with a lower loft," Adams says. "The 'downward' swing includes a fuller release of the hands and wrists through impact, so ultimately it's a more powerful swing."

Chapter 3 includes a chart to guide you in matching the right driver loft to your swing speed.

How Far Do You Really Hit It?

You can make a start toward selecting the right equipment by objectively determining just how far you hit the ball with your various clubs.

Many people seem to consider a driver shot of 250 yards as being not particularly impressive, as in the oft-heard statement, "Oh, I guess I hit my average drive around 250." Perhaps the average golfer has occasionally hit a drive 250 yards—but has conveniently neglected to take into account that the shot was downhill, downwind, and landed on a hard, dry fairway.

Given the "normal" conditions of flat terrain, little or no wind, and an average roll on the ball after landing, 250 yards is an *extremely substantial hit.* To put it another way, the average drive length on the PGA Tour is about 263 yards. Go visit any PGA Tour event. Do you really think you can stay within 13 yards of those guys?

Similarly, golfers speak very casually about hitting a 5-iron 175 or 180 yards. That's a very long 5-iron for the average golfer. As Barney Adams, whose company specializes in custom-fitting its customers, says, "In testing golfers, I have *never* met a golfer who underestimates how far he or she hits the ball. I have met a fair number of golfers who, after telling me how far they averaged with certain clubs, actually went out and hit the ball about as far as they said. But I believe that over 70 percent of the golfing population substantially overestimates how far they hit the ball."

Two points here: First, forget about trying to match some monstrous yardage figure you may have heard a certain PGA Tour player hit the ball with a certain club. That's not what golf is about. For that matter, forget about trying to match shot lengths with someone else in your foursome. Secondly, by measuring your shots objectively and knowing how far you really do hit a driver, a 5-iron, or a pitching wedge, you're much more likely to make a better club purchase.

Get a "Dynamic" Reading of the Proper Lie for You

Most golfers don't realize it, but the lie of the golf club can have a very significant effect on the accuracy of their shots. (This is an area we will cover in more detail in Chapter 5 on irons.) Most people who have heard about the desirability of obtaining the correct lie for their clubs have attempted to do this by measuring the club's lie *statically,* that is, at the address position rather than measuring the lie of the club at impact—when it counts. The "static" measurement is usually done by checking to see if the sole or bottom of the club is flat on the floor when you address the ball normally. But Barney Adams notes,

"Very few golfers move the clubhead through impact with their hand and body positions identical to where they were at address. Most often, the golfer's hands are positioned a little higher at impact than they were at address." Adams points out that if the hands are indeed higher at impact, the tendency will be for the heel of the club to be "up" at impact—which can affect both the force and the direction of the shot.

Determine the Right Makeup for Your Fourteen-Club Set

In the past, there was a more or less "standard" configuration that made up a set of fourteen clubs, which is the limit you are allowed to carry by the Rules of Golf of the United States Golf Association. (Yes, there are probably a goodly percentage of golfers who have added a club here or there, without removing another from their bags. Yes, they may be getting away with carrying more than fourteen clubs in casual rounds. The recommendation here is to play with a maximum of fourteen clubs in your bag at all times—then you won't ever feel shorted when you're in a competition.)

At any rate, the most common set makeup might have looked like this:

- Three woods (or, more accurately for most golfers today, metalwoods): a driver, a 3-wood, and either a 4- or a 5-wood
- Eight irons, normally numbered 2 through 9
- Two wedges (a pitching wedge and a sand wedge)
- The putter

While a fourteen-club set with this makeup might serve you well, the time when you're considering new clubs is also the time when you should consider whether the makeup of your set is right for you. Since the time you last bought clubs, you certainly have aged, and in some cases, this may mean you don't swing the club with the same speed or efficiency as you did five or ten years ago. On the other hand, if you're relatively young, you may be physically stronger than you were when your current set makeup was suitable for you. Or, through fine swing instruction and diligent practice, you may also be swinging the club much faster and more precisely than in past years.

Clubmaking experts agree that most amateurs, particularly those with slower swing speeds and those who consistently score over 90, tend to carry sets that make the game harder than it needs to be. For example, you may be carrying a driver that is difficult for you to get airborne and also to hit straight; you may be carrying one or more long irons (numbers 2, 3, or possibly 4) that you also have trouble getting well airborne; and there may be "gaps" in the lofts of your wedges that prevent you from playing all your short-game shots as efficiently as you could. (This, as we'll see in Chapters 5 and 6, is often not the golfer's fault as much as it is the manufacturers', in that lofts of the irons and wedges have changed dramatically in the last decade.)

Every golfer is different, but if you fall into the general category of the golfer described above, you'll probably do well to consider a set that includes the following:

- A driver with *plenty of loft*
- At least *three* fairway/utility woods (numbers 3, 5, and 7; possibly also a 9-wood)
- Irons starting with no longer than a 4-iron, or possibly a 5
- Three wedges instead of two, most likely adding a lob wedge, which carries greater loft than the sand wedge (approximately 60 degrees of loft, as compared to 55 or 56 degrees for the sand wedge, as we'll see in Chapter 6)
- The putter

Now's the time to be realistic about what clubs will benefit you most. Barney Adams of Adams Golf says, "If I'm working on a new set with a golfer whose average score is 100, the first thing I'd like to do is convince him or her to take the driver out of the bag completely!" The driver is the least-lofted club in the bag. The less loft on the club, the less backspin on the ball. And the less backspin there is on the ball, the more it's going to hook or slice when the player makes a mistake. "The reason most 100 shooters shoot 100," Adams asserts, "is that they hit tee shots out of bounds, lose balls in the water or woods, and take several penalty strokes per round. In addition, they have to waste shots chipping the ball out of trouble when they do find the ball after bad tee shots.

"I'd much rather see such a golfer use more loft from the tee, such as in a 3-wood or even a 4-wood. They should be teeing off with a club with 15 or even more degrees of loft rather than one with, say, 10 degrees, which is about average for a man's driver. Since they'll also put more backspin on the more-lofted 3-wood, their bad shots won't curve as much. They'll wind up maybe in the rough with a playable shot, rather than in the woods or out of bounds."

This solid advice does not even take into account that many golfers lack sufficient swing speed to obtain an optimum trajectory with a driver, even when they do hit it straight.

Similarly, many golfers would benefit greatly from the addition of at least one more lofted fairway wood in the bag, and the removal of at least one of the long irons. Although the lofts of clubs like the 5-, 7-, and 9-woods overlap in terms of loft with the lofts of the 2-, 3-, and 4-irons (generally, lofts on all these

---

"Alternates" to Your Set

We've discussed a number of options regarding your set makeup. A final thought here: If you can afford it, you may benefit from owning a couple of "alternate" clubs to your fourteen-club set. These are clubs that can usefully be inserted into your set when you are playing under course conditions that are abnormal, or which may give you an edge at those times when your swing is not at its best.

For example, if you're going to be playing an amateur tournament on a relatively flat, open course, in windy weather, even though you don't carry a 3-iron as a rule, it might be good to have one to replace your 7-wood, with which you hit the ball nice and high but might be at a disadvantage in a brisk wind.

Alternatively, suppose you are playing in very heavy, wet, sloppy conditions. It might not be as crucial to be carrying a 60-degree lob wedge, because the greens will be much slower than normal and the ball won't run far on the short shots around the greens. Having a lofted 9-wood to put in your bag in its place to simplify your medium-length approach shots from wet rough may save you strokes.

---

clubs are in the 19–26-degree range), the lofted woods are much easier for the average player to hit. Why? Mainly because the center of gravity on a lofted fairway wood is much lower than it is on a long iron clubhead. With the fairway wood, most of the weight is contacting the ball below its equator, and so the ball gets airborne much more easily. The lofted woods are also particularly useful when you need to get some distance on shots from out of long rough.

"Macho" Golfers Usually Score Worst

Although the "stigma" of carrying a number of lofted woods instead of the long irons is waning to some degree, it still exists. It's not considered "macho" for a male golfer to carry a 9-wood, or even a 7-wood. If a super-lofted utility wood is more beneficial to you than a longer iron, what's the big deal? As Golfsmith's Tom Wishon puts it, "The golfer who puts a 9-wood in his bag may get a little ribbing about it at first. But after you start taking money from the others in your group by hitting shots you couldn't pull off with a long iron, you'll probably see a similar club in their bags before too long."

Many amateurs should consider the addition of one more wedge in their bags, at the expense of a little-used long iron, as well. Let's face it: The higher your handicap, the more greens you will miss on your approach shots. Therefore, you're likely to have to play more touchy recovery shots around the greens. A 60-degree lob wedge may prove a boon for those situations where your ball is in a poor lie off the green, and the pin is tucked close so there's not much green to land the ball on. Ordinarily, you'd have little alternative but to chop the ball onto the green and watch it run well past the hole. With a lob wedge, you'll have a much better chance to make the ball land softly so that it stops within one-putt range.

This should give you some good general food for thought as to what you should be thinking about as you consider purchasing your next set of clubs.

What About Used Clubs?

Although in most cases clubs can be purchased for less than the suggested retail price, the bottom line may still be beyond what is reasonable for you. This may be particularly true if you are someone who only plays, say, ten or twelve times a year. Price may be even more of a factor for the beginning golfer who may be asking, "I'm not completely sure I'm going to continue to play golf. Why should I pay big bucks for clubs when I might not play the game for very long?"

Hopefully, all newcomers to golf will find its challenge well worth continuing. Meanwhile, a recommendation: *Learn as much as you can about your golf swing, then shop for a set of used clubs that will allow you to play competently as your game develops.*

Find a teaching center or retail outlet where you can learn your average swing speed with the driver. Practice at the driving range enough so that you know what your basic shot pattern is. Say you have an average swing speed of 80 mph; your most common shot with the driver slices 25 yards and travels 180 to 190 yards; and your most prevalent shot with a 5-iron slices 10 to 15 yards and travels 135 yards. Well, you know from this (or will know, after reading this book) that you would definitely want clubs that have fairly flexible shafts as opposed to stiff ones. You would also benefit from clubs that had relatively high rather than low lofts on them, particularly with the driver; maybe you don't even need a driver until you have developed your swing for another year or two.

Once you have some parameters of your game, shop around, either in stores or through newspaper ads. If you find a used set you think might work for you, ask if you can leave a deposit, *then go out and hit shots with the clubs.* Do the clubs feel relatively easy to swing, or does it seem like hard work? Does the length of the club seem comfortable to you when you grip it with your top hand just below the butt end of the grip? How does the flight of the ball compare with that obtained from other clubs you may have used before?

continued

What About Used Clubs? *(continued)*

If at all possible, do this testing with a local professional observing and providing an opinion on how these clubs might work for you over a one- or two-year period, in conjunction with the development of your swing over that same span. His or her fee for this observation will be a worthwhile investment. At the very least, have an experienced, competent player watch you try out the used set.

Remember that there's no rule that says you must play with fourteen clubs. If you're a beginner, a used set that includes the 3-, 5-, and 7-woods, irons 4 through 9, two wedges, and a putter—twelve clubs in all—may do just fine.

While the age and condition of used sets will vary greatly, it's reasonable to expect to find a set for between $200 and $400 that serves you well during your golf apprenticeship.

One last tip. You might find a nice-fitting used set that has one small problem— the grips feel old and slick. If all else seems right and you decide to buy the clubs, make a small investment in having new grips installed (we'll talk about grips in Chapter 9). Most golfers don't replace their grips often enough, and it's unlikely that there will be "fresh rubber" on any used sets you're contemplating buying. A new set of grips might just make that used set feel great in your hands.

CHAPTER 2

The Right Shafts Can Make the Game Easier

The shaft of the golf club can readily be likened to the transmission of an automobile. The golf shaft "transmits" the energy produced by your body, arms, and hands during the swing to the clubhead, which strikes the golf ball and sends it away on its flight. In addition to transmitting velocity to the clubhead, the golf shaft, because of its particular flexion characteristics, has an effect on the attitude of the clubface as it is delivered to the ball. Depending on what shaft you're using, it can cause the clubface to be either more open or more closed (pointing right or left, respectively) in relation to the target at impact, and it can also cause the clubface to strike the ball with a greater or lesser degree of loft, thus affecting the trajectory of the shot.

Most club experts would agree that the shaft is the most important component of the golf club. Getting the right one can be a very tricky proposition for the consumer. It's much easier to look at the clubhead design of a metalwood, iron, or wedge and make a visual judgment of whether it appeals to you and to your shotmaking tendencies. But you can't visualize in a golf shop just how a shaft is going to perform in delivering that clubhead to the ball. There is some information provided by clubmakers that is supposed to help you learn the flex characteristics of the shafts in a given set, but this information can be misleading.

There are literally hundreds of shaft options available to you. Most manufacturers offer their metalwoods and irons in a selection of shaft materials (usually steel or graphite) and with a wide offering of shaft flexes within each material.

In almost all cases, there is a shaft that will perform well for you in the club models offered by the major manufacturers. The problem is that the information on shafts *is not standardized* from one company to the next. You must learn what really counts about the golf shaft and know what you're getting in a shaft before you make a buying decision.

Pick Your Shaft Material—Graphite vs. Steel

Undoubtedly shaft material is one of the hottest—and most important—topics to the golf club consumer. The two materials that dominate the clubshaft market are steel and graphite. There are no official breakdowns of the percentage of steel shafts versus graphite shafts in the overall marketplace, but it is a certainty that the traditional material since about 1940—steel—is gradually losing its domination of the market share to graphite. Generally, graphite has become more and more popular in drivers and fairway metalwoods, but steel still comprises the higher percentage of shafts in sets of irons and wedges.

No doubt an entire book could be written on the benefits of graphite shafts as opposed to those of steel, and more will be said as we go along. For now, let's look at a basic summary of advantages and disadvantages of each.

Advantages of Steel Shafts

Steel shafts are very consistent. Steel is an isotropic substance. This means, in layman's terms, that it is molecularly consistent throughout its structure. As such, in the entire process of forming steel into a golf shaft, manufacturers are able to produce shaft after shaft very consistently. Thus, when you buy a set of clubs with steel shafts made by one of many reputable manufacturers, you can reasonably expect that your set's 8-iron will perform with very similar flex and torque characteristics to the shaft in your 4-iron, or in your driver. *Consistency* is probably steel's biggest benefit.

Graphite shafts are a composite material, made up of graphite fibers that are held together by various forms of epoxy resin. On average, most graphite shafts are comprised of about 67 percent graphite and 33 percent epoxy resin. However, Golfsmith's Tom Wishon notes, "The suppliers of the graphite sheets from which shafts are eventually made try to be very consistent in their ratios of the materials, but they can easily vary by plus or minus 2 percent. And that can definitely make a difference in the consistency of the final product."

Steel shafts are relatively inexpensive. While a steel shaft may cost a club manufacturer $5 or $6, graphite will vary greatly, from as little as $6 to $50 per shaft or more. As you look through the list of iron sets that appear in

Chapter 5, you'll notice how this translates into cost to you for a set of eight irons. The differential between steel- and graphite-shafted sets can easily be $320, or $40 per iron. In drivers and fairway woods, the cost differences between steel and graphite are greater: You'll see many drivers in the table in Chapter 3 showing a graphite/steel cost differential of greater than $100 *per club*. Is the difference worth it? Ultimately, you must be the judge.

Advantages of Graphite Shafts

Graphite shafts are usually much lighter than steel shafts. The heaviest steel shafts, for example those in the True Temper Dynamic Gold series, weigh approximately 125–128 grams, or 4.4–4.5 ounces, each. The lightest at the time of this writing was the True Temper True Lite (at 89 grams, or 3.1 ounces). While the heaviest graphites weigh more than the lightest steel shafts, Golfsmith's Wishon points out, "Several graphite manufacturers have broken the 50-gram mark. That's a tremendous difference. The number-one factor that controls the weight of the club is the golf shaft. If you have a lower total-weight club, you will be able to swing that lighter total weight faster. The player potentially gains distance," Wishon concludes. (UST offers a shaft in its Competition Lite Series that is currently the lightest at 45 grams, or 1.6 ounces.) Wishon adds, however, that "the difference in the shot's distance as based on lighter total weight has been proved *not to be all that substantial.* If you went from a driver shaft that weighed, say, 120 grams to a shaft that weighed 55 to 60 grams, which is more than *2 full ounces* lighter, you might expect an increase in distance of 8 to 10 yards—that's all." Of course, a player making such a change will also need to determine if a club this much lighter will affect his or her swing rhythm adversely. This could conceivably affect the quality of club-to-ball contact, which could negate that distance advantage and possibly also result in less accurate shots.

Graphite offers increased dampening of the feel of club-to-ball impact. When you hit an iron shot poorly, say off the toe of the club, there is a greater jarring effect through the hands and arms. "Sort of like hitting a brick with a hammer," says Barney Adams. This jarring sensation is particularly unpleasant in cold weather. Graphite can soften the sensation caused by mishit shots in general and can be a help to golfers with arthritic joints. Some Tour pros and top amateurs who practice a great deal also favor graphite based on the fact that using graphite shafts during the striking of thousands upon thousands of shots is good preventative medicine against joint problems down the road.

That said, it should be added that steel is still the shaft material of choice for most pros, at least in the irons. "Consistency in the shaft from club to club is paramount to the Tour player," says Wishon. Of course, it's not a bad thing for a golfer of any ability level.

Shaft Flex Ratings: How They Can Fool You

Let's make sure you understand how companies label their clubshafts regarding flex. The majority (but not all companies) do so as follows:

- The most flexible shaft in the company's line is labeled **L**, for "Ladies."
- The next most flexible shaft, or the shaft with the next higher "stiffness" rating, is usually labeled **A**, and is also referred to as a "Senior" flex.
- The shaft with the next highest stiffness rating is labeled **R**, for "Regular."
- The shaft with the next highest stiffness rating is labeled **F**, for "Firm." (Note: The **F** rating is a more recent flex rating refinement. You will see this letter rating far less frequently than the other five listed.)
- The shaft with the next highest stiffness rating is labeled **S**, for "Stiff."
- The shaft with the highest stiffness rating carries the letter **X**, for "Extra Stiff."

It should be noted that some companies, such as Ben Hogan, label their shafts numerically from 1 to 5, with 1 corresponding to an L flex and 5 corresponding to an X flex. For simplicity's sake, shaft flexes listed in the product tables are uniformly stated by the letter system, regardless of any different method used by an individual company.

All this sounds pretty good so far, doesn't it? And if every shaft labeled L actually had the same flex characteristics as every other shaft marked L, and so on, you could feel confident, assuming you had determined which flex worked best with your swing, that you were buying the right shaft. Unfortunately, this is not the case.

How Flex Is Rated

The most popular method by which shaftmakers rate the flex of a shaft is by measuring its *frequency*. Frequency refers to the number of reverberations or *cycles per minute* (cpm) the shaft will register when its tip end is pulled down or "tweaked" and then released, while the butt end is clamped in place at 5.25 inches from the butt. A *frequency analyzer* is used to provide this reading of the shaft's cpm.

The more reverberations, or cycles, a shaft makes per minute, the stiffer it is. Conversely, the fewer cycles per minute, the more flexible the shaft. According

Other Shaft Flex Rating Methods

The system of letter-coding golf shafts as L, A, R, S, or X is by no means universal. Some companies use words to describe the shaft flex, for example, "Flexible," "Seniors," or "Strong."

Perhaps the most sensible and precise way of designating shafts is that of FM Precision, which manufactures the stepless, steel Rifle shaft, which has become quite popular. FM Precision rates the Rifle shaft numerically, with sixty flexes available in a range from 2.0 to 8.0. A shaft rated 2.0 is extremely flexible; each succeeding flex is .1 higher than the previous one.

According to Kim Braly, FM Precision's manager of technical services and product development, each of these flex listings corresponds directly with its readout on a frequency testing machine. "For example, on our scale, a 4.0 shaft means that the shaft reads out at 240 cycles per minute," Braly says. "A person buying a 6.5 shaft will be getting a shaft that registers 265 cycles per minute." This numeric method makes a lot more sense than a letter-code rating in which what constitutes an "L" or an "R" shaft varies greatly from manufacturer to manufacturer.

Golfsmith's Tom Wishon, meanwhile, is a strong advocate of another system currently used by a minority of manufacturers, in which the shaft label recommends it for players whose driver swing speed is within a certain range. Instead of labeling a shaft with S for Stiff, it might carry a label that refers to a driver swing speed of "92 to 104 mph." "From our testing, we have found out so far that shafts labeled with a swing-speed recommendation by companies such as Taylor Made, Top Flite, and Nicklaus, for example, do indeed carry frequencies that should perform reasonably well for players with the swing speed recommended. Assuming you can obtain an accurate reading of your swing speed with the driver, I believe this is a much better way of fitting the golf shaft to the individual."

to Golfsmith's Tom Wishon, based on a finished driver with a length of 43.5 inches, the five basic flexes described should yield the following range of cpm:

SHAFT FLEX LETTER RATING	CYCLES PER MINUTE
L (Ladies)	Up to 230
A (Seniors)	231–240
R (Regular)	241–255
S (Stiff)	256–265
X (Extra Stiff)	266–275

The big problem, according to Wishon and others in the industry, is that *there is no absolute standard for shaft flex throughout the entire industry.* "Every company is free to make its R flex or its S flex with as many or as few cpm as it wants," Wishon reports. "The letter code means very little. One company's R shaft can conceivably be as flexible as another company's L, yet as stiff as a third company's X."

Wishon adds that two of the very top sellers of drivers today have taken advantage of the ambiguity of the current letter codes, to make drivers with relatively "soft" or flexible shafts with labeling that does not reflect this fact. "Callaway's Big Bertha and Taylor Made's Bubble Burner both have a flex in graphite that's marked R, that in reality is quite flexible," he reports. When Wishon's company tested the "regular" shafts of these two models in 1995, their cpm readings were 236 and 237 cpm, respectively—the most flexible R shafts of any of the top-rated clubs. Indeed, according to the ranking of letter flex ratings shown above, both of these R shafts, at least at the time they were tested, fell into the flex range of most A (Seniors) shaft flexes.

Graphite/Steel Flex Ratings Rarely Match

Wishon believes that in terms of knowing what you're getting in frequency, you can be a lot more confident about the letter-code ratings if you are considering steel as opposed to graphite. "Among the most commonly purchased flexes by men, which are R, S, and X, the actual cpm readings by major steel-shaft makers such as True Temper, Brunswick, and Apollo are all going to be quite similar to each other," he says. "You can be pretty confident that they'll all feel and perform similarly.

"However, if the consumer looks at a number of graphite shafts with, say, an R flex made by different manufacturers, he or she will find that there's no close relationship as to cpm reading. Readers should know that more and more of the major manufacturers are having their shaft flexes made much softer than they were ten years ago."

Wishon says his testing has shown that the band or spectrum of shaft flex in graphites, from most flexible (L) to stiffest (X), is much wider than it is for steel shafts. "If you get a readout on an X shaft in graphite and an X shaft in steel, they're likely to show similar flex characteristics. But there is a far wider range of flexibility in the graphites than the steels, so that a graphite R is likely to be substantially more flexible than a steel R, and a graphite L will be far more flexible than a steel L," he concludes.

A Personal Observation on Graphite Flexibility and Related Performance

In my own irons, I have used the True Temper Dynamic Gold shaft since 1985. This is the heaviest steel shaft on the market. The flex designation is "S300." (In True Temper's flex rating system for the Dynamic Gold line, there are five divisions of flex within each letter rating. Within the S range, for example, there is an S100, S200, S300, S400, and S500.)

I like this shaft because I feel I have the best possible control of my irons in terms of direction and flight. Although I may try to draw or fade a shot as needed, I expect to get only a little bend in either direction. Moreover, the tendency is for the ball to fly medium-low, which is helpful in controlling the ball in windy conditions; again, a personal preference.

Recently, I had the opportunity to test out several top brands of irons with graphite shafts. Among these were the Ram FX Pro Set, Titleist DCI, and Lynx Black Cat irons. In each case, I used a graphite shaft rated as Stiff. I have found that with all of these graphite shafts, there is a tendency to hit the ball in a more *right-to-left* pattern and also to hit the ball *a little higher than normal.* This implies that these graphite S shafts are more flexible than my own—a more flexible shaft makes it a little easier for the clubface to close through impact, encouraging a draw, and it also causes the bottom of the clubshaft to bow forward more through impact, which means there will be a bit of additional loft on the clubface.

I'm stating this not in a judgmental way; it's just an observation I've made every time I've hit a stiff graphite iron as compared to the True Temper Dynamic Gold steel. It's an observation in keeping with the assertion by Golfsmith's Wishon that most graphites will play "softer" than steel shafts with the same flex designation. If you hit most of your poor shots low and/or to the right, it's something to keep in mind.

The "Torque" Factor—How Important Is It?

You may or may not have heard club or shaft manufacturers describe a feature known as the shaft's *torque.* This refers to a slight, rotary twisting movement of the shaft through the impact zone, as opposed to the bending and unbending of the shaft along its length, which defines the shaft's flex.

To understand torque better, hold a driver with one hand firmly on the grip. Then exert pressure on the clubhead with the other hand so that it would close the clubface. The degree to which this twisting motion occurs through impact, given a certain specific amount of swing force, represents the degree of torque in the shaft.

Torque is referred to in degree measurements. The higher the degree of torque, the more the clubhead will twist through impact. The lower the reading, the more stable the clubhead will be. Experts tell us that readings for torque in graphite shafts can vary greatly, anywhere from 1.8 degrees up to 12 or 13 degrees. However, for most reputable manufacturers, the upper-end torque reading is about 7 degrees. There is usually a correlation between the degree of torque and the flex rating of the shaft. The stiffer the shaft, the lower the torque reading, and the more flexible the shaft, the higher the torque.

It might sound as though torque, because it represents a degree of twisting of the clubhead through impact, is an undesirable trait, as it could affect the accuracy of your shots. This is not completely true. "If a shaft doesn't have any torque, or even if it has very little torque, the feeling at impact is very stiff or 'boardy.' Golfers generally won't like it," Barney Adams reports. "A shaft with more torque gives a better feel, but there's a bit of a trade-off here. I don't believe it's a good idea to give the poorer golfer a shaft with a high degree of torque, because that is like saying, 'More twist is good for you.' As regards torque and its relationship with flex, I'd prefer that the higher handicapper use a shaft that's more flexible, but with a moderate amount of torque."

Adams believes that torque is a somewhat overrated factor in the golf shaft. "It's mostly a marketing tool," he says. "It does exist, but it's not crucial. It's another feature for manufacturers to sell to the consumer. For example, you'll find that the cheaper graphite shafts will usually carry the highest torque readings, because the materials are put together in a looser weave. Well, what does the manufacturer of this cheaper shaft that has, say, 7 degrees of torque now get to say? He says, 'Here's our special high-torque shaft, which is designed to aid the senior player.' He gets to justify this inexpensive shaft."

Golfsmith's Tom Wishon, meanwhile, warns the consumer that there is a much wider range for torque in graphite shafts than there is in steel shafts. "If you were to check the torque reading for any of the steel R flex shafts in the industry, you'd find that there is almost no difference in their readings, maybe half a degree at most. Even if you were to measure the most flexible steel shaft available versus the stiffest X shaft in steel, the range of difference in torque is only 1.5 degrees according to our testing." In other words, if you're going with steel shafts, don't sweat the torque factor. If, on the other hand, you elect to play graphite, you do have that torque range of from 1.8 to 7.0 degrees to consider (although the majority of high-quality graphite shafts will tend to be between 3.5 and 5.0 degrees in this measurement). So most definitely, try to find out the torque rating. Remember that the greater the torque, the better the shot may feel through impact, but you'll have slightly more clubhead twist through impact and thus slightly less control of the shot.

Kick Out "Kickpoint"!

You may have heard of the term *kickpoint* or *flexpoint* in the shaft. Shaft and/or club manufacturers like to announce that a certain shaft has a "low kickpoint" and that such a flexing action at a low point on the shaft aids the player who needs help getting the ball up in the air. Conversely, shafts with a "high kickpoint," it is claimed, have their maximum flex at a higher point up the shaft, and this higher kick- or flexpoint "helps the stronger player keep the ball down." So the scratch player who averages 260 yards with the driver rushes to purchase clubs with a high-kickpoint shaft, and the short-hitting senior eagerly pays the tab for a low-kickpoint shaft design.

In reality, forthright club experts admit, the concept of kickpoint is basically a myth. Dick Murtland, vice-president of operations for Adams Golf, explains, "Kickpoint is defined as the apogee of the curve on the shaft when it's under stress—it's the point at which the shaft flexes the most. In any given shaft we've seen, the apogee of the club's flex *doesn't vary by more than one inch up or down the shaft*. If you have a shaft that's flexible, its flex- or kickpoint will be just a shade lower than the kickpoint on a stiff shaft." In other words, if you need a high-frequency or stiff-shafted club, its kickpoint will be a touch higher on the shaft than if you were to choose a very whippy shaft—but the difference in the positioning of these kickpoints *is both automatic and a negligible factor.* Don't make a decision on a certain shaft based on a salesperson's pitch about its low or high kickpoint.

Judging Graphite Shaft Quality Is Difficult

Tom Wishon of Golfsmith reports that in 1996, at least, the original equipment manufacturers (also known as OEMs) were putting substantial pressure on graphite shaft companies to lower the price of their various offerings. "What most OEMs understand is that if a graphite shaft has a nice coat of paint and a nice multiple-colored logo, the public can't tell whether it's a $6.50 shaft or a shaft using very high grade materials that costs $40 or $50 to manufacture."

It would be great if you knew, in whatever brand of clubs you were considering, who the maker of the shaft was. Quite often you won't know unless you ask, because the company will stipulate in its agreement with the shaftmaker that the shaft will *not* be identified by the maker's name. "The OEMs are going more and more in this direction," says Wishon, "because they don't want to be in the position of having to rely on only one shaft supplier. They usually have two or three sources, but they don't want some of their product going out with shafts that say 'Aldila' and others that say 'Unifiber,' or whoever. That would confuse the public." If the brand of shaft does not appear on the clubs you are considering, ask the salesperson to find out. If you like the physical factors in the club-shaft and find out that it's made by a respected shaftmaker—True Temper, FM Precision, Aldila, Grafalloy, UST, Apollo, Unifiber, or A. J. Tech, for instance—you have reason to expect consistent performance from the golf shaft.

Shaft/Clubhead Quality Control: Why Sets Are Imperfect

In discussing the flex characteristics and overall quality of a golf shaft, it's worth noting that the shaft is one of only three components of any club, the clubhead and grip being the other two. The performance of the shaft will be affected by any irregularities in either the clubhead or the grip attached to it—and, to a slight degree, irregularities are almost "par for the course."

Why does this happen? you ask. Because for golf shafts, clubheads, and grips, there are weight variances or tolerances that are deemed acceptable when the club is assembled. As Barney Adams of Adams Golf explains, when shafts are labeled by the L-A-R-S-X method, within any one of those flex ranges, the club manufacturer's shipment of shafts will likely cover a range of frequencies that can span about twelve readings—from 254 through 265, say, for a Stiff shipment. "Meanwhile," Adams says, "the company's 5-iron heads are expected to weigh 261 grams, but it's usually understood that there is a plus or minus 2-gram differential in the weight of the clubhead as delivered from the foundry. So one 5-iron head may weigh 263 grams, another 259." (For the record, there are 28.35 grams in 1 ounce. A 261-gram clubhead weighs approximately 9.2 ounces.) There may also be slight variation in the weight of the grips, but this is usually minor and will be left out of the equation for the moment.

Now, Adams says, suppose a certain manufacturer does *not* check the weights of the delivered 5-iron heads and clubshafts. The 5-iron heads are in one bin and the S shafts are in another. "A worker who is assembling 5-irons reaches for a shaft and draws one that is at the *high* end of the stiff range, maybe 265 cpm," Adams says. "Next the worker selects a clubhead, and it's one of those that is 2 grams *light*. When you put a light clubhead onto a shaft that is at the top of the Stiff range, because the weight at the end of the shaft is just a shade lighter than it should be, during the swing that shaft is going to flex just a little *less* than it would have if the head weight were perfect. What you wind up having," Adams concludes, "is an *Extra Stiff* 5-iron in a set that's marked Stiff!"

If you happen to be really unlucky, you could be buying a 6-iron that's assembled with the opposite tolerances coming into play. That is, the worker pulls out a shaft that's on the flexible end of the spectrum for the stiff shafts in the bin. Then he/she pulls out a 6-iron head that's 2 grams on the *heavy* side. When this club is assembled, Adams asserts, you may have a head that will bend an already somewhat more flexible shaft even more. This means that despite the S labeling on the clubshaft, it's very possible that you can end up with an *Extra Stiff* 5-iron and a *Regular* 6-iron. "It happens all the time," says Adams. "I've heard many golfers tell me they hit a friend's brand-new, top-name driver on the practice tee and were just killing it. They ran to a retail outlet or pro shop and bought the club with exactly the same specifications. Then they find out, they don't hit the club nearly as proficiently. It just doesn't feel the same. Well, it's because even though they think they are, they're not playing with the same club!" Conclusion: No matter what brand or model you're buying, you must hit the club to make sure it performs like you think it will.

It should be added that the extreme example given above should not happen very often. Many companies claim to measure the weights of all their shafts, clubheads, and grips, and to sort them according to the plus or minus variations described. That way, they claim, the heavy clubhead will not wind up on the marginally too-flexible shaft, nor will the light clubhead be attached to a slightly stiffer-than-desirable shaft so that it plays even "stiffer." Still, inaccuracies occur that can make clubshafts (or, more precisely, the club in its entirety) feel and swing a little differently than expected. Is there anything you can do about this? Fortunately, there is.

Know the Frequency of the Clubs You're Buying

Always insist on hitting some balls with the brand of clubs you're considering. If buying at a golf course, hopefully you will be allowed to hit some demo clubs on the range. If purchasing from a retail outlet, make sure that you visit one that has an indoor driving net so that you can at least get a sense of the club's feel at impact. You might also consider contacting any of the major companies listed at the end of this book. Many companies arrange "Demo Days" across the country. You may be able to attend one near you and hit plenty of shots with the clubs you're considering.

This aside, heed Tom Wishon's advice: "Before you visit a retail outlet or pro shop, call and ask, 'Does your shop have a frequency machine?' This is one of the best ways to find out how the shafts compare in clubs you're considering.

"A frequency reading is not going to provide you with the total feel of the golf club, but getting a reading should give you a good feeling about whether you're on the right track," Wishon says. He recommends that you bring along an older club that you've had success with. Ask the retailer to measure its reading on the frequency analyzer. Suppose this club's shaft reads out at 252 cpm. Ideally, the clubs you're considering, which hopefully you've been allowed to hit and which you judge positively so far, will have a reading within several cpm of the club you brought along. You now have good reason to feel confident that this club or set will work well for you.

If you're considering buying a graphite-shafted club or set, the availability of a frequency analyzer is even more important. Why? *Because the analyzer can give you an indication of the quality of the construction of the graphite shaft in question.* "With a steel-shafted club, the frequency reading for any given club is going to be very consistent, no matter what angle you set the shaft in the machine," Wishon explains. "That may *not* be the case with a graphite shaft if it isn't of high quality." Wishon advises that you do this: Ask the person who is showing you the clubs to give the graphite club in question *four* frequency readings: first, with the toe of the club pointing down; then with it pointing up; third, with the toe pointing to the left; and finally, with the toe pointing to the right. "If you get four separate readings that are within two to three cycles per minute of each other, then you've got a good-quality shaft in terms of its consistency," Wishon says. "If you get a difference of *four or more cpm* between the readings at any of these positions, you should look for something else. This isn't a very consistent graphite shaft."

The recommendation that you find a club retailer who can allow you to hit shots with various models, and who will allow you to get an actual reading of the frequency of the clubshafts, admittedly requires that the retailer put more time and effort into the sale. If you're serious about getting a new set of clubs that performs consistently and that feels right, you should demand this level of service.

It may well be that when you do business with someone who makes these resources available, you'll end up paying a little more for the set than you would from another retailer. But on a full-set investment that will certainly cost upwards of $1,000, isn't an additional $25 to $50 worth the peace of mind and confidence that you've got a well-made and well-matched set of clubs?

A Final Recommendation on Pricing and Shaft Selection

A set of top-of-the-line metalwoods and irons can be a big investment. You can easily spend over $1,000 for four metalwoods, and over $1,200 for a set of nine irons and wedges. That's $2,200 before you've outfitted yourself with a putter, bag, shoes, balls, gloves, and other accoutrements. But if you're trying to limit your purchase to $1,000 for a full set, I strongly suggest you *go with the best set you can find with steel shafts.*

As Tom Wishon points out, "For the golfer on a budget, to go into a Wal-Mart or a Kmart and try to pick up a full set of clubs, eight irons and three woods, all with graphite shafts for somewhere in the $250 to $300 range, that's where you could really get into trouble. You are very likely to be buying shafts that will perform inconsistently. And, in that buying environment, you won't have any chance to find out by hitting the clubs or testing them for their frequency, to get any feel for what you're actually getting."

The two factors of lower price and more predictable performance of the shaft, whether it's the shaft in an inexpensive or a top-name club, make steel the smart "budget" buy. Look at it this way: It's still what the majority of Tour professionals play!

CHAPTER 3

Choosing a Driver: Pick What's Right, Not What's "Hot"

It's time to examine the clubs that are on the market today, and to make the choices that help your game the most (while not finding it necessary to raid your IRA account).

In the next six chapters, we will discuss the various segments of the clubs that make up a full set, along with the golf ball you'll be striking with those clubs (Chapter 8). A substantial portion of each chapter will consist of tables of information on offerings by the major manufacturers for each particular club. This will allow you, as you learn from the text, to browse through the tables and begin to pick out manufacturers and models that have design specifications that appeal to you. Each of these chapters will also include a healthy selection of photographs of the top offerings. Thus, you will be able to use what you learn, technically and visually, as an initial weeding-out process on what clubs to test for a possible purchase.

In this chapter, the subject is drivers. Before we begin, a few words on the tables in this chapter (and those following) might be helpful.

The table material in this chapter includes the most pertinent technical stats provided by the various manufacturers on their driver models. The specifications in the driver tables are the most detailed of any in the book. There are two reasons for this: First, the driver is the longest club in the bag. The longer the clubshaft, the more critical that it be well fitted to your swing. It's much more likely that you could adapt to a sand wedge that had a shaft that was too stiff for you, and which you'd use from a maximum distance of 80 to 90 yards out,

Callaway Great Big Bertha (above left)
Cobra King Cobra Ti (left)
Taylor Made Burner Bubble Titanium
(above)

than you could to a too-stiff driver that you hope to boom 260 yards down the fairway.

Secondly, it's unnecessary to repeat all the elements regarding the golf shaft used in a particular model from the driver through the wedge chapters. So you'll get the information about shafts in this chapter and can refer back to this table if necessary when studying later chapters.

Certain information will be provided across the board for all segments of clubs, such as the lofts and lengths available, type of grips used, whether women's and/or left-handed clubs are available under a given model name, and the suggested retail price of the club or set in question.

As was mentioned earlier, every effort was made to obtain complete information from each manufacturer in the specific formats designed. Some manufacturers provided less complete specs than others.

At the bottom of each table page, there's a legend to explain the abbreviations that appear in the tables.

The Clubhead: Is There a "Magic" Material for Your Driver?

In 1995 and 1996, in the United States, the most significant addition to the driver marketplace was clubheads made from *titanium*. This is a very light, very strong, very expensive aerospace-oriented material (although it is actually said to be the fourth most plentiful metal in the world). In the past couple of years, the use of titanium has been praised at some point or another as a cure-all for just about any type of lousy tee shot, as well as generally providing added distance. The most prominent titanium-headed drivers on the market are the Callaway Great Big Bertha, Cobra's King Cobra Ti, and Taylor Made's Burner Bubble Titanium (see table listings for others).

The other predominant clubhead material for drivers today is stainless steel. Aluminum is another material that makes up a small percentage of metal driver clubheads; additionally, there are clubheads made of graphite and of natural or laminated wood.

The use of stainless steel in driver and fairway wood heads began to attract attention around 1980, and through the decade of the 1980s stainless steel steadily overcame the use of wood, which had been used almost universally in all "wood" clubs prior to that time.

When stainless steel overtook wood as the material of choice in driver and fairway wood clubheads during the 1980s, its chief benefits were that metal heads could be manufactured with much greater consistency than wood; that metal heads could be shaped and weighted in specific ways that would encourage different types of ball flights as needed by different golfers; that metal heads were more economical than wood, particularly wood heads made of relatively scarce natural persimmon; and, finally, that metal heads could be designed in larger sizes than in the past. This boom in "oversize" drivers, which supposedly create a larger "sweet spot" on the clubface and allow more forgiveness on errant shots, started around 1991 in the United States.

Since 1995, titanium has elbowed its way into the marketplace mainly by expanding on the advantages of stainless steel: Since titanium is lighter than stainless steel, it can be formed into a larger clubhead still while still weighing the same amount. (As you'll see in the ensuing tables, the size of the clubhead is measured in cubic centimeters, or ccs.)

In the past, most wood-headed drivers measured around 150 to 155 ccs. The first metal drivers in the early 1980s were of similar size. Gradually, the advantage of stainless steel's "hollow head" and the opportunity to enlarge the clubhead came into play so that now an "average-size" metal driver clubhead is about 190 to 200 ccs. By comparison, most titanium heads are huge—often around 250 ccs and sometimes more. If you remember the craze for Callaway's "oversize" Big Bertha (which measures about 195 ccs) in the early 1990s, and realize that the titanium 250-cc Great Big Bertha is about 28 percent larger than *that*—well, you're getting the picture of just how radical the changes have been.

"Weighing In" the Metals

The three most used metals in the manufacture of drivers and fairway woods are stainless steel, titanium, and forged aluminum. You may have heard a lot of claims regarding the physical advantages of each in terms of their respective strengths and weights. According to a report by research physicist Leon J. Seltzer of San Diego here's how the three three metals stack up in terms of yield strength (in pounds per square inch):

Aluminum	75,000
Titanium	120,000
Stainless Steel	160,000

While stainless steel is the strongest, it is also by far the heaviest of the three materials. The heavier a metal is, the fewer options club designers have in terms of the size and weight distribution that can be built into the clubhead. Here's how the same three materials measure up in terms of their weight or density (in pounds per cubic inch):

Aluminum	0.101
Titanium	0.163
Stainless Steel	0.290

While aluminum metalwood heads are in the minority right now, as the lightest and therefore the most "workable" of the three metals, it's possible that aluminum may become more prominent in future designs.

Debunking Some Myths

Granted, titanium heads can be made substantially larger than those of stainless steel. Yet, there's a lingering doubt among some designers that titanium will prove to be no more than a substantial fad. "In Japan, a titanium driver is a status symbol, absolutely," says Golfsmith's Tom Wishon. "You can tell a titanium driver by its sound—from what I've seen, most titanium investment casters make the walls of the clubhead just a little thicker than they do with stainless steel. So the sound is not quite so clangy as it is with stainless steel. It's more of a 'tink' sound. In Japan, if a guy hits a driver and it doesn't make that tink sound, he's a 'low-rider'—he doesn't have the status of the rest of the guys who do have titanium. But the sound at impact can't be considered a true performance feature; and I don't think Americans are being quite so vain about this whole thing."

Adams Golf's Barney Adams, whose company offers titanium as well as stainless steel–headed driver models, raises the question of how much easier it really is to hit the ever-larger driver clubheads made of titanium. "I know that millions of dollars are being spent to sell the public on the notion that bigger is better," says Adams. "I believe the benefit is more psychological than anything—if the golfer looks down and sees a bigger driver head, he or she might feel more confident. But if you're talking about pure performance, that's another story. Clubmakers say they're 'enlarging the sweet spot' all the time. But the sweet spot by definition is still an infinitesimal spot which is the optimum meeting point of clubface and the center of the ball. You can't enlarge it! So in terms of enhanced performance, at that moment of truth, I don't believe that titanium brings anything to the party."

Perhaps of more concern than the value of the larger head made of titanium is the idea that titanium is capable of making the ball take off faster from the clubface. "Rebound velocities—that's where the real myths are about titanium," says Tom Wishon. "I've heard a number of manufacturers tell customers that a titanium clubface actually rebounds backward at impact, then snaps forward, as if to 'slingshot' the ball off the clubface. *This is a load of hogwash!* The material in a clubhead has a totally different coefficient of restitution than the golf ball does. Even if a clubface deformed somewhat at impact, which it doesn't, the ball would be gone before the clubface had a chance to re-form outward. This is something that does not happen, cannot happen, and is a total myth. *There is no inherent difference in the way the ball comes off the face of a stainless-steel versus a titanium driver."*

There is one advantage of titanium-headed drivers that might cause golfers to think that the material itself helps them gain some yardage. As Wishon points out, a clubhead that is larger from toe to heel and from top to bottom will usually be larger from face to rear as well. When this is the case, the clubhead's *cen-*

Cleveland VAS Titanium

Vulcan X-Wing

Don't Buy the "Drag" Theories

You've probably read or seen ads for drivers that promote a head design that is "aerodynamically efficient." Club manufacturers purport that certain of their designs can be swung faster because there is "less drag or wind resistance" to the clubhead during the swing, the implication being that with this reduced drag, you'll get more distance.

According to Tom Wishon of Golfsmith, such claims of aerodynamic advantages in certain driver clubheads are "without doubt, a bunch of baloney. We're talking about golf clubs here, not some race cars at the Indy 500. The amount of drag that golf clubs create as they are swung is an absolutely infinitesimal factor in the club's performance.

"Talking about stuff like air drag is a way to justify some weird-looking head design, and to fool the consumer into thinking something is worthwhile that isn't," Wishon states.

You've got plenty of other factors to consider—don't waste your time on "drag."

---

ter of gravity is located farther behind the clubshaft than it is with a smaller clubhead. Without attempting a physics lesson here, suffice it to say that when the center of gravity is farther back, the effective loft of the clubface at impact is slightly greater. This in turn gives the shot a little greater loft. And, as we'll see, the majority of amateurs are not using enough loft on their drivers to begin with. In sum, when the average player gets a slightly higher trajectory, he or she ends up carrying the ball a little farther. Which is great! In such a situation, though, it's the *design* of the clubhead that is aiding a player's distance, not the titanium itself.

Three Top Concerns for Your Driver: Accuracy, Accuracy, and Accuracy

---

I'm highly prejudiced. If there's one thing I would like to help readers to do, it's to find a driver with which *you hit the most accurate tee shots possible*. Even— gasp!—if it means you end up using a driver that you hit 4 or 5 yards shorter than the longest-hitting driver you can find.

Think about it. When you go for that "big number," that 8 or 9 that balloons your score and wrecks your confidence for the rest of the round, you'll

Mizuno T-Zoid Diamondface

Kenneth Smith KS 2000

find that almost every time, it was an errant tee shot that started everything downhill. Sometimes this is obvious, as when you knock the ball out of bounds and accrue a stroke-and-distance penalty, or duck-hook two balls into a lake. But often it's a less obviously wild tee shot that sets off a sorry chain of events.

Say you've pushed a drive into the right rough. You still have a shot to the green, but you must keep it extra low to stay under tree branches 25 yards ahead. You hit the shot well, but the ball catches the last branch and ricochets into the woods. Next you try to recover through a tiny opening, smack the ball into a tree trunk, and wind up needing a guide instead of a caddie to find your way out.

After you've walked off the green with your 9, you realize that if your not-that-bad drive had been a mere 4 or 5 yards closer to the fairway, you'd have had clear access to the green. You'd likely have made a par-4, and even allowing for some miscue, a bogey-5. You'd have been four or five shots better off and enjoyed the rest of your round a lot more.

In terms of obtaining distance versus accuracy with the driver, *pick the more accurate club if you want to score your best*. Say you have one driver that you can hit 10 yards longer than another. However, you know from experience that you also hit the "longer" driver more erratically. Ask yourself this: How much farther do I have to hit the ball off every tee, to make up for one or two tee shots that end up costing me two or more strokes on a hole? There's no precise answer, but believe me, you'd have to hit it a *lot* farther! Much more than 10 yards, to make up the difference in strokes you lose via two "foul balls."

Barney Adams describes the dilemma that many club manufacturers face with regard to balancing what's best for the golfer with the reality of selling clubs, particularly drivers. "If I could talk honestly to the 100-shooter who is all over the course, I'd ask this player to start teeing off with a 3-wood instead, or possibly even a 5-wood!" he says. "If the 100-shooters could just learn to keep the ball in play all the way around the course, I have no doubt that they could learn to break 90 very quickly."

Driver Testing: How's Your First Shot?

We've recommended that for the driver or for any club, if at all possible you hit full shots with the club(s) you're considering purchasing. According to Barney Adams of Adams Golf, you should assess the results with any test club as follows:

Step up to the tee and visualize the type of shot you want to play as if you're on the golf course. Then address the ball and try to execute that tee shot. What was the result of that first shot? Was it what you expected? *If the club fits you, you should be able to hit it well immediately!* As Adams puts it, "There are no tees on golf courses that have a bucket of balls sitting on them, for you to hit extra shots. If you don't hit a club well right off the bat, move on to the next one, because it doesn't fit you. It's not a matter of you finding a way to hit the driver in question effectively after hitting fifty to seventy-five balls. That would be saying, 'Here's a driver I can *adjust* to.'"

Sounds like a harsh test of a club. There's a chance (assuming, of course, you're not a PGA Tour member) that you might top that first ball with a driver that really would have been good for you. So, okay, maybe you can give it *two* or *three* test swings before drawing a conclusion—but that's it.

Unfortunately, golfers' egos, fueled no doubt by barrages of TV ads showing golfers hitting drives that traverse oceans, get in the way of the real object of the game, which is to shoot the best possible score. "If I invented a set of clubs that was so accurate that it would *guarantee* the golfer a handicap reduction of five strokes, with the proviso that they would hit the ball 20 yards shorter, well, I wouldn't be able to *give* them away!" Adams laments.

What makes a driver more accurate? It's impossible to write a prescription for each individual. But one factor regarding the accuracy you can obtain is the length of the driver's clubshaft. There's a "right" maximum clubshaft length with which each individual can make solid contact, which is the key ingredient to accuracy. And there's no doubt that the shorter the clubshaft, the greater your chance for accuracy. The length of the shaft and the amount of loft on the clubface are the reasons few golfers have severe problems with a wedge, but many hit their drivers "off the world."

If you decide that accuracy is a prime element in what you're looking for in your next driver, check the lengths that drivers are offered in. You're more likely to hit it straight with a club that's 43 inches in length than you are with one that's 45 or longer.

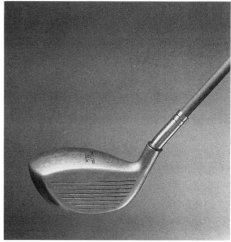

Cobra King Cobra (above left)
Cobra King Cobra Offset (above right)
RTS Driver (right)

Forget It! I Want to Hit It as Far as I Can!

Okay, so you haven't quite bought that argument, at least not yet. You want to play better *and* you want to be the longest hitter in your foursome. If so, you need to investigate all lengths of drivers to see what gives you the best combination of length and reasonable accuracy.

In general, drivers are getting longer. Until perhaps 1990, the generally accepted average driver length was 43 inches. As you'll see in the table, for men's clubs virtually everyone offers models in some length longer than 43 inches, and for men there are no drivers shorter than this length.

It's ironic, if you stop to think about it, that most manufacturers will entice you to buy their drivers because of certain vaguely stated characteristics that guarantee you longer distance. While they're doing this, though, how many go out of their way to tell you that the clubshaft they're offering is 1 or 2 or more inches longer than standard? Few, if any. "Everyone tries to tell the consumer that this new shaft with magical properties they've developed will add so much distance to their drives," Adams says. "The main piece of 'magic,' which they avoid stating, is that the new club is 45½ inches long, or 2½ inches longer than the one you've been using!"

Experts recommend that you tread carefully with longer-shafted drivers. "I believe that for every golfer, there's an optimum driver length to which he or she will react by making the purest possible swing, rather than by trying to hit the ball hard. That's the length he or she should play with," Adams contends. "It's ironic: The people who can adapt to long-shafted drivers the best are the ones who need them the *least*—the golfers who are gifted with excellent athletic skills and coordination, who can hit the ball long to begin with." Golfsmith's Wishon concurs. "Longer drivers are no guarantee of increased distance whatsoever—for some players, they can become a big headache," he says. "We've seen just as many cases where golfers have picked up distance by going to a *shorter* driver than a longer one, because they hit the shorter-shafted club much more solidly."

A few years ago, I conducted a study on how far golfers hit their tee shots with different-length drivers. A group of twelve golfers of various skill levels tested drivers that were identical except for their lengths, which were 43, 44, and 45 inches. The differences in distances they achieved with the three different lengths were very slight; and the players actually obtained the best total distance with the 44-inch driver in this test.

From a design standpoint, there's one more interesting note regarding club length. If you look at driver lengths in the table, you'll notice that for the majority of companies, drivers offered with graphite shafts are slightly longer than those with steel, usually by ½ inch. The majority of amateurs who go to a graphite-shafted driver don't realize it's longer—they may get the impression they're hitting the ball slightly farther, attributing this length to the fact that the shaft is graphite.

Why do graphite shafts tend to be longer? There's a specific reason. When the manufacturer puts a graphite shaft (which as we've seen will usually be lighter than steel) into a clubhead that was originally designed for a steel shaft, the club's feel, or "swingweight," actually becomes a bit heavier. In order to adjust the club's swingweight to its originally intended level, the lighter graphite shaft is lengthened slightly. "Lengthening the shaft is the only way the companies can get their swingweights right when using graphite shafts," says Wishon. Actually, another alternative is the expensive process of casting a different clubhead for graphite-shafted clubs than for steel ones. This would allow the shafts to be the same length in either material. However, "This is not what most com-

Confidence Titanium

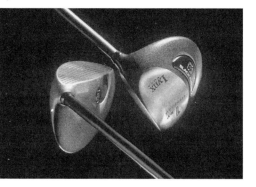

Lynx Black Cat

The Golden Bear's Driver History

What has the greatest player in the history of the game used as his driver over the course of his career? Jack Nicklaus's personal clubmaker for more than twenty years, Jack Wulkotte, tells us the following.

Throughout the 1960s, when Nicklaus was known as the longest and best driver in the game, and into the 1970s, he used a persimmon-headed driver that was the standard length for that time, 43 inches (Extra Stiff steel shaft). The loft on this driver was 11 degrees—also about standard when driver heads were made of wood. In no sense did Nicklaus use a club of exotic materials or specifications when achieving his most prodigious length.

In the early to mid-1970s, Wulkotte reports, although Nicklaus was hitting this driver very straight, he wasn't happy that some other players were beginning to out-distance him. In 1975 he went to a persimmon-headed driver that was 43½ inches in length and carried between 9.0 and 9.5 degrees of loft. He used this driver until approximately 1988.

Wulkotte notes that all of Nicklaus's drivers since 1975 have been "counterbalanced"; that is, there is ½ ounce of lead added under the *grip* end of the club. Nicklaus does this because he wants to keep the total weight of the club *up*.

Since 1988, Nicklaus has experimented substantially with various drivers and has used drivers up to 45 inches in length. He has reduced his loft even more, to between 8 and 9 degrees, since the graphite shafts he's been using are more flexible than in the past and make it easier to get the ball airborne.

Nicklaus still uses counterbalancing in his drivers and likes the club to have a relatively heavy swingweight (measured at D-5) and a heavy (by today's standards) total weight of about 13 ounces.

panies choose to do," Wishon says, "and it's certainly not the best way to run the army, so to speak, because companies are in effect forcing the consumer into swinging a longer club. And it's absolutely true that the longer the club, the harder it will be to hit it right on center."

Driver Loft: Err on the "High" Side

As we touched on in Chapter 1, every golfer has a minimum amount of loft on the driver clubface that he or she will be able to hit efficiently. It's true that there are factors in various clubhead designs, such as the exact location of the center

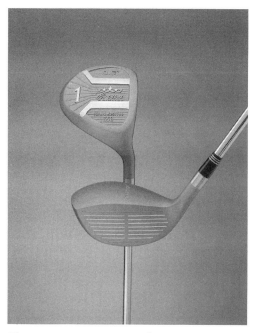

Slazenger Crown Limited

Gary Player Black Knight Titanium

of gravity, which also affect the trajectory of the tee shot. But clubface loft is the most important thing to look at in terms of obtaining your optimum trajectory off the tee.

Loft is more important for the driver than on your irons. If, for example, your 6-iron happened to carry a loft of 32 degrees instead of 33, this would not be a major problem. It would simply mean that your 6-iron shots would fly just a shade lower and that you would obtain an extra yard or two on the shot. However, consider what happens if everything about a driver's design works well for you, except that you choose the club with a loft that's 1 degree lower than your optimum. This is not unusual—in fact, many golfers try to hit drivers that have 2, 3, or even 4 degrees too little loft for them. The general reasoning seems to be that the lower the loft, the more the ball will shoot out on a line drive, the more it will roll upon landing, and the longer the shot will be.

But as we mentioned in Chapter 1, in order for a tee shot to carry optimally when launched at a low angle, the clubhead must contact the ball while moving at a very substantial speed. If clubhead speed at impact is relatively low, the ball will not take on enough backspin or "lift." Instead, it will nose-dive, and you'll get a much shorter carry than you would with a little more loft.

Clubmaking experts agree that golfers with slower swing speeds will obtain their maximum distance with substantially higher-lofted drivers than the strongest players. In addition, if you're swinging a driver that's too straight-faced for you, you'll instinctively sense this and feel as though you have to "lift" the ball off the tee rather than swing through it. Too little loft on a driver can contribute greatly to a golfer making his or her *worst* swing with the club that requires the best one!

Again, every driver that has, say, 10 degrees of loft will not necessarily launch the ball identically, because of variations in the clubhead's center of gravity based on its design and shape. While various driver clubheads "play" a little differently, the following table should provide you with a reasonable guide as to the *minimum* loft you should use on your driver (or shall we say, tee-shot club?) depending on your swing speed.

DRIVER SWING SPEED (mph)	MINIMUM CLUBFACE LOFT NEEDED (degrees)
110	8.0
100	9.5
90	11.0
80	12.5
70	14.0

Driver Weights: How Low Should You Go?

While drivers have been getting longer, at the same time a major trend is to make them as light as possible, too. The theory here is that the lighter the total weight, the faster you can swing the clubhead and the greater distance you will automatically obtain. A leader in this area of development is Goldwin Golf, whose AVDP drivers are advertised as weighing in the 9–9.5-ounce range—a full 4 ounces, or 30 percent, lighter than what would have been considered the average driver weight not long ago.

Most of the reduction in weight in these drivers is due to the remarkable variance in shaft weights on the market today. Golfsmith's Wishon reports that if a driver's total weight is between 12.0 and 12.75 ounces, its shaft weight will be between 86 and 109 grams. Drivers weighing between 11.25 and 12.0 ounces will have shafts weighing in the 70–85-gram range. "If your driver weighs less than 11.25 ounces, the shaft is almost sure to weigh less than 70 grams," Wishon reports.

Certainly, there is merit in finding a driver that is light and easy to swing. Wishon advises that if the average golfer is using a driver that weighs more than 12 ounces, it's probably heavier than he or she needs. "The average person who is not 'golf strong,' who plays just once a week and rarely practices, would ben-

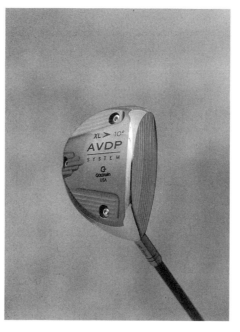

PowerBilt T-Minus 1 (above)
Goldwin AVDP (right)

efit most from a driver that's in the 11-ounce range, or even slightly lighter," he advises.

A word of warning about seeking an ultralight driver for added distance: Take your own swing tempo and the rest of your set into account. If you have a very quick swing tempo to start with, it will probably speed up even more with a very light driver, so that you may have trouble making optimum contact with it. "Any weight changes should be slight, not radical," Barney Adams suggests. "It's more important that your set be consistent in all respects. If all your clubs are light, that might be good, but if they're all relatively heavy, that might work well, too. Somebody once asked Jack Nicklaus why he took an ultralightweight driver out of his bag, even though he hit it quite far. Nicklaus's answer was, 'The problem is, I have to go back and swing all the other clubs, too.'"

What's the Right Driver Worth?

At the time this book went to press, in the U.S. market you could pay up to $1,000 for the driver of your dreams (see Ram's FX Ti-Forged or Maruman's Power Titan in the table listings). These, of course, are one-of-a-kind (well, two-of-a-kind) prices—and if you're willing and able to pay them, more power to you.

Tommy Armour Hot Scot

At the beginning of 1996, a price tag of $500 for a top-brand titanium driver seemed to be the "magic number" that the manufacturers believed was attainable. This has not proved to be the case, as Cobra then came out with a suggested retail of $367 for its King Cobra Ti driver, while other top manufacturers reduced their asking price to under the $400 mark.

It is my own opinion, but one that is shared by many others involved in club design, that there are plenty of stainless steel–headed driver models available that can improve your tee shots just as well as titanium.

As to the nontitanium drivers, some top-name graphite-shafted models may still command $300 or more. Steel-shafted driver models are usually far less expensive. An example is the Wilson Invex, which carries a suggested retail of $299 in graphite (with stainless-steel head), as opposed to $185 with a steel shaft. If you're thinking about going with a graphite shaft only in the driver, a price differential such as this might not cause much concern. Just hit enough test shots to make sure you've found the graphite shaft that provides better overall results than you can get with steel.

You'll also find some budget buys among the driver listings. For example,

Can You Mix Graphite and Steel Shafts?

Many golfers who experiment with different shafts find that they like the lightness that graphite offers in the driver and/or in the fairway woods, but maybe not as much in their irons. Also, for many golfers, the cost of having an entire set of graphite-shafted clubs is beyond their means. In cases such as these, what about the strategy of using graphite in the driver and steel in the irons?

Most experts believe it's fine to use graphite in the driver alone, or just in the driver and fairway woods, as long as they have clearly determined that the performance values of the steel and graphite shafts are similar. This goes back to the point made by experts in the industry that letter codes on shafts of different materials and/or made by different companies can be misleading. You can't assume that the R graphite shafts in your woods made by Company A will perform similarly to the R steel shafts in your irons that are produced by Company B. You need to know about the different shafts' frequencies and torque factors in terms of actual readings, as well as to watch the results of your well-hit shots using the different shafts.

Tom Wishon points out that in addition to the shaft's flex, "Golfers need to watch for the weight differentials between any different shafts they use. If a player uses an ultralight graphite shaft in the driver which reduces its total weight to 10 ounces, but has a heavy steel shaft in the 3-wood that gives it a total weight of 14 ounces, for most golfers that's going to be disruptive."

*Yonex Super ADX Titanium
(above)
Titleist Howitzer Supersize Drivers
(right)*

Dynacraft, a maker of club components, offers completed driver models for as low as $45 with steel shafts and $65 with graphite. If you're on a tight budget, there's no reason you shouldn't look into them.

Is Good Old Persimmon Dead?

You'll find some listings for "real" wood-headed drivers and fairway woods in the tables, but not many. Since the mid-1980s, various types of metal-headed "woods" have predominated.

The beauty and in some cases the playability of a finely crafted wooden club is undeniable. But in addition to the scarcity and expense of quality persimmon, it's also undeniable that the consistency from clubhead to clubhead in factory-made metal-wood heads is much greater than it could be in any natural material. You could never tell precisely how any two identically crafted persimmon driver heads would perform at the end of a shaft, because the degree of density of the wood and its center of gravity could not be absolutely defined. Two outwardly identical heads could make the ball fly somewhat differently.

"If any good player had a persimmon driver they really liked, it would be like searching for the Holy Grail to find a good backup club," notes Barney Adams. "Manufacturers would go out on the range with a huge selection of drivers, and players would keep trying different ones until they hit upon one where the heads felt exactly the same.

"With metal, once you get a good design, you can make a million heads exactly the same way. The consumer is bound to get a better product. That's why I really don't think wood heads can come back."

DRIVER PRODUCT INFORMATION

MANUFACTURER	MODEL	CLUBHEAD MATERIAL	CLUBHEAD SIZE (cc)	LENGTHS (in.)	LOFTS (deg.)
Adams Golf	Air Assault	17-4 ss	195	43.5 s, 44 g	7, 9, 10.5, HT (offset high trajectory)
	Air Assault	Titanium	230	45	11
	Comments: Patented design lowers center of gravity.				
Tommy Armour	855s Hot Scot	Steel	190	43.5 s, 44 g	9, 10, 11
	855s Golden Scot	Steel	190	44	11
	855s Diamond Scot	Steel	190	43	12
	Tommy Gun	Titanium	260	45	8.5, 10
Black Ice Golf	Tour Balance	17-4 ss w/ ceramic clubface	Midsize	Custom lengths from 41 to 52	9, 10, 11

Comments: All models custom fit. Black Ice facing can be applied to other metal-faced drivers.

Legend:	g=graphite (in "Shaft Materials/Weights" column only, g=grams)	A=Seniors' shaft flex ratings
		R=Men's Regular shaft flex ratings
	s=steel	F=Firm
	ss=stainless steel	S=Men's Stiff shaft flex rating
	L=Ladies' shaft flex rating	X=Men's Extra Stiff shaft flex rating

Shaft Materials/ Weights	Shaft Flexes/ Frequencies	Torque (*deg.*)	Grip Style	Left-Handed	Women's	Suggested Retail
Filament-wound graphite (88g), extra-light graphite (70g)	L 225, R 238, F 248, S 260	L (4.0), R (3.5), F (3.0), S (2.8)	Golf Pride, Royal	Y	Y	$142 steel $239 graphite
Ultralight graphite (58g)	L, R, F, S	2.5–4.0	Golf Pride, Royal	N	Y	$460
Dynamic steel	R, S	2.3	Golf Pride Tour Wrap	Y	N	$265 graphite
Tour Step II steel	R, S, X	2.3				
G-Force 2 Tour graphite	R, S, X	2.9				
G-Force 2 Tour graphite	Single Flex	4.5	Golf Pride Tour Wrap	N	N	$265
G-Force 2 Tour graphite	Single Flex	6.09	Diamond Perf Wrap	N	Y	$265
Grafalloy Pro Lite	R, S	3.5	Golf Pride Tour Wrap	N	Y	$350
Dynamic Gold steel (125g), Penley graphite/ boron (80g), A. J. Tech Duration 4000 graphite (47g)	L, A, R, F, S, X (210–280 depending on other specs)	Not supplied	Griptec Tour Wrap	Y	Y	$160 steel $215 Penley graphite $215 A. J. Tech graphite

continued

DRIVER PRODUCT INFORMATION *(continued)*

MANUFACTURER	MODEL	CLUBHEAD MATERIAL	CLUBHEAD SIZE *(cc)*	LENGTHS *(in.)*	LOFTS *(deg.)*
Black Rock	Killer Bee Titanium	6AL 4V Titanium	260	46, 48, 50	8, 10
	Killer Bee	ss	240	46, 48, 50	10
	Comments: 50-inch driver weighs only 11.2 ounces.				
Bridgestone	Precept Titanium	Titanium	275	45	11
	Precept Tour	ss	Midsize	44	9, 10.5
	Precept Extra	Aluminum alloy	Midsize	Not supplied	9.5
Bullet Golf	Invincible	Titanium alloy	290	45	8, 10.5
	.444	ss	250	44	9, 10.5, 12
	.444T	Titanium	Not supplied	Not supplied	Not supplied
Callaway Golf	Great Big Bertha	Ruger titanium	250	45 (men) 44 (women)	6, 5, 7.5, 8, 8.5, 9, 10, 11, 12
	Big Bertha War Bird	17-4 ss	190	44 (men) 43 (women)	8, 9, 10, 11, 12

Legend:	g=graphite (in "Shaft Materials/Weights" column only, g=grams)	A=Seniors' shaft flex ratings
		R=Men's Regular shaft flex ratings
	s=steel	F=Firm
	ss=stainless steel	S=Men's Stiff shaft flex rating
	L=Ladies' shaft flex rating	X=Men's Extra Stiff shaft flex rating

Shaft Materials/ Weights	Shaft Flexes/ Frequencies	Torque (*deg.*)	Grip Style	Left-Handed	Women's	Suggested Retail
High modulus graphite	46" R, S 48", 50" S	R 3.7 S 3.4	Golf Pride Tour Wrap	Y	N	$349.95– $399.95
High modulus graphite	46" R, S 48", 50" S	Not Supplied	Golf Pride Tour Wrap	Y	Y	$199.95– $249.95
High-modulus graphite (65g)	R, S	Not supplied	Royal Tour Wrap	N	N	$299
Brunswick Precision steel, high-modulus graphite (65g)	R, S	Not supplied	Royal Tour Wrap	N	N	$145 steel $210 graphite
High-modulus graphite	R, S	Not supplied	Royal Tour Wrap	N	N	$170
Grafalloy graphite (70–90g), ceramic Kevlar (75g)	Grafalloy, 4 flexes; ceramic Kevlar, 1 flex	2.5–4.0 g, 3.0 Kevlar	Golf Pride Tour Wrap	N Y	Y Y	$170 ceramic Kevlar $220 graphite $120 ceramic Kevlar $150 graphite
Not supplied				N	N	Not supplied
BBVL graphite	L, A, R, F, S	Not supplied	Proprietary All-Weather	Y	Y (Ladies' Gems)	$500
RCH 96 graphite, Memphis 10 steel	L, A, R, F, S	Not supplied	Proprietary All-Weather	Y	(Ladies' Gems)	$185 steel $285 graphite

continued

DRIVER PRODUCT INFORMATION *(continued)*

MANUFACTURER	MODEL	CLUBHEAD MATERIAL	CLUBHEAD SIZE (cc)	LENGTHS (in.)	LOFTS (deg.)
Cleveland Golf	VAS Titanium	Titanium	250	45	8, 10, 12
Cobra Golf	King Cobra Titanium	Titanium 6AL 4V	210, 225, 235	44, 45, 46	8.5, 9.5, 10.5, 11.5
	King Cobra Offset	17-4 ss	197	44 g, 43.5 s	9 (deep face), 10.5, 12
	Senior King Cobra	17-4 ss	190	44 g, 43.5 s	10.5 offset, 12 regular
	Tour King Cobra	17-4 ss	185, 195	43.5	9 (deep face), 10.5
	Lady Cobra	17-4 ss	190	43 g, 42.5 s	10.5 offset, 12 standard
Confidence Golf	Titanium	Titanium	260	45	9, 10, 11
	Zoom Hydro Wing	ss	210	42, 43, 44	9.5, 10.5
	Visa	ss	210	42, 43, 44	9.5, 10.5

Legend:	g=graphite (in "Shaft Materials/Weights" column only, g=grams)		A=Seniors' shaft flex ratings
			R=Men's Regular shaft flex ratings
	s=steel		F=Firm
	ss=stainless steel		S=Men's Stiff shaft flex rating
	L=Ladies' shaft flex rating		X=Men's Extra Stiff shaft flex rating

Shaft Materials/ Weights	Shaft Flexes/ Frequencies	Torque (deg.)	Grip Style	Left-Handed	Women's	Suggested Retail
Graphite	A, R, S, X	Not supplied	Golf Pride Tour Wrap	N	N	$500
Lightweight graphite	A, R, S, X	2.8	Rubber Tour Wrap	N	N	$367
Lightweight graphite or lightweight steel	A, R, S, X	2.8 g, 2.5 s	Rubber Tour Wrap	Y	N	$159 steel $267 graphite
Lightweight graphite or lightweight steel	A	4.0 g, 2.5 s	Rubber Senior Tour Wrap	Y	N	$159 steel $242 graphite
Tour Weight graphite, titanium, True Temper Dynamic Gold steel (122g), Brunswick Rifle steel	R, F R, S, X R, S, X 5.0–7.0 (R, S, X)	1.8 1.8 2.5 2.5	Tour Full Cord or Rubber Tour Wrap	Y	N	$167 either steel shaft $309 Tour graphite $292 titanium
Graphite, steel	L	4.5 g, 2.5 s	Ladies Rubber Tour Wrap	Y	Y	$149 steel $217 graphite
High-modulus graphite (68g) for all models; steel available for Zoom and Visa	R, S	4.0	Golf Pride Velvet Cord	N	N	$500
	L, R, S	4.5 g, 3.7 s	Rubber Soft Wrap, Golf Pride Victory	Y	Y	$180 steel $310 graphite
	L, R, S			Y	Y	$240 steel $190 graphite

continued

DRIVER PRODUCT INFORMATION *(continued)*

MANUFACTURER	MODEL	CLUBHEAD MATERIAL	CLUBHEAD SIZE (cc)	LENGTHS (in.)	LOFTS (deg.)
Daiwa	Exceler Titanium	Titanium	250	45	9, 10.5
	Hi-Trac MF-100 "250"	Aluminum/ titanium	250	45	11
	Ballistic	A356 alloy	220	45	10.5
	Hi-Trac MF-110	630 ss	193	44	9.5, 10.5
Dunlop	Tour DG	17–4 ss	225	44	9, 10.5
	RMS	17–4 ss	225	44	9.5, 10.5
	DDH Tour	17–4 ss	240	44	10.5
	Tour Ti	6–4 titanium	280	44	9.5
	Revelation	ss w/forged titanium insert	Not supplied	45	10.5

Legend:	g=graphite (in "Shaft Materials/Weights" column only, g=grams)	A=Seniors' shaft flex ratings
		R=Men's Regular shaft flex ratings
	s=steel	F=Firm
	ss=stainless steel	S=Men's Stiff shaft flex rating
	L=Ladies' shaft flex rating	X=Men's Extra Stiff shaft flex rating

SHAFT MATERIALS/ WEIGHTS	SHAFT FLEXES/ FREQUENCIES	TORQUE (*deg.*)	GRIP STYLE	LEFT-HANDED	WOMEN'S	SUGGESTED RETAIL
Sheet-wrapped lightweight graphite (59g)	R, S	3.9–4.0	Rubber Perforated Wrap	N	N	$415
Sheet-wrapped lightweight graphite (59g)	R, S	3.9–4.0	Rubber Perforated Wrap	N	N	$250
Sheet-wrapped graphite (75g)	A, R, S	3.4–3.6	Rubber Perforated Wrap	N	Y	$265
Sheet-wrapped graphite (75g)	A, R, S	3.4–3.6	Rubber Perforated Wrap	Y	Y	$190
Tour EI graphite, steel	R, S	4.5 graphite	Golf Pride Tour Velvet	N	N	$225 steel, $330 graphite for set of 3 woods
Tour EI graphite, steel	R, S	4.5 graphite	Golf Pride Tour Velvet	N	Y	$225 steel, $315 graphite for set of 3 woods
Tour EI graphite, steel	R, S	4.5 graphite	Dunlop Perma Wrap	Y	Y	$141 steel, $207 graphite for set of 3 woods
Graphite (51g)	S	5.0	Golf Pride Tour Velvet	N	N	$285
Graphite (51g)	R, S	5.0	Golf Pride Tour Velvet	N	N	$148

continued

DRIVER PRODUCT INFORMATION *(continued)*

MANUFACTURER	MODEL	CLUBHEAD MATERIAL	CLUBHEAD SIZE *(cc)*	LENGTHS *(in.)*	LOFTS *(deg.)*
Dynacraft	Copperhead	17-4 ss	205	43, 44	9.25, 10.5, 13.25
	Limited	17-4 ss	204	43, 44	9, 11, 10 (deep face)
	Ti	6-4 titanium	250 or 285	44, 45, 46	10.5
	Comments: Custom fitting available for all clubs.				
Goldwin Golf	AVDP Jumbo XL	7075-T6 heat-treated aluminum	260	44	8, 9, 10, 11
	AVDP Tour Milled		200	44	8, 9, 10, 11
	AVDP Seniors XL		260	45	12
	AVDP Seniors Standard		200	44	8, 9, 10, 11
	AVDP Lady XL		260	44	12
	AVDP Lady Shallow		190	43	12
	Comments: AVDP system features extreme weight reduction in grip and top of clubshaft.				

Legend:　g=graphite (in "Shaft Materials/Weights" 　　A=Seniors' shaft flex ratings
　　　　　　column only, g=grams)　　　　　　　　　　R=Men's Regular shaft flex ratings
　　　　　s=steel　　　　　　　　　　　　　　　　　　F=Firm
　　　　　ss=stainless steel　　　　　　　　　　　　　S=Men's Stiff shaft flex rating
　　　　　L=Ladies' shaft flex rating　　　　　　　　　X=Men's Extra Stiff shaft flex rating

SHAFT MATERIALS/ WEIGHTS	SHAFT FLEXES/ FREQUENCIES	TORQUE (*deg.*)	GRIP STYLE	LEFT-HANDED	WOMEN'S	SUGGESTED RETAIL
True Temper Dynamic Gold steel (122g), Aldila Low Torque graphite (80g)	Steel R 255, S 265, X 271; graphite L 235, A 240, R 255, S 270	2.5 s, 4.0 g	Golf Pride Tour Velvet	Y	Y	$75 steel $100 graphite
True Temper Dynamic Gold steel (122g), Aldila Low Torque graphite (80g)		2.5 s, 4.0 g	Golf Pride Tour Velvet	Y	Y	$75 steel $100 graphite
Fenwick Energy sheet-wrapped graphite (55g)	R 255, S 265	4.5	Golf Pride Tour Velvet	N	N	$250
Unifiber/Goldwin high-modulus lightweight graphite (55 g)	A, R, F, S, X	Not supplied	Winn Ultra-Light Grip	N	Y	$395
	R, F, S, X	Not supplied	(weighs 7 grams)	N	N	$295
	A	Not supplied		N	N	$395
	A	Not supplied		N	N	$295
	L	Not supplied		N	Y	$375
	L	Not supplied		N	Y	$275

Total club weight 9.3 ounces, grip weighs only 15% of standard weight grips.

continued

DRIVER PRODUCT INFORMATION *(continued)*

MANUFACTURER	MODEL	CLUBHEAD MATERIAL	CLUBHEAD SIZE (cc)	LENGTHS (in.)	LOFTS (deg.)
Golfsmith	Titanium 260	Titanium 6AL 4V	260	43.5 s, 45 g	9.5, 11
	Harvey Penick Master	17-4 ss	180	43.5 s, 44 g, 43 ultralight graphite	10, 12
	XPC Plus	17-4 ss	205	43.5 s, 44 g	9.5, 11, 13
The GolfWorks	Tarantula	17-4 ss	201	44	11
	Bio-Mech II	17-4 ss	203	44	9.5, 11
	Kinetic II	17-4 ss	207	41	10
Ben Hogan	Edge GCD Titanium	Titanium	Oversize	Not supplied	Not supplied
	Edge GCD	Not supplied	Midsize	43.25 s, 43.75 g	9, 10.5, 12
	Apex Persimmon	Persimmon	Standard	43.25 s, 43.75 g	10

Comments: Hogan shafts use 1–5 numerical flex rating system

Legend:	g=graphite (in "Shaft Materials/Weights" column only, g=grams) s=steel ss=stainless steel L=Ladies' shaft flex rating	A=Seniors' shaft flex ratings R=Men's Regular shaft flex ratings F=Firm S=Men's Stiff shaft flex rating X=Men's Extra Stiff shaft flex rating

Shaft Materials/ Weights	Shaft Flexes/ Frequencies	Torque *(deg.)*	Grip Style	Left-Handed	Women's	Suggested Retail
Ultralight graphite (66g), steel (119g)	L, A, R, S 238 graphite R 250 steel R	4.5 g	Golfsmith Rubber Wrap	Y	Y	$290 steel $345 graphite
Ultralight graphite (64g), graphite (85g), steel (116g)	L, A, R, S 241 ultralight graphite R, 250 graphite R	4.5 g, 4.2 ultralight g	Penick Wrap (standard, midsize, lightweight)	Y	Y	$110 steel $145 graphite $169 ultralight graphite
Graphite (92g), steel (119g)	L, A, R, S 251 graphite R, 250 steel R	5.5 g	XPC Plus Wrap	Y	Y	$100 steel $135 graphite
Tarantula graphite (98g)	R, S	3.5	Rubber Wrap Style	N	N	$45 steel $74 graphite
Bio-Mech II graphite (87g)	L, A, R, S	4.3	Rubber Wrap Style	N	Y	$45 steel $65 graphite
Distance Master graphite (87g) (all available w/steel)	R, S, X	4.5	Rubber Wrap Style	N	N	$45 steel $64 graphite
Not supplied	Not supplied	Not supplied	Apex V-Trac Cord	N	N	$460
Apex steel L, A, R, S, X; Apex graphite, L, A, R, S, X	Not supplied	Not supplied	Apex V-Trac Cord	N	Y	$150 steel $250 graphite
Apex steel L, A, R, S, X; Apex graphite L, A, R, S, X	Not supplied	Not supplied	Apex V-Trac Cord	N	Y	$185 steel $300 graphite

(corresponds to L, A, R, S, X flexes as shown).

continued

DRIVER PRODUCT INFORMATION *(continued)*

MANUFACTURER	MODEL	CLUBHEAD MATERIAL	CLUBHEAD SIZE *(cc)*	LENGTHS *(in.)*	LOFTS *(deg.)*
Izzo	Duranium	Duranium	260	45	10.5
	Titanium	6AL 4V titanium	260	45	10.5
Javelin Blue	Titanium	Titanium	236	44	9, 10.5
	Stainless	17-4 ss	188	43.5	8.5, 9.5, 10.5
Kunnan Golf	EXT	Metal composite	220	44 (men) 42.5, 43 (women)	9.5 (men) 11.5 (women)
	IGS 2000M	Metal composite	230	44 (men) 43 (women)	9, 10.5 (men) 14 (women)
	Tribute	Metal	Not supplied	43.5, 44 (men) 42 (women)	10, 11 (men) 12 (women)

Comments: *Clubhead is stainless steel encased in graphite.*

Legend:	g=graphite (in "Shaft Materials/Weights" column only, g=grams)	A=Seniors' shaft flex ratings
		R=Men's Regular shaft flex ratings
	s=steel	F=Firm
	ss=stainless steel	S=Men's Stiff shaft flex rating
	L=Ladies' shaft flex rating	X=Men's Extra Stiff shaft flex rating

Shaft Materials/ Weights	Shaft Flexes/ Frequencies	Torque (*deg.*)	Grip Style	Left-Handed	Women's	Suggested Retail
Izzo LT graphite (75g)	R, S, X	Not supplied	Golf Pride Tour Velvet Wrap	N	N	$320
FM Precision steel (100g); Izzo LT graphite (75g)	R, S, X (steel and graphite)	Not supplied	Golf Pride Tour Velvet Wrap	N	N	$320 steel $375 graphite
Flex-matched graphite (72g)	Graphite available in 9 flexes, JW1 through JW9	Not supplied	Tour Wrap, Tour Cord, Ladies Tour Wrap	N	Y	$395
Flex-matched graphite (72g)	Graphite available in 9 flexes, JW1 through JW9	Not supplied	Tour Wrap, Tour Cord, Ladies Tour Wrap	N	Y	$300
Micro Tip graphite (85g)	L, A, R, S	3.0–6.0	Golf Pride Tour Wrap	Y	Y	$350
Autocure graphite (60g)	L, R, S, X	5.5–7.0	Golf Pride Tour Wrap	N	Y	$250
Boron-reinforced graphite (75–94g)	L, A, R, S	5.5–7.0	Golf Pride Tour Wrap	Y	Y	$120

continued

DRIVER PRODUCT INFORMATION *(continued)*

MANUFACTURER	MODEL	CLUBHEAD MATERIAL	CLUBHEAD SIZE (cc)	LENGTHS (in.)	LOFTS (deg.)
Lynx	Black Cat Titanium	Titanium	Oversize	45	9, 10.5, 12
	Black Cat	17-4 ss	Midsize	43.5	9, 10.5, 12
	Tigress 6	17-4 ss	Midsize	42	11
MacGregor	Superlite Titanium	Titanium 6V 4AL	260	45	10.5
	VIP Titanium	Titanium 6V 4AL	210	44	9, 10.5

Legend:	g=graphite (in "Shaft Materials/Weights" column only, g=grams	A=Seniors' shaft flex ratings R=Men's Regular shaft flex ratings
	s=steel	F=Firm
	ss=stainless steel	S=Men's Stiff shaft flex rating
	L=Ladies' shaft flex rating	X=Men's Extra Stiff shaft flex rating

Shaft Materials/ Weights	Shaft Flexes/ Frequencies	Torque (*deg.*)	Grip Style	Left-Handed	Women's	Suggested Retail
Flare 650 light graphite (65g)	A, R, S, X	Not supplied	Golf Pride Standard Wrap	N	N	$435
Flare graphite Dynamic Flare steel, Lynx Lite Flare steel	A, R, S, X R, S, X R, S	Not supplied	Golf Pride Standard Wrap	Y	N	$185 steel $265 graphite
Lynx Powertune graphite	L	Not supplied	Golf Pride Victory	N	Y	$158
Grafalloy Ultralite graphite (60g)	A, R, S	Not supplied	Golf Pride Tour Wrap Cord	N	N	$350
Exel Flex Profile graphite	L, A, R, S, X	Not supplied	Golf Pride Tour Wrap Cord, Tour Wrap (women)	Y	Y	$310

continued

Driver Product Information *(continued)*

Manufacturer	Model	Clubhead Material	Clubhead Size *(cc)*	Lengths *(in.)*	Lofts *(deg.)*
Maruman Golf	Power Titan	Beta and 16-4 titanium	209	44	10.5
	M301T "Big"	Titanium	230	44	11.5
	Verity G	17-4 ss	190	43.5	11

Comments: Clubface in Power Titan formed from rarely used beta titanium.

Manufacturer	Model	Clubhead Material	Clubhead Size *(cc)*	Lengths *(in.)*	Lofts *(deg.)*
Maxfli Golf	VHL Oversize	17-4 ss	215	44 g, 43.5 s	9, 10.5, 13
Merit Golf	Tour International	Persimmon	Standard	43.5	10
	Fusion	17-4 ss	194–209	43.5 s, 44 g	9.5, 10, 10.5
	Prophecy	17-4 ss	178	43.5 s, 44 g	9.5, 10.5

Comments: Custom orders at no additional cost.

Legend:	g=graphite (in "Shaft Materials/Weights" column only, g=grams)	A=Seniors' shaft flex ratings
		R=Men's Regular shaft flex ratings
	s=steel	F=Firm
	ss=stainless steel	S=Men's Stiff shaft flex rating
	L=Ladies' shaft flex rating	X=Men's Extra Stiff shaft flex rating

Shaft Materials/ Weights	Shaft Flexes/ Frequencies	Torque (deg.)	Grip Style	Left-Handed	Women's	Suggested Retail
Carbofit SL-1 graphite (54g)	R, S	4.6	Cord Tour Wrap	N	N	$990
Carbofit HV graphite (69g)	R, S	5.0	Proprietary by Maruman	N	Y	$595
Carbofit HV graphite (74g), Parsec high-elastic graphite/Kevlar (65g)	R, S	5.2–5.9	Proprietary by Maruman	Y	Y	$195 Carbofit shaft $325 Parsec shaft
VHL graphite (87g), VHL steel (115g)	L, A, R 265; S 275	4.7 g L, 4.5 g A, 4.0 g R, 3.5 g S	Golf Pride Tour Velvet	Y (10.5 loft only)	Y (13 loft only)	$158 steel $241 graphite $216 women's/ seniors' graphite
True Temper Dynamic Gold steel (122g)	R300, S300	Not supplied	Golf Pride Tour Wrap, All Cord	N	N	$200
True Temper Dynamic Gold steel (122g), Dynalite Gold, Aldila Synchro Flex graphite	R, S Dynamic; A, R, S Dynalite; A, R, S graphite	Not supplied	Golf Pride Tour Velvet	N	N	$130 steel $170 graphite
True Temper Dynalite steel (114g), Aldila graphite	L, A, R, S	Not supplied	Golf Pride Tour Wrap	Y	Y	$94 steel $128 graphite

continued

DRIVER PRODUCT INFORMATION *(continued)*

MANUFACTURER	MODEL	CLUBHEAD MATERIAL	CLUBHEAD SIZE (cc)	LENGTHS (in.)	LOFTS (deg.)
Mitsushiba Golf	MTS	17-4 ss, titanium insert	220	44	9, 10.5
	Curare	17-4 ss	220	44	10.5, 12
	Integrity	17-4 ss	190	44	10.5, 12
	Verdict	Alloy	215	44	11
Mizuno USA	T-Zoid Titanium	Titanium	240	46	9, 10.5, 11.5
	T-Zoid	17-4 ss	200	44.25 g, 43.25 s	8.5, 9.5, 10.5, 11.5, 13
	TC Mid Plus	17-4 ss	189	44 g, 43.25 s	9.5, 11, 13

Comments: T-Zoid driver offered in five different lofts; internal rails create lower center of gravity,

Legend:	g=graphite (in "Shaft Materials/Weights" column only, g=grams)	A=Seniors' shaft flex ratings
		R=Men's Regular shaft flex ratings
	s=steel	F=Firm
	ss=stainless steel	S=Men's Stiff shaft flex rating
	L=Ladies' shaft flex rating	X=Men's Extra Stiff shaft flex rating

Shaft Materials/ Weights	Shaft Flexes/ Frequencies	Torque (deg.)	Grip Style	Left-Handed	Women's	Suggested Retail
Graphite (85g)	Not supplied	3.5	Lamkin Perma-Wrap	N	N	$259
Wrapped graphite (75g)	Not supplied	5.0–6.0	Lamkin Perma-Wrap	Y	Y	$80
Wrapped graphite (75g)	Not supplied	5.0–6.0	Lamkin Perma-Wrap	Y	Y	$72
Wrapped graphite (75g)	Not supplied	5.0–6.0	Lamkin Tru-Tac	Y	Y	$60
Turbo Gold graphite, True Temper Dynamic Gold (122g) or Dynalite (118g) steel	L, A, R, S, X graphite; R, S steel	1.8–5.3 g	Golf Pride Tour Velvet	N	N	$650
Turbo Lite graphite (58–61g)	R, S	5.4	Royal Sand Wrap	N	N	$200 steel $300 graphite
Exsar V graphite, True Temper Dynamic Gold (122g) or Dynalite (118g) steel	L, A, R, S, X graphite; R, S steel	2.5–4.5 g	Golf Pride Tour Velvet	Y	Y	$100 steel $165 graphite

higher launch angle.

continued

DRIVER PRODUCT INFORMATION *(continued)*

MANUFACTURER	MODEL	CLUBHEAD MATERIAL	CLUBHEAD SIZE *(cc)*	LENGTHS *(in.)*	LOFTS *(deg.)*
Nicklaus Golf	Air Bear	17-4 ss	200	44	9.5, 10.5
	Air Bear Offset	17-4 ss	200	44	10.5
	Air Bear Titanium	Titanium	220	44.5	9.5, 10.5
Ping	Zing II	17-4 ss	Not supplied	Custom lengths	9, 10.5, 12, 14
Gary Player Golf	Black Knight Titanium	100% pure titanium	255	44.5	9, 10.5
	Comments: Super oversize head creates increased hitting area; cambered nondrag sole.				
Players Golf	Tiger Titanium	Forged titanium	275	45	9.5, 10.5, 13
	Prozema	17-4 ss	Not supplied	43.5 s, 44 g	10.5

Legend:	g=graphite (in "Shaft Materials/Weights" column only, g=grams)	A=Seniors' shaft flex ratings
	s=steel	R=Men's Regular shaft flex ratings
	ss=stainless steel	F=Firm
	L=Ladies' shaft flex rating	S=Men's Stiff shaft flex rating
		X=Men's Extra Stiff shaft flex rating

Shaft Materials/ Weights	Shaft Flexes/ Frequencies	Torque (deg.)	Grip Style	Left-Handed	Women's	Suggested Retail
Vapor Ultralight graphite (56g), Driveshaft standard graphite (75g); True Temper Crankshaft steel	A, R, S, X Vapor graphite; L, A, R, S Driveshaft graphite; R, S steel	3.5 Vapor	Golf Pride or Griptec Tour Wrap	Y	Y	$160 steel $290 graphite
		4.5 Drive-shaft	Golf Pride or Griptec Tour Wrap	N	N	$160 steel $290 graphite
		2.0 s	Golf Pride or Griptec Tour Wrap	N	N	$499
JZ steel, Z-Z65 steel, graphite	Single flex in steel shafts; 6 flexes in graphite	Not supplied	Ping DylaGrip or Textured Spiral; others optional	Y	Y	$190 steel $265–$300 graphite
Ultra-lightweight graphite (60g)	R 270, F 280	4.3	Golf Pride Tour Wrap	N	N	$499
Kevlar boron graphite	L, R, S	2.5	Rubber Tour Wrap	N	N	$399
True Temper Dynamic steel, graphite	R, S	Not supplied	Full Cord	N	N	$113

continued

DRIVER PRODUCT INFORMATION *(continued)*

MANUFACTURER	MODEL	CLUBHEAD MATERIAL	CLUBHEAD SIZE *(cc)*	LENGTHS *(in.)*	LOFTS *(deg.)*
Power Bilt	TPS Oversize	17-4 ss	200	43.5, 44 (men) 42.5, 43 (women)	9, 10.5, 12
	T-Minus 1	Titanium/ aluminum alloy	270	45	10.5
Comments: TPS includes Sims Shock Relief insert, revised face bulge, rounded sole.					
Pro Select	Prism Ti	Titanium	230 or 280	44.5	10.5
	SE Jumbo	17-4 ss	195	43.5 (men) 42.5 (women)	9.5, 10.5, 13
	NXT One Offset	17-4 ss	190	43.5 (men) 42.5 (women)	10.5, 12
	NXT One Titanium	Alloy w/titanium insert	210	44.5	11
Rainbow Golf	Sealed Power	Titanium 6AL 4V	225	44	9, 10, 11, 13
	Sealed Power 250	Titanium 6AL 4V	250	45	11
Comments: One of the first producers of titanium-head drivers (since 1988).					

Legend:	g=graphite (in "Shaft Materials/Weights" column only, g=grams) s=steel ss=stainless steel L=Ladies' shaft flex rating	A=Seniors' shaft flex ratings R=Men's Regular shaft flex ratings F=Firm S=Men's Stiff shaft flex rating X=Men's Extra Stiff shaft flex rating

Shaft Materials/ Weights	Shaft Flexes/ Frequencies	Torque (*deg.*)	Grip Style	Left-Handed	Women's	Suggested Retail
True Temper Dynamic Gold steel (125g), Dynasty Plus steel (120g), UST Tour Weight graphite (108g), Dynasty Plus graphite (80–97g)	Steel S300, S400, X100, X200; graphite L, A, R, S	2.3–2.6 s, 2.9–4.9 g	Golf Pride Tour Velvet	Y	Y	$185 steel $250 graphite
Extra-light graphite	R, F	5.0	Golf Pride All Weather	Y	Y	$125
Power kick filament-wound graphite	R, S	3.5	Tour Tech Wrap	N	N	$250
Titanium and graphite	L, R, S	4.0	Tour Tech Wrap	Y	Y	$150
Tour Series graphite	L, A, R, S	4.5	Tour Tech Wrap	Y	Y	$99
Power kick filament-wound graphite	R, S	3.5	Tour Tech Wrap	N	Y	$150
High-modulus graphite-boron (80g)	L, L+, A, A+, R, R+, S, S+, X	3.0	Lamkin Pro, Golf Pride Tour Wrap	Y	Y	$400
High-modulus graphite-boron (70g)				N	Y	$450

continued

DRIVER PRODUCT INFORMATION (continued)

MANUFACTURER	MODEL	CLUBHEAD MATERIAL	CLUBHEAD SIZE (cc)	LENGTHS (in.)	LOFTS (deg.)
Ram Golf	FX-Ti Forged	3-piece forged titanium	260	45	10.5
	Big Eye	Titanium alloy	260	45	11
	FX-Oversize (standard and low trajectory)	ss	200	44	10.5 standard, 9 low
Comments: Company claims forged titanium is 1.5 times stronger than cast titanium.					
Rawlings	FT 190	Forged titanium	200	44.5, 45	10.5
	Persimmon	Persimmon	Classic or midsize	44	10
	Catapult	Titanium alloy	225	46	10
	Pure Ti	Forged titanium	245	44.5	8, 10
RTS Golf	RTS	17-4 ss	212	44, 45 (men) 43 (women)	9.5, 10.5, 12
Comments: "Reduced Torque System" exemplified by center-shafted design.					

Legend:	g=graphite (in "Shaft Materials/Weights" column only, g=grams)	A=Seniors' shaft flex ratings
	s=steel	R=Men's Regular shaft flex ratings
	ss=stainless steel	F=Firm
	L=Ladies' shaft flex rating	S=Men's Stiff shaft flex rating
		X=Men's Extra Stiff shaft flex rating

Shaft Materials/ Weights	Shaft Flexes/ Frequencies	Torque (*deg.*)	Grip Style	Left-Handed	Women's	Suggested Retail
Ultralight high-modulus graphite (58g)	R, S	3.5–4.0	Genuine Leather Wrap	N	N	$1000
Ultralight graphite (60g)	R, S	3.5–4.5	Ram Wrap	N	N	$199
Tempo weight graphite (84g)	R, S	3.5–4.5	Ram Wrap	Y	Y	$150
True Temper Dynalite graphite (85g), Extralite graphite (60g)	R, S, X	Not supplied	Rubber Tour Wrap	N	N	$450
True Temper Dynamic Gold steel (122g), Dynalite graphite	R, S	Not supplied	Rubber Tour Wrap	N	N	$210 steel $285 graphite
Ultralight graphite (58g)	R, S	Not supplied	Rubber Tour Wrap	N	N	$150
Aldila graphite (85g)	L, A, R, S	Not supplied	Rubber Tour Wrap	N	Y	$299
FM Precision steel (104g), FM Precision Fibermatch graphite (84g)	Kick+ 230, R 240, F 250, Tour 260, Tour+ 270	Not supplied	Griptec Tour Wrap	Y	Y	$275

Custom lie and face angle available.

continued

DRIVER PRODUCT INFORMATION *(continued)*

MANUFACTURER	MODEL	CLUBHEAD MATERIAL	CLUBHEAD SIZE *(cc)*	LENGTHS *(in.)*	LOFTS *(deg.)*
Slazenger	Crown Limited	17-4 ss	185	43.5 standard (41 to 46.5 available)	8.5, 10.5, 12, 14
Kenneth Smith	KS 2000	17-4 ss	210	Custom lengths	10.5
	Royal Signet 90	Persimmon or laminated maple	200	Custom lengths	Custom lofts (9–12)
	Royal Signet CIB	Persimmon or laminated maple	175	Custom lengths	Custom lofts (9–12)
	Comments: All driver models are custom made with personalization included.				
Snake Eyes Golf	Snake Eye Driver	Combined ss, titanium, and other metals	205	44, 45	9, 10, 11

Comments: White-gold chrome finish—very durable.

Legend: g=graphite (in "Shaft Materials/Weights" column only, g=grams)	A=Seniors' shaft flex ratings
s=steel	R=Men's Regular shaft flex ratings
ss=stainless steel	F=Firm
L=Ladies' shaft flex rating	S=Men's Stiff shaft flex rating
	X=Men's Extra Stiff shaft flex rating

Shaft Materials/ Weights	Shaft Flexes/ Frequencies	Torque (*deg.*)	Grip Style	Left-Handed	Women's	Suggested Retail
FM Precision Rifle (steel), FM Precision high-modulus and filament-wound graphite	Spectrum of flexes offered, frequency range 206–271	Torque dictated by frequency	Golf Pride (all models available)	N	Y	$140–$150 steel $195–$250 graphite
Ultralight graphite (60g), boron graphite (85–90g), steel (110–120g), titanium (105g); available all models	L 235, A 250, R 260, S 270	4.0 g, 3.0–3.5 boron, 2.5 s, 2.2–2.6 titanium	Golf Pride, Royal, Griptec in various styles; Leather Perforated Wrap	N	Y	$180 steel $235 graphite $260 titanium
	L 240, A 250, R 260, S 270, X 280			Y	Y	$255 steel $285 graphite $310 titanium
	L 240, A 250, R 260, S 270, X 280			Y	Y	$255 steel $285 graphite $310 titanium
Viper graphite (76–84g), Python graphite (60g)	R, S, X	2.5 Viper 4.2 Python	Golf Pride Tour Wrap	N	N	$350

continued

DRIVER PRODUCT INFORMATION *(continued)*

MANUFACTURER	MODEL	CLUBHEAD MATERIAL	CLUBHEAD SIZE (cc)	LENGTHS (in.)	LOFTS (deg.)
Taylor Made	Titanium Bubble	Titanium 6AL 4V	230	44, 45	8.5, 9.5, 10.5, 12
	Champagne Titanium Bubble	Titanium 6AL 4V	230	43.5	12
	Burner Bubble	17-4 ss	200	44	8.5, 9, 9.5, 10.5, 12
	Champagne Burner Bubble	17-4 ss	200	43, 43.5	10.5, 12
	Burner Metalwood	17-4 ss	200	43	8.5, 9, 9.5, 10.5, 12
	Comments: "Bubble" shaft is widest just below the grip.				
Titleist	Howitzer	Titanium	250	43.5, 44, 45 (men) 42.5 (women)	8, 10, 12
	DCI Starship	ss	170	43.5	9, 10.5, 12
	Know Right	ss	Not supplied	43.5 (men) 43 (women)	12
Top-Flite	Intimidator	ss, titanium face	230	44	9, 10.5

Legend:	g=graphite (in "Shaft Materials/Weights" column only, g=grams)	A=Seniors' shaft flex ratings
		R=Men's Regular shaft flex ratings
	s=steel	F=Firm
	ss=stainless steel	S=Men's Stiff shaft flex rating
	L=Ladies' shaft flex rating	X=Men's Extra Stiff shaft flex rating

Shaft Materials/ Weights	Shaft Flexes/ Frequencies	Torque (deg.)	Grip Style	Left-Handed	Women's	Suggested Retail
Bubble graphite (60–85g)	L 220, A 230, R 240, S 255, X 270	3.0 g X, 3.5 g S, 4.0 g R, 5.0 g A, 4.5 g L, 3.0 s	Rubber Tour Wrap	Y	N	$400
Bubble graphite (60–85g)	L 220		Rubber Tour Wrap	N	Y	$400
Bubble graphite (60–85g)	A 235, R 245, S 260, X 270		Rubber Tour Wrap	Y	N	$300
Bubble graphite (60–85g)	L220		Rubber Tour Wrap	N	Y	$300
True Temper Dynamic Gold steel (122g); Dynalite steel (118g)	R 245, S 260, X 275		Rubber Tour Wrap	Y	N	$180
Fuse lightweight graphite (60–107g), Fuse ultralight graphite (56–58g)	L 235, A 245, R 255, S 275, X 300	2.2–6.0	Golf Pride Buffed Tour Wrap	Y	Y	$375
Tri-Spec graphite, Tri-Spec steel	L 245, A 250, R 255, S 265, X 275	4.0–4.5	Golf Pride Buffed Tour Wrap	Y	Y	$130–$160 steel $205–$250 graphite
Tri-Spec graphite	L, A, R	Not supplied	Golf Pride Air Cushion	N	Y	$260
Aldila sheet-wrapped graphite (84–92g)	A 249, R 254, S 265, X 275	2.9–3.6	Golf Pride Buffed Tour Wrap	Y	N	$275

continued

DRIVER PRODUCT INFORMATION *(continued)*

MANUFACTURER	MODEL	CLUBHEAD MATERIAL	CLUBHEAD SIZE *(cc)*	LENGTHS *(in.)*	LOFTS *(deg.)*
Vulcan	X-Wing	17-4 ss	190	24 custom lengths	8.75, 10.5
	Q-Pointe	17-4 ss	185		8.75, 10.5
Comments: Wide range of custom-fitting options.					
Wilson	Invex	17-4 ss w/titanium hosel	175	44	8.5, 9, 10.5, 12
	Invex Titanium	Titanium	210	45	9, 10.5, 12
Comments: Unique aerodynamic design with large crown, narrow sole.					
Wood Brothers	Texan	Persimmon	Midsize	43.5 s, 44 g	10
	Kool Kat	Cork-filled persimmon	Midsize	43.5 s, 44	10.5
	F-300	Metal	Midsize	44	9.5, 10.5

Legend: g=graphite (in "Shaft Materials/Weights" column only, g=grams)
s=steel
ss=stainless steel
L=Ladies' shaft flex rating

A=Seniors' shaft flex ratings
R=Men's Regular shaft flex ratings
F=Firm
S=Men's Stiff shaft flex rating
X=Men's Extra Stiff shaft flex rating

Shaft Materials/ Weights	Shaft Flexes/ Frequencies	Torque (deg.)	Grip Style	Left-Handed	Women's	Suggested Retail
Ultralight graphite (58g)	10 flexes offered, frequency range 225–270	Not supplied	Royal, Lamkin, Golf Pride Tour Wrap in 7 custom sizes	N	Y	$225
Ultralight graphite (58g), high-modulus graphite (85g)				Y	Y	$160
Steel (110g), graphite (79–91g)	Graphite LL 230, L230, A 230, R 240, S 250, X 260	2.0–5.0 g and s	Royal Sand Wrap	Y	Y	$185 steel $299 graphite
Graphite (60g)			Royal Sand Wrap	N	Y	$400
True Temper Dynamic Gold steel (125g); VST 2600 graphite (73g)	R, S, X	3.0–5.0 g	Golf Pride Tour Wrap	Y	N	$320 steel $390 graphite
True Temper Dynalite steel (118g), G Loomis and UST graphites (80–85g)	L, A, R, S, X	3.0–5.0	Golf Pride Tour Wrap	N	Y	$175 steel $225 graphite
UST graphite	R, S, X	3.0–5.0	Golf Pride Tour Wrap	Y	N	$196 graphite

continued

DRIVER PRODUCT INFORMATION *(continued)*

MANUFACTURER	MODEL	CLUBHEAD MATERIAL	CLUBHEAD SIZE (cc)	LENGTHS (in.)	LOFTS (deg.)
Yonex	Super ADX Titanium	Titanium	250	45	9.5, 11
	Super ADX	Graphite, ss face	220 or 300	44, 45, 46, 48	7, 9, 10, 11
	Super ADX Senior	Graphite, ss face	220 or 300	44	11,12
	Super ADX Ladies	Graphite, ss face	220–250	43, 43.5	12, 13
	ADX 100i	Graphite	Not supplied	43.5, 44, 45	9, 11, 13
	Tour	Graphite	Not supplied	44	9
Zevo	lob	ss	210	43–48	10.5, 13
	Air Zevo Oversize	ss	210	43–48	9, 10.5, 13
	Air Zevo Comp Equipe	ss	195	43–48	9, 10.5

Legend:	g=graphite (in "Shaft Materials/Weights" column only, g=grams)	A=Seniors' shaft flex ratings
		R=Men's Regular shaft flex ratings
	s=steel	F=Firm
	ss=stainless steel	S=Men's Stiff shaft flex rating
	L=Ladies' shaft flex rating	X=Men's Extra Stiff shaft flex rating

Shaft Materials/ Weights	Shaft Flexes/ Frequencies	Torque (*deg.*)	Grip Style	Left-Handed	Women's	Suggested Retail
High-modulus graphite	R, S, X	Not supplied	Tour Weave Cord	Y	Y	$420
Ultralight graphite	R, S, X	Low	Rubber Tour Wrap	Y	N	$350
Ultralight graphite	A	Not supplied	Not supplied	Y	N	$350
Ultralight graphite	L	Not supplied	Not supplied	N	Y	$350
High-modulus graphite	L, R, S	Not supplied	Not supplied	Y	Y	$275
Graphite/boron	R, S, X	Not supplied	Not supplied	Y	N	Not supplied
Graphite (55–95g)	7 flexes available	2°–6°	Zevo Pro Wrap	N	Y	$225–$350
Graphite (55–95g) steel (110–125g)	7 flexes available	2°–6°	Zevo Pro Wrap	Y	Y	$175–$200 steel $285–$350 graphite
Graphite (55–95g) steel (110–125g)	7 flexes available	2°–6°	Zevo Pro Wrap	N	Y	$175–$200 steel $285–$350 graphite

CHAPTER 4

The Fairway Woods: A Growing Segment of the Savvy Player's Set

This book has a chapter devoted to drivers and another devoted to the fairway/utility woods because this setup mirrors a change in the consumer's buying habits in recent years.

In the past it was more common for golfers to buy their woods or metalwoods together in a set. When "wooden" woods were still predominant through the 1960s, 1970s, and early 1980s, it was fairly standard practice for most amateurs who owned a full set to carry a total of three woods. Most commonly, these would be a driver, 3-wood, and 4-wood, or a driver, 3-wood, and 5-wood. Most golfers would also carry irons numbered 2 through 9, a pitching wedge, sand wedge, and putter to total fourteen clubs, the USGA limit.

Buying patterns have changed in recent years. The driver has taken on particularly special importance, as well it should. Consumers tend to buy the driver separately from the other metalwoods. For a number of reasons, they are also tending to put more fairway metalwoods in their bags than in years past.

Callaway Big Bertha Ely Would

This chapter will examine and report on all fairway metalwoods with greater loft than the driver. This can include clubs known as fairway drivers, with lofts in the 12–13-degree range, which are designed to be used from both the tee and the fairway, and clubs such as Callaway Golf's Ely Would, a catchy moniker for an 11-wood. With such a club you can loft shots into the greens that look similar in flight to most 7-iron shots.

Let's look at why the role of fairway and utility woods is increasing, and what you should consider carrying in your bag.

Mizuno T-Zoid Fairway Woods

Lofted Woods Are Unquestionably "Easier to Hit"

If you have played golf for a number of years, and particularly if you are a middle-to-high-handicap golfer, you have no doubt had your share of struggles trying to strike solid, well-flighted shots with the 2- and 3-irons. (This statement overlooks even the existence of the 1-iron, a club that is readily available through most manufacturers, but is usually carried only by top amateurs and professionals.) Quite possibly, you are still struggling with the long irons today. Why is it that these clubs present such problems for all but the best amateur players? Basically, it has to do with the loft and the design of the long irons as compared with the lofted metalwoods.

If we look at the lofts of the various clubs as they have been traditionally constructed, it would appear that there is a great deal of overlap between the longer irons and the lofted fairway woods. According to highly respected club designer Ralph Maltby in his book *Golf Club Design, Fitting, Alteration & Repair* (4th ed., Ralph Maltby Enterprises, 1995), the standard loft for fairway woods and the modern standard loft for the irons numbered 1 through 4 (men's clubs) are as follows.

Fairway Wood	Standard Loft (degrees)	Iron	Standard Loft (degrees)
3-wood	16	1-iron	16
4-wood	19	2-iron	19
5-wood	22	3-iron	22
6-wood	25	4-iron	25
7-wood	28		
8-wood	31		
9-wood	34		

Dynacraft Copperhead 3-Wood

As you can see, the standard loft on a 3-wood and a 1-iron is the same (16 degrees); and the loft on a 5-wood and a 3-iron is the same (22 degrees). Yet most golfers don't even carry a 1-iron; and almost all handicap players would agree that they can hit a 5-wood higher, longer, and more easily than they could ever hit a 3-iron. Why? Basically, there are four factors.

First and most significant are the design features inherent in the metal fairway wood clubhead. In almost all cases, the metalwood's center of gravity will be lower in the metalwood than it will be on the long iron. If you have a 2-iron available, take it out and stand it on a tabletop, then place a golf ball against the face. Particularly if the club is a more traditional, forged-style iron, it's likely you'll see that the top of the clubface is even with or perhaps slightly above the top of the ball. Now take out a 4-wood and make the same comparison. If it's like most fairway wood designs, you'll see that the top line of the clubface is slightly below the top of the ball. This virtually guarantees that the metalwood's center of gravity is below the ball's equator. "It's largely because the center of gravity on most metalwoods is lower than that on the long irons that most amateurs find a lofted metalwood much easier to hit," says Mark Young, formerly product manager of pro clubs for Wilson Sporting Goods.

On many of today's metalwood designs, the center of gravity is lowered even more than you might surmise from its outward appearance. This is because the metal in the sole of the club may be thicker than that on its top or crown. (It should be noted that in the past, with wooden fairway woods, the same effect was often obtained by placing a relatively heavy, brass sole plate on the wooden head. This also served to lower the center of gravity substantially and helped golfers get the ball airborne easily.)

On some metal fairway woods, you may see two "rails" built into the sole, which run perpendicular to the clubface. "These rails serve to further lower the center of gravity of the club, as well as to improve the club's ability to move through rough grass in the impact zone without twisting," Young says. Many companies now use various offshoots of the rail concept in the soles of their metalwoods, such as Taylor Made's "K" sole and Callaway's War Bird sole design.

Callaway Big Bertha War Bird 3-Wood

Secondly, although the lofts may be similar, most fairway metalwood shafts are substantially longer than those in the long irons. This is significant in terms of the relationship between clubface loft and clubhead speed needed at impact in order to send the ball out on an optimum trajectory, as we talked about with the driver. Although fairway woods/long irons have greater loft than the driver, significant clubhead speed is still necessary to get the ball airborne with clubs in the 15–24-degree-loft range—particularly since these clubs are usually hit off the ground as opposed to hitting the ball off a tee with the driver. At any rate, you'll see in looking through the table in this chapter that most of today's fairway metalwoods (men's models) are between 41 and 43 inches in length. Meanwhile, even though all clubs are getting longer in general, men's 2-, 3-, and 4-irons are usually between 38 and 40 inches in length (more on iron length in Chapter 5).

The point is that the fairway metalwoods are, on average, *about 3 inches longer than corresponding irons with the same loft*. Because of the longer shaft, you will generate more clubhead speed with the fairway metalwood, and that additional speed also contributes to your ability to get the ball airborne more easily.

The third reason the metalwoods are easier to hit than the long irons is one that we'll get into in more detail in the next chapter. While club manufacturers have created many iron head designs that do in fact make it easier to get the long irons airborne, this has been more than offset by the fact that *most companies have lowered the loft on their long irons.* Virtually all irons numbered 1 through 4 actually have *less* loft than the standard lofts that were listed on page 85. And keep in mind, the lofts listed there are lower still than what club designer Ralph Maltby refers to as "traditional" iron lofts of twenty or more years ago.

The final reason fairway woods are easier to hit is mostly psychological. As Young points out, the larger, more substantial look of a fairway wood clubhead, in itself, will increase most amateurs' confidence. While iron manufacturers have made substantial efforts to modify long iron designs to make them more user-friendly, still, most golfers feel more secure with a fairway wood in hand. And, anytime you have more confidence in any shot, your chances of executing it well will increase.

Golfsmith Posi-Trac

Is a Fairway Driver for You?

Several companies, such as Top Flite, Taylor Made, Mizuno, and Kunnan, offer clubs known as fairway drivers, which do double duty as drivers from the tee and as long-hitting clubs from the fairway. Fairway drivers generally have about 13 degrees of loft—more than on the average driver but less than the average 3-wood.

Should a fairway driver be part of your arsenal, either in addition to a lower-lofted driver or perhaps as your longest club? You might benefit from one if either of the following conditions apply.

If you generate medium to low clubhead speed with the driver (85 mph or less), you should have ample loft on your driver to begin with. Thus the fairway driver *as your regular tee-shot club* will help you off the tee. Just be sure that if you opt for a 13-degree fairway driver, you also adjust your next-most-lofted fairway wood. There would be little need for you to also carry a 15- or 16-degree 3-wood. A 4- or 5-wood with loft in the 17–19-degree range would be your logical "next" fairway wood.

If you're a strong but somewhat erratic driver, you might do well to own a fairway driver in addition to a lower-lofted regular driver (say in the 9-degree range). You'll get double duty from the fairway driver in that you'll be able to effectively hit the club from good fairway lies, and you can tee off with the fairway driver on holes that require a fairly accurate tee shot as well as respectable distance. By learning to use the "big stick" only on the longest, most open holes, you will score better.

If, however, you are among the majority of amateurs who obtain the best combination of length and accuracy with a driver in the 10.0–11.5-degree range of loft, a fairway driver should not be necessary.

Some Oddities Regarding Fairway Wood Numbering

Add up all these factors, and for the vast majority of golfers, lofted metalwoods are a boon to all but perhaps the strongest, lowest-handicap amateur golfers. On average, a lofted fairway wood will give the player a loftier flight, greater total carry, and more stopping power when the ball hits the green than will an equally lofted long iron.

More and more golfers are realizing this fact and moving toward a set that adds one or possibly two fairway metalwoods to the bag, while removing one or two long irons. Generally, women players are less hesitant to do this than male amateurs. But no golfer should place a stigma upon himself or herself for deciding to add a lofted fairway wood. Some of the very best Tour pros, such as Ray Floyd, have made the 5-wood a permanent part of their arsenals, and

Titleist Women's DCI
Starship Fairway Woods

with very beneficial results. Mark Young points out, "It's a rare trend when improvement shown by the average golfer, as has happened with the addition of more fairway woods, has influenced the *professionals* to alter their sets in that direction, rather than vice versa."

With the number of fairway woods available, there probably is no longer a need to draw a distinction between "regular" fairway woods and "utility" woods. Until recently, a "utility" wood was a club that was considered something beyond the normal range of fairway woods, which in years past usually stopped at the number 5-wood. Utility woods, such as the Stan Thompson Ginty or the Cobra Baffler, were highly lofted, very small-headed, low-center-of-gravity models that were designed to extract the ball from virtually any lie.

Goldwin 6-Shooter
Goldwin
Magnificent 7

However, if you look at the table in this chapter, you'll note that almost all major manufacturers now offer lofted fairway woods up to a 7-wood; a fair number of companies have 9-woods available; and a few, such as Callaway, even offer an 11-wood. For most companies, then, there really is no set point at which to differentiate between a fairway wood and a utility wood.

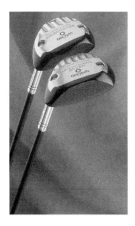

In a sense, manufacturers may have confused the issue for consumers with regard to fairway woods. Looking through the table, you'll notice that the vast majority of manufacturers offer their metalwoods in odd numbers only: 3, 5, 7, 9. A few, such as Daiwa, offer a 4-wood, while Goldwin Golf offers a 6-wood (known as the Six Shooter) in its AVDP line. A minority of companies give their metalwoods specific names rather than numbers. For most, though, it's odd numbers only. This means that if you have been carrying a 1-3-5 met-

---

Hit the 3-Wood Downwind

Most amateurs who carry a 3-wood don't use it as often as they should. You'd benefit from taking a page out of the book of the PGA Tour pros on using this club. Watch closely when you attend an event or when watching TV, and you'll notice that the Tour players will hit a 3-wood rather than a driver a surprising percentage of the time. This tends to go unnoticed because even with a 3-wood, the Tour pros still hit it plenty long.

You, too, should take advantage of the opportunity to use your 3-wood off the tee when the conditions warrant it. Most often, you should take advantage of the opportunity to tee off with a 3-wood *when the wind is at your back*.

As we've already seen, anytime you use a club with greater loft, you will put more backspin on the ball, which means any amount of hook or slice will be reduced. So, your odds of hitting the fairway with the 3-wood are always better. What many amateurs don't realize, in addition, is that with a respectable tailwind, *you'll hit your 3-wood just as far as or farther than your driver anyway*. Any tailwind will reduce the amount of backspin on the ball and thus tend to "knock the shot down." Thus a tee shot with, say, a 10-degree driver may not get high enough in the air to benefit from the tailwind. A shot hit with a 3-wood that has about 15 degrees of loft will get up in the air and ride the wind's benefit—to at least where your normal driver shot would land.

---

alwood configuration in the past, you would need to jump to a 7-wood to add one fairway wood, and to a 9-wood if you wished to add two.

However, you should note that although there is a number gap from one club to the next, in most cases *the basic specifications between the 5-wood and the 7-wood or the 7-wood and the 9-wood are not that much different*. A good example is Daiwa's Hi-Trac MF 110 model. The men's 5-, 7-, and 9-woods are only 2 degrees apart in lofts (19, 21, and 23 degrees, respectively); and these three clubs *are all the same length* (41.5 inches). The lofts just mentioned, incidentally, show the differentiation between "standard" lofts for fairway woods shown earlier in this chapter and the actual lofts on many current models. Most of these high-numbered fairway woods do not have as much loft as you might expect, given the fact that they are numbered two clubs apart.

Why have companies gone to numbering the fairway woods two numbers rather than one number apart? There's no good explanation, at least that I can see. Perhaps some golfers would feel better about buying a metalwood with, say, 19 degrees of loft if it were called a 4-wood rather than a 5-wood; or a

26-degree-lofted club if it were called a 7-wood rather than a 9-wood. However, don't be put off by this; if the club fits, play it!

Where Lofted Fairway Woods Help the Most

In general, if you do not generate a great deal of clubhead speed, you'll benefit most from an additional lofted fairway wood. Additional fairway woods will also prove a tremendous benefit if you play a course that has a substantial amount of rough, from which you must play a fair number of medium-long approach shots. It's a tough deal, even for PGA Tour pros, to hit effective long irons from anything more than light rough. These clubs must be swung through rough at very high speeds, or else the longer grass will wrap around the club's hosel through the impact zone. This will both slow down and close

Kunnan IGS 2000M 3-Wood

Use "Alternate" Fairway Woods Depending on Conditions

If you have bought into the idea of using a larger number of fairway woods, it might be wise to alternate what you carry in your bag depending on the course and the conditions you're playing.

Assume in addition to your driver you own a 3-wood, 5-wood, and 7-wood (and you have a total of more than fourteen clubs altogether, so you can't just leave everything in). If you are playing in wet conditions after a heavy rain, you'll want to hit your long shots high and soft, since you won't get any roll on your shots. Also keep in mind that when it's wet, water gets between clubface and ball at impact and tends to reduce the amount of backspin; therefore, shots fly a little lower than in dry conditions. In a case like this, you might want to leave out your 3-wood, which would be difficult to control and to get sufficient carry with off the wet grass. This suggestion is even more appropriate if your course is a hilly one, where odd lies make shots with the 3-wood even more problematic.

Conversely, you might be playing on a relatively flat course, in very dry midsummer conditions but on a windy day. Here you might decide that your 7-wood is not of as much use because you'd like to hit the ball a little more "under" the wind on your approach shots. You'll probably be more accurate by choking up slightly on your 5-wood and playing a controlled, three-quarter shot (which will keep the ball lower than even your regular 5-wood shot) in instances where you're a 7-wood distance from your target.

Should You Add to Your Fairway Wood Arsenal?

Let's say you currently play with three metalwoods in your set, none of them with a loft greater than 19 degrees (by today's standards, either a 4- or a 5-wood). You should seriously consider adding one or two lofted fairway woods (say a 7- or a 7- and a 9-wood) if you answer yes to most of the following statements about your own game and the course you most often play.

Your swing:
- Your swing speed with a driver is 85 mph or less.
- You cannot carry the ball in the air with a 3-iron more than 160 yards from a good fairway lie.
- You have trouble hitting a 3-iron from the fairway onto a green, and making the ball hold the green.
- You must use at least a 6-iron loft in order to confidently hit a shot from medium rough.

Your course:
- Has rough that would be considered "medium" to "difficult" to contend with.
- Is relatively hilly so that you must hit lofted shots from some awkward lies.
- Has relatively firm and/or smallish greens that are difficult to hold.
- Is long enough so that you frequently play shots of between 160 and 200 yards on par-3s and par-4s.

---

the clubface through impact; a smothered shot that remains in the rough is the most common result.

The design of a lofted metalwood, by comparison, helps flatten out the taller grass through impact—the grass doesn't grab the hosel nearly as much, and the shot can be struck with greater clubhead speed and with the face remaining on target.

These conditions favoring lofted woods from rough are all the greater when conditions are wet and heavy.

"Trade-offs" with the Fairway Woods

When you trade in your 2- and 3-irons for, say, a 5-wood and a 7-wood, you do concede a few things. For one, long irons can be quite useful if you are playing in windy conditions and on a relatively open golf course where you can run the ball onto the greens. It's helpful to be able to hit the ball low so that the wind doesn't blow it off line as much as it might a lofted wood. Many golfers find that they are more accurate with long irons on par-3s, where they also have the advantage of hitting the ball off a tee, or off the tee on short par-4s that require accurate shot placement.

Generally, though, these advantages are going to prove more important only to players who hit the ball hard enough with long irons to consistently obtain a nice trajectory, so that shots can hold most greens; and who get substantial distance from their long irons, for example 200 yards or more from a 2-iron. These are capabilities that probably no more than 10 to 20 percent of the golfing population possess.

Callaway Great Big Bertha 3-Wood

What to Watch for Regarding Fairway Wood Designs

If you are in the market for some new or additional fairway woods, there are several things you should be aware of regarding the clubhead design (in addition to finding the right shaft characteristics, of course). While the aesthetics of one clubhead design over another are very much an individual choice, there are a couple of important points to keep in mind. Golfsmith's Tom Wishon warns, "What with all the oversize drivers taking precedence in the marketplace, you want to make sure that you don't get fairway woods that are too deep-faced, that is, too tall from the top to the bottom of the clubface. It's not a problem for most golfers if they have an oversize, deep-faced driver, because the ball is teed up, and you can adjust the height that you tee it. But you'll most often be hitting the fairway woods off the grass. Make sure that you don't get a 'companion' fairway wood to an oversize driver in which the center of gravity makes it hard for you to get the ball airborne." This advice is especially pertinent if you happen to have a relatively slow swing speed, say 80 mph or less with the driver. Slow swing-speed players would be well advised to look for fairway woods that, if anything, are a little more shallow-faced than the fairly strong player might require.

On the other hand, Mark Young points out that the player who is a talented shotmaker will benefit if his or her fairway woods are a little more on the deep-faced side. "While the shallow-faced fairway wood is easier to get the ball up with, a little deeper face is better for the golfer who can 'shape' his or her shots, hitting the ball either low or high, right to left or left to right, because the player can deliver more clubface to the ball in the manner needed for the particular shot," he says.

*MacGregor VIP Titanium
7-Wood*

Meanwhile, you may be among the legions of golfers who, rather than being "shotmakers," can depend on one specific shot shape to show up consistently: a slice. If so, you might want to consider some of the newer "offset" fairway wood designs. These offset fairway woods, such as the King Cobra Offset and the Titleist Know Right, place the clubhead farther behind the centerline of the clubshaft. This, as we mentioned earlier, moves the center of gravity of the clubhead farther back and results in the tendency for the clubface to move through impact both with greater loft and in a more closed position. Such clubs may not totally eliminate your slice, but they very likely will reduce it.

Another point regarding clubhead shape or size is that, unlike with the driver, for most golfers a really big clubhead in terms of overall volume in cubic

Titleist Know Right Fairway Woods

centimeters is *not* likely to help your shotmaking. You'll be hitting fairway woods off a tee at times, to be sure; but more often, you'll be playing them from a variety of different lies. This will include many uneven or sidehill lies, where an extra-large head might prove cumbersome in terms of making nice clean contact. Many manufacturers have designed the soles of the fairway woods to be quite a bit more rounded than might have been true in the past, to prevent the sole from catching when playing from hilly lies or from the rough in general. Most amateurs will benefit from a relatively rounded as opposed to a flat sole on the fairway woods.

The tendency of oversize fairway woods to hinder shotmaking to some degree raises a serious question regarding the value of titanium as a clubhead material in the fairway woods. We know that titanium is a beneficial material in creating oversize drivers; we also know that titanium does not inherently make a golf ball go farther. Why, then, should you spend a great deal of extra money on two, three, or four titanium-headed fairway woods? Unless for some reason you've decided you prefer a larger-headed fairway wood and find more of them among the offerings that are available in titanium, the recommendation here is that you not spend extra money on something that won't inherently help you. Go buy yourself a few dozen extra golf balls or a lesson instead.

FAIRWAY/UTILITY WOOD PRODUCT INFORMATION

MANUFACTURER	MODEL AND NUMBERS	CLUBHEAD MATERIAL	CLUBHEAD SIZE	NUMBERS	LENGTHS (*in.*)
Adams Golf	Air Assault (3, 5, 7)	17-4 ss	Midsize	3	42.5 s, 43 g
				5	42 s, 42.5 g
				7	41 s, 42 g
	Tight Lies (4)	17-4 ss	Midsize w/ shallow face	N/A	42.5 s, 42.75 g
	Comments: Patented design lowers center of gravity for higher flight.				
Tommy Armour	855s Hot Scot (3, 5, 7)	Steel	Oversize	3	42.5 s, 43 g
				5	42.5 s, 43 g
				7	41 s, 42 g
	855s Golden Scot (3, 5, 7)	Steel	Oversize	3	43
				5	42
				7	41.5
	855 s Diamond Scot (3, 5, 7)	Steel	Oversize	3	42
				5	41.5
				7	41
	Tommy Gun (3, 5)	Titanium	Oversize	3	44
				5	43
Black Ice Golf	Tour Balanced (3, 5, 7)	17-4 ss, ceramic face	Midsize	3	Custom lengths
				5	
				7	
Bridgestone	Precept Tour (3, 5)	ss	Oversize	3	43
				5	42

Legend:
g=graphite
s=steel
ss=stainless steel
L=Ladies' shaft flex rating
A=Seniors' shaft flex ratings

R=Men's Regular shaft flex ratings
F=Firm
S=Men's Stiff shaft flex rating
X=Men's Extra Stiff shaft flex rating

Lofts (deg.)	Shaft Materials and Flexes	Grip Style	Left-Handed	Women's	Suggested Retail
13	Steel, filament-wound graphite, compression molded graphite L, R, F, S (all models)	All Golf Pride and Royal styles available	N	Y	$142 steel $239 graphite
19.5					
24					
16			Y	Y	$142 steel $239 graphite
14, 16	Tour Step II steel R, S, X; G-Force 2 Tour sheet-wrapped graphite R, S, X	Golf Pride Tour Wrap	Y	N	$265
19					
23					
16	G-Force 2 Tour sheet-wrapped graphite, one flex	Golf Pride Tour Wrap	N	N	$265
19					
23					
16	G-Force 2 Tour graphite R, S	Diamond Perf Wrap	N	Y	$265
19					
23					
13	Grafalloy Pro-Lite R, S	Golf Pride Tour Wrap	N	N	$399
15					
14	Steel R, S; graphite L, A, R, F, S, X	Golf Pride Tour Wrap	3-wood only	Y	$130 steel $215–$250 graphite
19					
24					
14	FM Precision steel R, S; high-modulus graphite R, S	Royal Tour Wrap	N	N	$145 steel $210 graphite
20					

continued

FAIRWAY/UTILITY WOOD PRODUCT INFORMATION *(continued)*

MANUFACTURER	MODEL AND NUMBERS	CLUBHEAD MATERIAL	CLUBHEAD SIZE	NUMBERS	LENGTHS *(in.)*
Bullet Golf	Invincible (3, 5, 7)	ATS titanium alloy	Oversize	3	43
				5	42
				7	Not supplied
	444 (3, 5, 7)	ss	Oversize	3	43
				5	42
				7	42
	Tour (3, 5, 7)	ss	Oversize	3	43
				5	42
				7	42
	444 T (3, 5, 7)	ss, titanium face	Oversize	3	43
				5	42
				7	42

Legend: g=graphite   R=Men's Regular shaft flex ratings
              s=steel   F=Firm
              ss=stainless steel   S=Men's Stiff shaft flex rating
              L=Ladies' shaft flex rating   X=Men's Extra Stiff shaft flex rating
              A=Seniors' shaft flex ratings

Lofts (deg.)	Shaft Materials and Flexes	Grip Style	Left-Handed	Women's	Suggested Retail
16	Ceramic Kevlar, Grafalloy Speed Flex graphite (flexes not supplied)	Golf Pride Tour Wrap, Bullet Double Diamond (women)	N	Y	$170 ceramic Kevlar $220 graphite
21					
Not supplied					
15	Ceramic Kevlar, Grafalloy Speed Flex graphite, steel		Y	Y	$95 steel $120 ceramic Kevlar $150 graphite
21					
25					
15	Ceramic Kevlar, Grafalloy Speed Flex graphite, steel		N	Y	$80 steel $100 ceramic Kevlar
21					
25					
15	Not supplied		N	N	Not supplied
21					
25					

continued

FAIRWAY/UTILITY WOOD PRODUCT INFORMATION *(continued)*

MANUFACTURER	MODEL AND NUMBERS	CLUBHEAD MATERIAL	CLUBHEAD SIZE	NUMBERS	LENGTHS *(in.)*
Callaway Golf	Great Big Bertha (3, 4, 5, 7)	Ruger titanium	Oversize	3	43.5m, 42.5w
				4	43m, 42w
				5	42.5m, 41.5w
				7	42m, 43w
	Big Bertha War Bird (2, strong 3, 4, 5, 7, 9, 11)	17-4 ss	Midsize	2	43.5m, 42.5w
				strong 3	43m, 42w
				3	43m, 42w
				4	42.5m, 41.5w
				5	42m, 41w
				7	41.5m, 40.5w
				9	41m, 40w
				11	41m, 40w

Legend:	g=graphite	R=Men's Regular shaft flex ratings
	s=steel	F=Firm
	ss=stainless steel	S=Men's Stiff shaft flex rating
	L=Ladies' shaft flex rating	X=Men's Extra Stiff shaft flex rating
	A=Seniors' shaft flex ratings	

Lofts (deg.)	Shaft Materials and Flexes	Grip Style	Left-Handed	Women's	Suggested Retail
14.5	BBUL graphite L, A, R, F, S; Memphis 10 lightweight steel (single flex)	Proprietary All-Weather	Y	Y (Ladies' Gems)	$500
13.25					
16					
18.5					
13.5	RCH 96 graphite L, A, R, F, S; True Temper Memphis 10 steel (single flex); Sandvik Titanium R, S	Proprietary All-Weather	Y	Y (Ladies' Gems)	$185 steel $285 graphite
13.5					
15					
16.5					
18					
20					
24					
27					

continued

FAIRWAY/UTILITY WOOD PRODUCT INFORMATION (continued)

MANUFACTURER	MODEL AND NUMBERS	CLUBHEAD MATERIAL	CLUBHEAD SIZE	NUMBERS	LENGTHS (in.)
Cobra Golf	King Cobra Ti Titanium (3, 5, 7)	100% 6-4 titanium	Oversize	3	43
				5	42.5
				7	42
	King Cobra Offset and Standard (3, 5, 7, 9)	17-4 ss	Midsize	3	43
				5	42.5
				7	42
				9	41.5
	Senior King Cobra (3, 5, 7, 9)	17-4 ss	Midsize	3	43
				5	42.5
				7	42
				9	41.5
	Tour King Cobra (3,5,7)	17-4 ss	Midsize	3	42.5
				5	41.5
				7	41
	Lady Cobra (3, 5, 7, 9)	17-4 ss	Standard	3	42
				5	41
				7	40.5
				9	40

Legend: g=graphite
s=steel
ss=stainless steel
L=Ladies' shaft flex rating
A=Seniors' shaft flex ratings

R=Men's Regular shaft flex ratings
F=Firm
S=Men's Stiff shaft flex rating
X=Men's Extra Stiff shaft flex rating

Lofts (deg.)		Shaft Materials and Flexes	Grip Style	Left-Handed	Women's	Suggested Retail
15, 16		Lightweight graphite A, R, S, X	Rubber Tour Wrap	Y	Y	$367
18, 19						
23						
14		Graphite, steel A, R, S, X	Rubber Tour Wrap	Y	N	$159 steel $267 graphite
18						
22						
25						
16		Graphite, steel A	Rubber Senior Tour Wrap	Y	N	$159 steel $242 graphite
20						
24						
28						
14		Tourweight graphite, steel, titanium R, S, X	Tour Full Cord or Rubber Tour Wrap	Y	N	$167 steel $292 titanium $309 Tour graphite
18						
22						
16		Ladies' graphite, lightweight steel	Ladies Rubber Tour Wrap	Y	Y	$149 steel $217 graphite
20						
24						
28						

continued

FAIRWAY/UTILITY WOOD PRODUCT INFORMATION (continued)

MANUFACTURER	MODEL AND NUMBERS	CLUBHEAD MATERIAL	CLUBHEAD SIZE	NUMBERS	LENGTHS (in.)
Confidence Golf	Zoom Hydro Wing (3, 5, 7)	17-4 ss	Oversize	3	42 s, 43 g
				5	41 s, 42 g
				7	40.5 s, 42.5 g
	Visa (3, 5, 7)	17-4 ss	Oversize	3	42 s, 43 g
				5	41 s, 42 g
				7	40.5 s, 41.5 g
Daiwa	Hi-Trac MF-110 (spoon, 3, 4, 5, 7, 9)	SVS 630 ss	Midsize	Spoon	42.5
				3	42.5
				4	42
				5	41.5
				7	41.5
				9	41.5
	Ballistic (3, 4, 5, 7)	A356 alloy	Midsize	3	42.5
				4	42
				5	41.5
				7	41.5
	Strike Force (metalwoods not specifically numbered)	17-4 ss	Standard	N/A	42.5
				N/A	41.5
				N/A	41.5
				N/A	41.5

Comments: Hi-Trac MF 110 features railed soles; Ballistic features removable sole weight.

Legend:	g=graphite	R=Men's Regular shaft flex ratings
	s=steel	F=Firm
	ss=stainless steel	S=Men's Stiff shaft flex rating
	L=Ladies' shaft flex rating	X=Men's Extra Stiff shaft flex rating
	A=Seniors' shaft flex ratings	

Lofts (deg.)		Shaft Materials and Flexes	Grip Style	Left-Handed	Women's	Suggested Retail
	15	Dynalite steel L, R; Micro Tuned Lite graphite L, R, S; Confidence Lite steel L; Confidence Lite graphite L, R, S	Soft Wrap (men), Golf Pride Victory (women)	Y	Y	$180 steel $310 graphite
	20					
	26					
	16			N	Y	$140 steel $190 graphite
	21					
	26					
	13	Graphite L, A, R, S	Golf Pride Perf Wrap	Y	Y	$190
	15					
	17					
	19					
	21					
	23					
	15	Graphite L, A, R, S	Golf Pride Perf Wrap	N	Y	$265
	17					
	19					
	21					
	15	Graphite L, R, S	Golf Pride Victory	N	Y	$150
	19					
	23					
	26					

continued

FAIRWAY/UTILITY WOOD PRODUCT INFORMATION *(continued)*

MANUFACTURER	MODEL AND NUMBERS	CLUBHEAD MATERIAL	CLUBHEAD SIZE	NUMBERS	LENGTHS *(in.)*
Dunlop	Tour DG	17–4 ss	Oversize	3	N/A
				5	N/A
				7	N/A
	RMS	17–4 ss	Oversize	Fairway Driver	
				3	N/A
				5	N/A
				7	N/A
	DDH Tour	17–4 ss	Oversize	3	N/A
				5	N/A
				7	N/A
Dynacraft	Copperhead Machete	17-4 ss	Midsize	Machete	41.5
	BFC Rail Series	17-4 ss	Oversize	N/A	42
				N/A	41.5
				N/A	41.5
				N/A	41
	Fairway Driver	17-4 ss	Midsize	F. Driver	43

Legend:	g=graphite	R=Men's Regular shaft flex ratings
	s=steel	F=Firm
	ss=stainless steel	S=Men's Stiff shaft flex rating
	L=Ladies' shaft flex rating	X=Men's Extra Stiff shaft flex rating
	A=Seniors' shaft flex ratings	

Lofts (deg.)	Shaft Materials and Flexes	Grip Style	Left-Handed	Women's	Suggested Retail
N/A	Tour EI graphite, Steel R, S	Golf Pride Tour Velvet Wrap	N	N	$225 steel, $330 graphite for set of 3 woods
N/A					
N/A					
13	Tour EI graphite, Steel R, S	Golf Pride Tour Velvet Wrap	N	Y	$225 steel, $315 graphite for set of 3 woods
N/A					
N/A					
N/A					
N/A	Tour EI graphite, Steel R, S	Dunlop Perma Wrap	Y	Y	$141 steel, $207 graphite for set of 3 woods
N/A					
N/A					
23.5	True Temper Dynamic Gold steel R, S, X; Aldila Low Torque graphite L, A, R, S, X	Golf Pride Tour Velvet (all models)	Y	N	$75 steel $100 graphite
13			Y	N	$75 steel $100 graphite
18					
23.5					
26					
13			Y	N	$70 steel $95 graphite

continued

FAIRWAY/UTILITY WOOD PRODUCT INFORMATION (continued)

MANUFACTURER	MODEL AND NUMBERS	CLUBHEAD MATERIAL	CLUBHEAD SIZE	NUMBERS	LENGTHS (in.)
Goldwin Golf	AVDP Tour Milled (3, 4, 5, 6, 7)	7075-T6 heat-treated aluminum	Midsize	3	43
				4	42.5
				5	42
				6	42
				7	42
	AVDP Senior (3, 4, 5, 6, 7)	7075-T6 heat-treated aluminum	Midsize	3	43
				4	42.5
				5	42
				6	42
				7	42
	AVDP Ladies (3, 4, 5, 6, 7)	7075-T6 heat-treated aluminum	Midsize	3	42
				4	41.5
				5	41
				6	41
				7	41

Comments: One of the most stylish designs on the market.

Legend:	g=graphite	R=Men's Regular shaft flex ratings
	s=steel	F=Firm
	ss=stainless steel	S=Men's Stiff shaft flex rating
	L=Ladies' shaft flex rating	X=Men's Extra Stiff shaft flex rating
	A=Seniors' shaft flex ratings	

Lofts (deg.)	Shaft Materials and Flexes	Grip Style	Left-Handed	Women's	Suggested Retail
13, 15	Goldwin/Unifiber AVDP high-modulus graphite, steel R, F, S, X	Winn Lightweight Wrap Grip	N	N	$195 steel $295 graphic
17					
20					
22					
24					
13, 15	Goldwin/Unifiber high-modulus graphite A	Winn Lightweight Wrap Grip	N	N	$295
17					
20					
22					
24					
13, 15	Goldwin/Unifiber high-modulus graphite L	Winn Lightweight Wrap Grip	N	Y	$275
17					
20					
22					
24					

Revolutionary lightweight grip weighs 7 grams.

continued

FAIRWAY/UTILITY WOOD PRODUCT INFORMATION (continued)

MANUFACTURER	MODEL AND NUMBERS	CLUBHEAD MATERIAL	CLUBHEAD SIZE	NUMBERS	LENGTHS (in.)
Golfsmith	Harvey Penick Weed Cutter	17-4 ss	Standard	N/A	41.5m, 40.5w
	Posi-Trac	17-4 ss	Midsize	3	42 s, 42.5 g
				5	41 s, 41.5 g
				7	40 s, 40.5 g
	Tri-Rail Speed Sole	17-4 ss	Midsize	3	43
				5	42
				7	41
The Golfworks	Fairway Devil	17-4 ss	Oversize	F. Devil	42.5
	Dare Devil	17-4 ss	Oversize	Dare Devil	40.5
	Out-a-Sight Break Out	17-4 ss	Oversize	Out-a-Sight	41.5

Legend:	g=graphite	R=Men's Regular shaft flex ratings	
	s=steel	F=Firm	
	ss=stainless steel	S=Men's Stiff shaft flex rating	
	L=Ladies' shaft flex rating	X=Men's Extra Stiff shaft flex rating	
	A=Seniors' shaft flex ratings		

	Lofts (deg.)	Shaft Materials and Flexes	Grip Style	Left-Handed	Women's	Suggested Retail
	20	Steel, graphite L, A, R, S, X	Penick Wrap	N	Y	$100 steel $145 graphite
	20	Lightweight steel, Carbon Stick graphite L, A, R, S	Golfsmith Rubber Wrap Style	N	Y	$75 steel $105 graphite
	20					
	20					
	15	Steel, graphite L, A, R, S, X	Golfsmith Rubber Wrap Style	N	Y	$92 steel $125 graphite
	19					
	22					
	13	Steel L, A, R, S, X; graphite L, A, R, S, X	Rubber Wrap Style	N	N	$45 steel, $64 graphite for all men's;
	22			N	N	$54 steel, $71 graphite for all
	25			Y	Y	women's

continued

FAIRWAY/UTILITY WOOD PRODUCT INFORMATION *(continued)*

MANUFACTURER	MODEL AND NUMBERS	CLUBHEAD MATERIAL	CLUBHEAD SIZE	NUMBERS	LENGTHS (*in.*)
Ben Hogan	Edge GCD (strong 3, 3, 5, 7, 9)	Not supplied	Midsize	strong 3	42.75 s, 42.25 g
				3	42.25 s, 42.75 g
				5	41.25 s, 41.75 g
				7	40.75 s, 41.25 g
				9	40.25 s, 40.75 g
	Apex (3, 4, 5)	Persimmon	Standard	3	42.25 s, 42.75 g
				4	41.75 s, 42.25 g
				5	41.25 s, 41.75 g
	Comments: Hogan shafts use 1–5 numerical flex rating system				
Javelin Blue	Javelin Blue (3, 5, 7)	ss	Midsize	3	42.5
				5	41.5
				7	41
	Javelin Blue Titanium (3, 5, 7)	Titanium	Oversize	3	42.5
				5	41.5
				7	41

Legend: g=graphite
s=steel
ss=stainless steel
L=Ladies' shaft flex rating
A=Seniors' shaft flex ratings

R=Men's Regular shaft flex ratings
F=Firm
S=Men's Stiff shaft flex rating
X=Men's Extra Stiff shaft flex rating

Lofts (deg.)	Shaft Materials and Flexes	Grip Style	Left-Handed	Women's	Suggested Retail
14.5	Apex steel L, A, R, S, X	Apex V-Trac Cord	N	Y	$150 steel $250 graphite
16					
20					
23					
26					
15	Apex graphite L, A, R, S, X	Apex V-Trac Cord	N	Y	$185 steel $300 graphite
18					
21					

(corresponds to L, A, R, S, X flexes as shown).

Lofts (deg.)	Shaft Materials and Flexes	Grip Style	Left-Handed	Women's	Suggested Retail
14.5	Graphite available in 9 flexes, JW1 through JW9	Tour Wrap, Tour Cord, Ladies Tour Wrap	N	Y	$300
19.5					
24.5					
14.5			N	Y	$395
19.5					
24.5					

continued

FAIRWAY/UTILITY WOOD PRODUCT INFORMATION *(continued)*

MANUFACTURER	MODEL AND NUMBERS	CLUBHEAD MATERIAL	CLUBHEAD SIZE	NUMBERS	LENGTHS *(in.)*
Kunnan	EXT (Fairway Driver, 3, 5, 7)	Metal composite	Mid-oversize	F. Driver	43
				3	43
				5	42
				7	41
	IGS (3, 5, 7)	Metal composite	Oversize and Midsize	3	43
				5	42
				7	41
Comments: Clubheads are stainless steel encased in graphite.					
Lynx	Black Cat Titanium (3, 5, 7)	Titanium	Oversize	3	44, 44.5
				5	43
				7	42.5
	Black Cat (3, 5, 7)	17-4 ss	Midsize	3	43 s, 43.5 g
				5	41.5 s, 42 g
				7	41 s, 41.5 g
	Tigress (3, 5, 7)	17-4 ss	Midsize	3	41
				5	40
				7	39.5
MacGregor	VIP Titanium (3, 5, 7)	Titanium 6V 4AL	Midsize	3	43
				5	42
				7	41

Legend:	g=graphite		R=Men's Regular shaft flex ratings
	s=steel		F=Firm
	ss=stainless steel		S=Men's Stiff shaft flex rating
	L=Ladies' shaft flex rating		X=Men's Extra Stiff shaft flex rating
	A=Seniors' shaft flex ratings		

Lofts (deg.)		Shaft Materials and Flexes	Grip Style	Left-Handed	Women's	Suggested Retail
	13	Micro Tip diameter graphite L, A, R, S	Tour Wrap	N	Y	$250
	14					
	18					
	22					
	14.5	Autocure graphite L, R, S, X	Tour Wrap	N	Y	$350
	18.5					
	21.5					
	13, 15	Flare 650 Lite graphite A, R, S, X	Golf Pride Standard Wrap	N	N	$435
	18					
	22					
	13, 15	Flare graphite A, R, S, X; Dynamic Flare steel R, S, X; Lynx Lite Flare steel R, S	Golf Pride Standard Wrap	Y	N	$185 steel $265 graphite
	18					
	22					
	16	Lynx Powertune graphite L	Golf Pride Victory	N	Y	$158
	21					
	26					
	15	Exel Flex Profile graphite L, A, R, S, X	Golf Pride Tour Wrap Cord, Tour Wrap (women)	N	Y	$310
	20					
	25					

continued

FAIRWAY/UTILITY WOOD PRODUCT INFORMATION *(continued)*

MANUFACTURER	MODEL AND NUMBERS	CLUBHEAD MATERIAL	CLUBHEAD SIZE	NUMBERS	LENGTHS *(in.)*
Maruman Golf	Power Titan (3, 4, 5)	Beta and 6-4 titanium	Midsize	3	42.5
				4	42
				5	41.5
	M301T (3, 5)	Titanium	Midsize	3	42.5
				5	41.5
	Verity G (3, 5, 7)	17-4 ss	Midsize	3	42.5
				5	41.5
				7	41
Maxfli Golf	VHL Oversize (3, 5, 7)	17-4 ss	Oversize	3	43 s, 42.5 g
				5	42 s, 41.5 g
				7	41.5 s, 41 g

Legend: g=graphite
s=steel
ss=stainless steel
L=Ladies' shaft flex rating
A=Seniors' shaft flex ratings

R=Men's Regular shaft flex ratings
F=Firm
S=Men's Stiff shaft flex rating
X=Men's Extra Stiff shaft flex rating

Lofts (deg.)	Shaft Materials and Flexes	Grip Style	Left-Handed	Women's	Suggested Retail
16	Carbofit graphite R, S	Cord Tour Wrap	N	N	$990
19					
22					
17	Carbofit graphite R, S	Proprietary by Maruman	N	Y	$595 men's $550 women's
23					
17	Carbofit graphite R, S; Parsec high-elastic graphite/Kevlar R, S	Proprietary by Maruman	Y	Y	$325 Kevlar $195 graphite $175 women's
23					
25					
15	True Temper steel or graphite L, A, R, S	Golf Pride Tour Velvet	Y	Y	$158 steel $241 graphite
20					$215 women's/ seniors' graphite
23					

continued

FAIRWAY/UTILITY WOOD PRODUCT INFORMATION *(continued)*

MANUFACTURER	MODEL AND NUMBERS	CLUBHEAD MATERIAL	CLUBHEAD SIZE	NUMBERS	LENGTHS (*in.*)
Merit Golf	Tour International (3, 4, 5)	Persimmon	Standard	3	42.5
				4	42
				5	41.5
	Fusion (3, 5, 7)	17-4 ss	Midsize	3	43
				5	42
				7	42
	Prophecy (3, 5, 7)	17-4 ss	Midsize	3	43
				5	42
				7	42
Mizuno USA	T-Zoid (Strong 3, 3, 5, 7)	17-4 ss	Oversize	strong 3	43 s, 44 g
				3	42.5 s, 43.5 g
				5	42 s, 43 g
				7	41.5 s, 42.5 g
	TC Mid Plus (3, 5, 7)	17-4 ss	Midsize	3	42.5
				5	41.5
				7	41.25

Legend:	g=graphite	R=Men's Regular shaft flex ratings
	s=steel	F=Firm
	ss=stainless steel	S=Men's Stiff shaft flex rating
	L=Ladies' shaft flex rating	X=Men's Extra Stiff shaft flex rating
	A=Seniors' shaft flex ratings	

Lofts (deg.)	Shaft Materials and Flexes	Grip Style	Left-Handed	Women's	Suggested Retail
15 18.5 21	True Temper Dynamic Gold steel R300, S300	Golf Pride Tour Wrap, All Cord	N	N	$200
15 19 25	True Temper Dynamic Gold, Dynalite Gold steel, Adila graphite A, R, S	Golf Pride Tour Velvet	N	N	$130 steel $170 graphite
16 21 27	True Temper Dynalite, Aldila graphite L, A, R, S	Golf Pride Tour Wrap	Y	Y	$94 steel $128 graphite
13 15 18 21	TurboGold graphite L, A, R, S, X; True Temper Dynamic Gold or Dynalite steel R, S	Royal Sand Wrap	N	N	$200 steel $300 graphite
16 21 26	Exsar graphite L, A, R, S, X; True Temper Dynamic Gold or Dynalite R, S	Golf Pride Tour Wrap	Y	Y	$100 steel $165 graphite

continued

FAIRWAY/UTILITY WOOD PRODUCT INFORMATION (continued)

MANUFACTURER	MODEL AND NUMBERS	CLUBHEAD MATERIAL	CLUBHEAD SIZE	NUMBERS	LENGTHS (in.)
Nicklaus Golf	Air Bear (3, 5, 7)	17-4 ss	Oversize	3	43
				5	42
				7	42
Ping	Zing II (3, 5, 7)	17-4 ss	Midsize/low profile	3	Custom-fit for length
				5	
				7	
PowerBilt	TPS (2, 3, 4, 5, 7)	17-4 ss	Oversize	2	43
				3	43
				4	42.5
				5	42.5
				7	42.5
Pro Select	Prism Tour (3, 5)	17-4 ss	Oversize	3	42.5
				5	41.5
	Prism O/S (3, 5, 7)	17-4 ss	Oversize	3	41.5
				5	41.5
				7	40.5
	PS 2 (3, 5)	17-4 ss	Oversize	3	42.5
				5	41.5

Comments: TPS woods include Sims Shock Relief Insert.

Legend:	g=graphite	R=Men's Regular shaft flex ratings
	s=steel	F=Firm
	ss=stainless steel	S=Men's Stiff shaft flex rating
	L=Ladies' shaft flex rating	X=Men's Extra Stiff shaft flex rating
	A=Seniors' shaft flex ratings	

Lofts (deg.)	Shaft Materials and Flexes	Grip Style	Left-Handed	Women's	Suggested Retail
14, 16	Steel, single flex; graphite L, A, R, S	Golf Pride or Griptec Tour Wrap	Y	Y	$160 steel $290 graphite
19					
22					
14, 16	JZ steel, Z-Z65 steel, graphite in 6 flexes	Proprietary Ping DylaGrip or Textured Spiral is standard	Y	All available for women's specifica-tions	$190 steel $265–$300 graphite
19					
22					
12.5	True Temper Dynamic Gold and Dynasty Plus steel S300, S400, X100, X200; UST Tour Weight graphite S; Dynasty Plus graphite L, A, R, S	Golf Pride Tour Velvet	Y	Y	$185 steel $250 graphite
15					
17					
21					
23					
14.25	True Temper graphite (custom-fit)	Lamkin Wrap	N	N	$125
20.25					
15.75	UST Gold Graphite L, R, S	Tour Tech Wrap	Y	Y	$99
21.75					
23.25					
15	Tri-Core graphite, UST graphite, steel	Lamkin Wrap	N	Y	$50 steel $99 graphite
21					

continued

FAIRWAY/UTILITY WOOD PRODUCT INFORMATION *(continued)*

MANUFACTURER	MODEL AND NUMBERS	CLUBHEAD MATERIAL	CLUBHEAD SIZE	NUMBERS	LENGTHS (*in.*)
Rainbow Golf	Sealed Power (Fairway Driver, 3, 5)	Titanium 6AL 4V	Midsize	F. Driver	43.5
				3	43
				5	42
	Sealed Power 250 (Fairway Driver, 3, 5)	Titanium 6AL 4V	Oversize	F. Driver	43.5
				3	43
				5	42
Ram	FX Oversize (Standard and and Low Trajectory, 3, 5, 7)	ss	Midsize	3	43
				5	42
				7	42
	Zebra Scoring Wood	ss	Standard	Zebra	41.5
Rawlings	Faultless (3, 5, 7, 9)	ss	Oversize	3	43
				5	42.5
				7	42
				9	41.5
RTS Golf	RTS (3, 5)	17-4 ss	Oversize	3	43
				5	42

Legend:	g=graphite	R=Men's Regular shaft flex ratings
	s=steel	F=Firm
	ss=stainless steel	S=Men's Stiff shaft flex rating
	L=Ladies' shaft flex rating	X=Men's Extra Stiff shaft flex rating
	A=Seniors' shaft flex ratings	

Lofts (deg.)	Shaft Materials and Flexes	Grip Style	Left-Handed	Women's	Suggested Retail
13	High-modulus graphite, L, L+, A, A+, R, R+, S, S+, X (both models)	Golf Pride, Lamkin	Y (3-, 5-woods only)	Y	$400
15					
21					
13			N	Y	$450
15					
21					
13.5, 16	Ram Tempo Weight graphite, L, A, R, S, X	Ram Wrap	Y (Standard lofts)	Y	$150
18.5, 21					
25					
27	Ram EFT graphite L, R	Zebra Half Cord	Y	Y	$150
16	Stepless lightweight steel, Aldila graphite L, A, R, S	Rubber Tour Wrap	N	Y	$65 steel
22					
25					
28					
14	FM Precision steel A, R, F, S, X; FM Precision Fibermatch graphite A, R, F, S	Griptec Smooth Wrap	Y	Y	$195 steel $275 graphite
20					

continued

Fairway/Utility Wood Product Information (continued)

Manufacturer	Model and Numbers	Clubhead Material	Clubhead Size	Numbers	Lengths (in.)
Slazenger	Crown Limited (3, 4, 5, 7, 9)	17-4 ss	Midsize	3	42.5
				4	42
				5	41.5
				7	41
				9	41
Comments: Center channel area in sole raises center of gravity.					
Kenneth Smith	KS 2000 (3, 5, 7)	17-4 ss	Oversize	3	42.75
				5	41.75
				7	41
	Royal Signet 90 (3, 4, 5)	Persimmon or laminated maple	Midsize	3	42.75
				4	41.75
				5	41

Comments: Royal Signet C Model offers woods numbered 2–11, loft range 13–39 degrees.

Legend:	g=graphite	R=Men's Regular shaft flex ratings
	s=steel	F=Firm
	ss=stainless steel	S=Men's Stiff shaft flex rating
	L=Ladies' shaft flex rating	X=Men's Extra Stiff shaft flex rating
	A=Seniors' shaft flex ratings	

Lofts (deg.)	Shaft Materials and Flexes	Grip Style	Left-Handed	Women's	Suggested Retail
15.5	FM Precision FM and Rifle steel, FM Precision high-modulus and filament-wound graphite (multiple flexes)	Variety of grip styles	N	Y	$140–$150 steel $195–$250 graphite
18					
21					
24					
27					
14	Steel R, S; ultralight graphite L, A, R, S; boron graphite A, R, S; titanium A, R, S, X	Golf Pride, Royal, Griptec in various styles	N	Y	$180 steel $235 graphite $260 titanium
19					
21					
15, 16			Y	Y	$255 steel $295 graphite $310 titanium
18, 19					
20, 21					

All persimmon/laminated woods are custom-made for all specifications.

continued

FAIRWAY/UTILITY WOOD PRODUCT INFORMATION *(continued)*

MANUFACTURER	MODEL AND NUMBERS	CLUBHEAD MATERIAL	CLUBHEAD SIZE	NUMBERS	LENGTHS *(in.)*
Taylor Made	Titanium Bubble (3, 5)	Titanium 6AL 4V	Oversize	3	42.5
				5	42
	Champagne Titanium Bubble (3, 5)	Titanium 6AL 4V	Oversize	3	42
				5	41.5
	Burner Bubble (Fairway Driver, Tour Spoon, 3, 5, 7, Attack Wood)	17-4 ss	Oversize	F. Driver	43.5
				T. Spoon	42.5
				3	42.5
				5	42
				7	41.5
				Attack	41
	Burner Metalwood (Fairway Driver, Tour Spoon, 3, 5, 7, Attack Wood)	17-4 ss	Oversize	F. Driver	42.5
				T. Spoon	42
				3	42
				5	41.5
				7	41
				Attack	40.5
	Champagne Burner Bubble (Fairway Driver, 3, 5, 7, Attack Wood)	17-4 ss	Oversize	F. Driver	42.5
				3	42
				5	41.5
				7	41
				Attack	41

Legend:	g=graphite	R=Men's Regular shaft flex ratings
	s=steel	F=Firm
	ss=stainless steel	S=Men's Stiff shaft flex rating
	L=Ladies' shaft flex rating	X=Men's Extra Stiff shaft flex rating
	A=Seniors' shaft flex ratings	

Lofts (deg.)	Shaft Materials and Flexes	Grip Style	Left-Handed	Women's	Suggested Retail
15	Graphite A, R, S, X	Rubber Tour Wrap	N	N	$400
19					
15	Graphite L	Rubber Tour Wrap	N	Y	$400
19					
13	Graphite A, R, S, X	Rubber Tour Wrap	Y	N	$300
14					
15					
18					
21					
23					
13	Steel A, R, S, X	Rubber Tour Wrap	Y	N	$180
14					
15					
18					
21					
23					
13	Graphite L	Rubber Tour Wrap	N	Y	$300
17					
21					
23					
25					

continued

FAIRWAY/UTILITY WOOD PRODUCT INFORMATION (continued)

MANUFACTURER	MODEL AND NUMBERS	CLUBHEAD MATERIAL	CLUBHEAD SIZE	NUMBERS	LENGTHS (in.)
Titleist	DCI Starship (3, 5, 7)	ss	Midsize	3	42.5
				5	41.5
				7	41.5
	Know Right (clubs not specifically numbered)	ss	Traditional	N/A	43m, 42.5w
				N/A	42m, 41.5w
				N/A	41.5m, 41w
				N/A	41m, 40.5w
				N/A	40.5m, 40w
				N/A	40.5m, 40w

Comments: Offset hosel plus upright lie angle encourage shots that draw instead of slice.

Top Flite	Intimidator (Fairway Driver, 3, 5, 7)	ss w/titanium	Oversize	F. Driver	43.25
				3	42.75
				5	42
				7	41.25

Comments: Contoured leading edge for playability from poor lies.

Legend:	g=graphite	R=Men's Regular shaft flex ratings
	s=steel	F=Firm
	ss=stainless steel	S=Men's Stiff shaft flex rating
	L=Ladies' shaft flex rating	X=Men's Extra Stiff shaft flex rating
	A=Seniors' shaft flex ratings	

Lofts (deg.)		Shaft Materials and Flexes	Grip Style	Left-Handed	Women's	Suggested Retail
	15	Tri-Spec steel L, A, R, S, X; Tri-Spec graphite L, A, R, S, X	Golf Pride Buffed Tour Wrap	Y	Y	$135–$165 steel $205–$250 graphite
	20					
	23					
	14	Tri-Spec graphite L, A, R	Golf Pride Air Cushion	N	Y	$260
	15					
	17					
	20					
	23					
	27					
	13	Aldila sheet-wrapped graphite A, R, S, X	Buffed Tour Wrap	N	N	$275
	16					
	21					
	25					

continued

FAIRWAY/UTILITY WOOD PRODUCT INFORMATION (continued)

MANUFACTURER	MODEL AND NUMBERS	CLUBHEAD MATERIAL	CLUBHEAD SIZE	NUMBERS	LENGTHS (in.)
Vulcan	Q-Pointe (3, 4, 5, 7)	17-4 ss	Midsize	3	24 custom lengths for all clubs
				4	
				5	
				7	
	Comments: Wide range of fitting options.				
Wilson	Invex (3, 5, 7)	17-4 ss/titanium	Midsize	3	43
				5	42.5
				7	42
	Invex Titanium	Titanium	Oversize	FW17	43.75
				FW22	43.25
Wood Brothers	Texan (3, 4, 5)	Persimmon	Standard	3	42.5
				4	42
				5	41
	Kool Kat (3.5, 4.5)	Persimmon w/cork center	Standard	3.5	42.5
				4.5	42
	F-300 (3, 5, 7)	Metal	Standard	3	42.5
				5	42
				7	42

Legend:	g=graphite	R=Men's Regular shaft flex ratings
	s=steel	F=Firm
	ss=stainless steel	S=Men's Stiff shaft flex rating
	L=Ladies' shaft flex rating	X=Men's Extra Stiff shaft flex rating
	A=Seniors' shaft flex ratings	

Lofts (deg.)	Shaft Materials and Flexes	Grip Style	Left-Handed	Women's	Suggested Retail
16	Ultralight graphite or high-modulus graphite in 10 flexes	Royal Lamkin, Golf Pride Tour Wrap, 7 sizes	Y	Y	$160
19					
22					
27					
14, 16	Firestick steel or graphite LL, L, A, R, S, X	Royal Sand Wrap	Y	Y	$285 steel $299 graphite
20					
22					
17	Firestick graphite, R, S, X	Royal Sand Wrap	N	Y	$400
22					
15	True Temper Dynamic Gold steel R, S, X; graphite R, S, X	Tour Wrap	N	N	$320 steel $399 graphite
18					
21					
17	Steel R, S, X; graphite A, R, S, X	Tour Wrap	N	N	$175 steel $225 graphite
19					
15	Graphite L, R, S, X	Tour Wrap	N	N	$196
21					
24					

continued

FAIRWAY/UTILITY WOOD PRODUCT INFORMATION *(continued)*

MANUFACTURER	MODEL AND NUMBERS	CLUBHEAD MATERIAL	CLUBHEAD SIZE	NUMBERS	LENGTHS *(in.)*
Yonex	Super ADX titanium (3, 5, Fairway Wood)	Titanium	Oversize	Not supplied	Not supplied
	Super ADX (3, 5, 7, 9)	Graphite, ss face	Oversize	3	43
				5	42
				7	41.5
				9	41
	Super ADX Senior (3, 5, 7, 9)	Graphite, ss face	Oversize	3	43
				5	42
				7	41.5
				9	41
	Super ADX Ladies (3, 5, 7, 9)	Graphite, ss face	Oversize	3	42
				5	41
				7	40.5
				9	40
	ADX 100i (3, 4, 5, 7)	Graphite	Oversize	3	43
				4	42.5
				5	42
				7	41
	Tour (3, 4, 5)	Graphite	Midsize	3	43
				4	42.5
				5	42

Legend: g=graphite
s=steel
ss=stainless steel
L=Ladies' shaft flex rating
A=Seniors' shaft flex ratings

R=Men's Regular shaft flex ratings
F=Firm
S=Men's Stiff shaft flex rating
X=Men's Extra Stiff shaft flex rating

Lofts (deg.)	Shaft Materials and Flexes	Grip Style	Left-Handed	Women's	Suggested Retail
Not supplied	Low-torque, high-modulus graphite R, S, X	Tour Weave Cord	Y	Y	$420
15	Low-torque, high-modulus graphite R, S, X	Rubber Tour Wrap	Y	N	$350
19					
23					
26					
15	Ultralight graphite A	Rubber Tour Wrap	Y	N	$350
19					
23					
26					
17	Ultralight graphite L	Rubber Tour Wrap	N	Y	$350
22					
25					
38					
16	High-modulus graphite L, R, S	Rubber Tour Wrap	Y	Y	$275
19					
22					
26					
15	Graphite/boron	Rubber Tour Wrap	Y	N	Not supplied
18					
21					

continued

FAIRWAY/UTILITY WOOD PRODUCT INFORMATION *(continued)*

MANUFACTURER	MODEL AND NUMBERS	CLUBHEAD MATERIAL	CLUBHEAD SIZE	NUMBERS	LENGTHS (*in.*)
Zevo	Lob (3, 5, 7, 9)	ss	Oversize	3	42.5
				5	41.5
				7	40.5
				9	39.5
	Air Zevo Oversize (3, 5, 7)	ss	Oversize	3	42.5
				5	41.5
				7	41.5
	Air Zevo Comp Equipe (2, 3, 5)	ss	Midsize	2	43
				3	42.5
				3	42.5
				5	41.5
				5	41.5

LOFTS (deg.)	SHAFT MATERIALS AND FLEXES	GRIP STYLE	LEFT-HANDED	WOMEN'S	SUGGESTED RETAIL
16	Graphite, 7 flexes	Zevo Pro Wrap	N	Y	$225–$350
21					
25					
29					
15	Graphite, 7 flexes	Zevo Pro Wrap	Y	Y	$175–$200 steel $285–$350 graphite
19.5					
23					
12	Graphite, 7 flexes	Zevo Pro Wrap	N	Y	$175–$200 steel $285–$350 graphite
12.5					
14.5					
16.5					
18.5					

CHAPTER 5

The Iron Game: How Manufacturers' Aims May Steer Yours Off Course

The numbered irons are becoming a lesser part of the average golfer's set. Very, very few golfers carry all the irons numbered 1 through 9 in their bags anymore. Of this tiny percentage, almost all are playing professionals and top amateurs. Even among the pro ranks, the 2-iron is being sent to pasture by some players in favor of a lofted wood or an additional wedge (a development we'll discuss in the next chapter). Among higher-handicap amateurs, the 3-iron and in some cases the 4-iron are often being removed in favor of other clubs.

To a great extent, the demise of the long irons is a result of questionable modifications made by manufacturers in recent years, in which the design features they have built into these clubs have rendered them almost unhittable by the average player. Yes, there are counterbalancing factors to any club's design in terms of playability. And you've no doubt read or heard different companies' claims of certain features that make the irons, and particularly the long irons, easier to play. The trouble is, you only hear about the features that will make the irons more playable. You never hear about the ones that actually make the long irons *less* playable—after which these so-called playability benefits are tacked on, if you will.

A brief review of the recent history of iron club design will help you get a better understanding of why these clubs often play differently than they have in the past. Later we'll discuss current features that are predominant in clubs currently on the market. This information should help you in your decision not only about what iron model to buy but also how many of them.

Note: As you observe the listing of iron clubs that accompanies this chapter, you'll see that in most cases the irons include the pitching wedge, but not the sand wedge. The reason is that the design features of the pitching wedge, as opposed to the sand wedge, are still very similar to the 9-iron. All wedges that have a greater loft than the pitching wedge will be covered in the next chapter.

Evolution of the Iron Clubhead

Don Wood is vice-president of research and development for Zevo Golf, based in Vista, California. Referring to irons used by players in the eras of Bobby Jones, Byron Nelson, Sam Snead, and Ben Hogan, Wood says, "The iron heads back then were literally flat-backed, with no special weight distribution to speak of. The biggest influence on weight distribution was the hosel (the area connecting the shaft to the head), which was much longer than it is on most clubs today. The hosel weight made most irons 'heel heavy,' so you had to hit the ball on the heel side of the center of the face to get a really solid shot."

By the mid-1950s, hosels had gotten shorter and iron clubfaces had also become substantially shallower. "These changes by definition made the club more 'forgiving,' since the club's center of gravity moved slightly outward, toward the center of the face, and slightly lower as well," Wood continues. "Then around 1960, the era of the 'muscle back' iron came into being. The muscle back was essentially a bulge of metal at the lower rear of the sole. Its purpose was to further lower the center of gravity and help golfers get their iron shots airborne more easily."

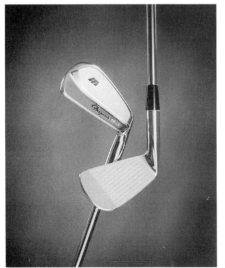

Mizuno MP-14

Tommy Armour
Ti 100

Basically, muscle-back irons dominated the scene until nearly 1980. The perimeter-weighted or "cavity back" style of iron clubhead, which most golfers are using today, hadn't yet taken over the market. This style of head places a much higher proportion of weight around the perimeter of the head, leaving relatively thin metal where the ball is actually struck. As you'll see in the iron listing that accompanies this chapter, close to 75 percent of the irons are cavity-back or perimeter-weighted clubs.

Why Bigger Isn't Always Better

All models in the table are listed as being standard size, midsize, or oversize. This information is provided because the size of iron clubheads, like that of the metalwoods, has become a significant design element in the past several years. There is no industry standard for specific size of a clubface by which it qualifies for one of these three categories; rather, the size designation is based on each individual company's judgment.

As a point of reference, a "standard size" iron will generally be one that mimics the size of classic iron designs of the 1960s (and will usually be similar in overall design—that is, a forged-steel iron as opposed to a cast cavity back). Examples are the Mizuno MP-14 and MP-29 forged blades. A "midsize" iron, usually cast and usually to some degree perimeter-weighted, is slightly larger but not glaringly so. An example is the Ping ISI. The Tommy Armour Ti 100 clubhead obviously takes up more area than either of the two previous clubs— it is the clearest example of an "oversized" iron.

Using these guidelines, of the irons listed there is almost an equal split between irons that are marketed as "oversize" and those marketed as "midsize"— roughly 40 percent for each. (There are several models that classify themselves as "progressively" sized, with specific size incrementation as the clubs move from long to short irons. These are included in the midsize count.) Irons listed as standard size, meanwhile, comprise just under 20 percent of all those listed.

One thing needs to be made clear to golfers who have been wooed by marketing claims to the effect that a larger clubhead will aid distance. "Advertisers would have you believe that a bigger head hits the ball farther, but this is *absolutely false*," Zevo's Wood says. "The opposite is true—smaller, denser clubheads will hit the ball farther.

"You could use this analogy," Wood continues. "You need to drive a nail, and you have two implements to drive it with, each of which weighs two pounds: a hammer and a frying pan. Which one would you use to drive the nail with? Of course you'd use the hammer, because the weight is concentrated at the point of impact.

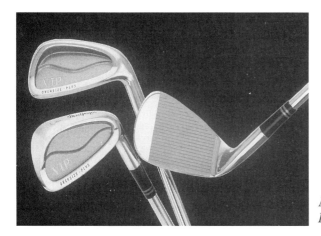

MacGregor VIP Oversize Plus

"In its purest form, an oversize clubhead, like the frying pan, generates less force at the point of impact. However, that's not to say there's no benefit to oversize iron heads," Wood says. "With a hammer, as with a smaller iron clubhead, you have to deliver the blow precisely to the object being hit. Some people aren't very precise in using a hammer, so they hit the nail with a mallet instead. Likewise, golfers who know that their delivery of the clubhead to the ball is erratic will benefit by hitting it with a larger clubhead that allows for more margin of error."

There are other reasons to think about your performance with iron clubs before you rush out and buy the biggest iron clubheads you can find. As Wood points out, a club described as "forgiving"also means that it is a little harder to put much sidespin on the ball, to make it curve in either direction. In other words, if you are interested in creative shotmaking with your irons, you should still consider a smaller, non-perimeter-weighted head. "Another benefit of standard-size iron heads, heads that are not too long in their heel-to-toe dimension," Wood adds, "is that they are easier to swing through lies in the rough. The larger the head, the greater the tendency for it to catch in the rough, so that the face gets slowed down or turned over." (Obviously, those of you who never hit a ball in the rough need not consider this factor!)

Cleveland VAS+

Wood believes that in terms of creating larger-size iron heads, the point of diminishing returns has already been reached. "The business of making super-size heads has a lot more to do with marketing goals than it does with the club's functionality," he candidly insists. "Manufacturers think, 'It worked with the metalwoods, so it should work with the irons.' Well, it won't work as well with the irons, because irons are a different animal. You have to hit precision shots with them, and do so out of all types of lies."

While oversize heads inherently diminish distance if the shot is hit perfectly squarely in a laboratory setting, they can actually help the player's distance on the course. As Wood points out, for many players, particularly those with higher handicaps, the oversize clubhead is an aid to confidence, and greater confidence encourages the player to swing harder. Again, though, the object with the irons is to hit the ball a precise distance to the flag, not simply pound it as far as you can. Therefore, this "oversize breeds confidence" factor seems more appropriate in relation to metalwoods than it does to irons.

Still, larger iron clubheads have been around for a time now. "Things are changing," Wood says. "By now you're getting a crop of good high school and college players who have grown up using oversize irons such as Ping Zings or Callaway Big Berthas. This size and the inherent playability features are normal to them."

Keep an Eye Out for a Suitable "Sole Mate"

One area of iron design that the average golfer pays little attention to, but which manufacturers work hard on and in which there's a great deal of variation, is the design of the sole. In older irons the club's sole tended to be flat when viewed from heel to toe. Such a design could cause a high degree of ground friction at impact, which would result in a loss of clubhead speed.

Most of today's models have a slight to substantial amount of sole radius from heel to toe. That is, the leading edge of the blade is rounded or "rockered," so that the center of the leading edge is lower than either the heel or the toe. The advantage of not catching the toe or heel in the ground probably outweighs a slight negative, which is that if you hit the ball off that heel or toe, which never gets quite to ground level, the shots will be hit slightly "thinner" than with a straight leading edge.

Callaway's Big Bertha irons demonstrate a particularly high degree of sole radius. They also show a high degree of *bounce angle,* another important factor in sole design.

Bounce angle, which we'll talk about in more detail in Chapter 6 on the wedges, basically means that an angle is built into the sole so that it rests on the ground in a condition that is other than perfectly flat. The sole may rest so that the leading edge of the club is slightly above the ground's surface. This helps assure that at impact it does not dig into the ground and produce the disastrously "fat" shot.

Most longer irons (2, 3, 4) will have very little bounce, or even negative bounce in the sole. (It's not as necessary here because the arc of the long irons through the ball is more sweeping than descending.) However, as the irons get shorter, they gradually display an increasing amount of bounce, to help elimi-

Callaway Big Bertha (above)
Daiwa Hi-Trac MF-110 (right)

nate the fat shot, which is more probable with a club swung on a steeper downward arc.

At any rate, as you inspect your potential new irons, observe the bounce angle in the soles (if any) and try to match it up well with your swing tendencies and your prevalent course conditions. "If you hit a lot of iron shots fat, you'll probably benefit from having a fairly noticeable degree of bounce in the sole," says Zevo's Wood. "Also consider course conditions. If the ground is normally hard, the club is going to 'bounce' more anyway, so you wouldn't need much bounce angle. Nor would you need as much of a heel-to-toe sole radius."

Clubface Material/Hardness Considerations

You'll note a column in the table listing the type of clubhead material used (in conjunction with the design style). Most cast iron designs are made of stainless steel, of which there are varying types and hardnesses. Customarily, 17-4 stainless steel is the hardest type; 431 stainless the next hardest; and the less-often-used 303 stainless steel the softest of the three. The majority of forged irons are made of carbon steel, which is significantly softer than any of the stainless metals. That's why forged irons that have seen a lot of rounds will be marked by more slight nicks and dents than a cast-stainless-steel club.

Many clubmakers and clubfitters believe that the relative hardness or softness of the material used is virtually impossible for most golfers to distinguish. This is not quite the same thing as saying that the type of metal in the clubface/hitting area has no effect on the shot's trajectory. "I'm a big believer in the use of

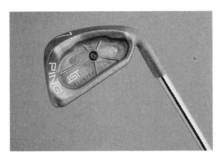

Ping ISI (nickel) (above left)
Ping ISI (copper) (left)
Lynx Black Cat Tour (above)

soft steel, particularly by the better golfer," says Zevo's Wood. "Soft steel such as carbon steel has certain restitution properties that allow the ball to stay on the clubface a fraction longer. This adds a degree of backspin to the shot, so the ball might land just a little more softly. Also, it's easier to curve the ball if desired. Beyond that," he adds, "feel is critical in the irons, which are designed to produce shots of precise distance on a precise line. The golfer who makes consistent contact should search for as much feel as he or she can get."

Wood also points out that softer carbon steel and 303 stainless steel have the advantage of being alterable. That is, you can adjust the loft or the lie of a carbon-steel clubhead by several degrees with little or no fear of breaking it. "People's games will often go through changes," he points out. "It's nice to be able to bend a club the way you need it, rather than having to buy a new set." If you were to choose a Wilson Staff RM (carbon steel) model, for example, loft and lie adjustments would be much safer than on a 17-4 stainless Tommy Armour 855s Silver Scot.

On the other hand, Wood states, "This is not to blast those companies that make hard metal iron heads. One advantage to these is that it helps the club to maintain its original specifications over a long period of time. Also, the golfer who is really not a good player is probably better off using a hard, 17-4 stainless steel, since he or she probably shouldn't *want* the directional problems that go along with a higher rate of backspin." Wood adds that this was one reason that extra-hard, heat-treated 431 stainless steel became very popular beginning in the 1980s.

Can Face Inserts Help Your Iron Game?

Several irons in the table listings feature clubfaces with a separate material inserted into the clubhead's hitting area—ceramic materials, several that use titanium inserts, brass, and others. Face inserts are far from new. After all, back when woods were actually made of wood, the intended hitting surface was always comprised of a fiber, plastic, or metal insert. The question is, might any of these face-insert iron designs be worth a look? Here our contributors are more optimistic. "I think a titanium-*faced* iron is a very interesting concept," says Barney Adams. "There you'd have a lighter and stronger clubface, allowing you to move the heavier stainless steel around the perimeter to get an optimum weight distribution. Actually," he continues, "I like graphite inserts in the irons even better than the idea of a titanium insert, except for one thing—graphite gets shredded very quickly, especially when hitting hard-range balls on a sandy practice tee."

Zevo's Wood suggests that another good possibility, one that has not been fully realized as of this writing, would be to use aluminum as the hitting area insert in irons, then surrounding it with a heavier metal. "Aluminum would provide a nice soft feel at impact, like some companies are promoting with putters, while lightening the middle of the clubface at the same time," he notes. "You could effectively kill two birds with one stone by using an aluminum insert."

An important additional note: Keep in mind that in the case of stainless steels, the number designation alone may not be a complete indicator of the material's hardness. Wood points out that, for example, 431 stainless steel can be heat-treated by a manufacturer so that the end product can be harder than 17-4 stainless steel, or that by an "annealing" heat treatment process, a 17-4 can be made to feel softer than some 431 stainless steels.

What about the hardness and feel attendant in that new kid on the iron block, titanium? (See sidebar, p. 145.) Wood explains that titanium is very hard, harder than 17-4 stainless steel. "It does not flex or bow whatsoever, which is another reason you can 'stretch' it to design extra-big clubheads."

Some Notes on Weight Distribution

A perimeter-weighted or cavity-back club is one in which the weight is amassed around the exterior of the head. This theoretically puts more weight behind the ball when it is hit away from the center of the face. Perimeter-weighted

Ray Cook Titanic

and cavity-back designs are often said to expand the sweet spot or enlarge the center of gravity. These are false claims. "A center of gravity does not contain any space at all, it's just a theoretical point. It can't be 'expanded,'" Wood points out. What does happen with a perimeter-weighted club is that, by definition, there will be more mass behind the mishit shot, so the result of a miss is likely to be better than on a more traditional muscle-back iron. However, it's the wise golfer who keeps in mind that there is never any completely free lunch. Since there is less mass behind the dead center of the face, it's only common sense that you'll get a little *less* out of those shots than out of a non-perimeter-weighted club. In sum, the more consistently you strike your irons, the less you need cavity-back/perimeter-weighted designs. And vice versa.

Keep in mind that weight distribution can be made to have an effect not only on the distance obtained with shots hit on various parts of the clubface but also on shot direction. As Don Wood explains, "If the clubhead's weight is located primarily on the heel end, the center of gravity is also closer to the heel, so that in effect the clubface will want to 'turn over,' or close, through the impact zone. The more material you see taken from the heel area and moved out toward the toe, the farther the center of gravity is toward the toe. In this case, the clubface will stay more open through impact, and thus the ball will tend to fly to the right." So, if you're a slicer like the majority of amateurs, a center of gravity a little toward the heel side of the clubhead will probably be a benefit.

The bigger the clubhead overall, the higher the center of gravity is likely to be in relation to the center of the ball. "Having a center of gravity that's too far 'up' and 'out' is something the average golfer should avoid, since it'll make his or her shots tend to go low and to the right," Wood advises.

What's the Deal About Titanium Irons?

In late 1995 and 1996, the titanium-headed iron has tried to shoulder its way onto the block in the iron marketing game. Foremost among these are the Ray Cook Titanic and the Tommy Armour Ti 100 models, both of which are highly oversize designs. Titanium being a highly expensive material to work with makes them very highly priced as well (see table at the end of this chapter).

As with titanium-headed metalwoods, this material allows manufacturers tremendous flexibility in the design of the clubhead. For example, titanium iron clubheads can be made far larger and with more radical designs, such as extremely deep cavity backs, because of its lightness in comparison to stainless steel. Do such opportunities make titanium worth the investment for you? Of course, this is an individual decision, both in terms of value for the dollar and also, perhaps, for the ego gratification that seems part and parcel of having "ti" throughout the bag. However, Zevo's Don Wood opines, "I really don't think titanium is going to offer much performance benefit. It's not necessary in a good iron. It's very hard. For some golfers this is good, but even there I don't think you can make a titanium iron head any harder than some heat-treated versions of stainless steel. In all, I think titanium irons are a form of overkill."

Barney Adams of Adams Golf is even more adamant on this subject. "The high cost of making a set of irons with 100 percent titanium heads is ludicrous. I don't believe there is any good reason for doing this. Jumbo, gigantic iron heads, which seem to be the main point in using titanium, may not help golfers because the taller the clubface is, the higher the center of gravity will be. That will hurt the average golfer, not help," Adams says. "Sure, you could keep the weight low by also putting a gigantic sole on every iron to offset the clubface height—but what's the point?"

Length and Lie

In the table is a column that provides the length, lie angle, and clubface loft for the 5-iron in each set listed. This gives you a clear idea as to how the entire set of one manufacturer compares to another with regard to these specifications. If a club has a longer shaft than average or a higher loft than average for a 5-iron, the same things will almost certainly hold true for the other irons. Incidentally, it's almost universal that the lengths of irons increase or decrease by ½-inch increments throughout the set.

In general, the iron clubs, like the metalwoods, have been slowly getting longer. In the past, according to information from Ralph Maltby's *Golf Club Design, Fitting, Alteration & Repair*, the traditional standard men's length for the

Taylor Made Burner Bubble

5-iron was 37 inches. Today's models, for the most part, run between 37.5 and 38 inches in length, and a fair number exceed 38 inches. In some cases where the iron is offered in both steel and graphite, the graphite shaft is ½-inch longer. Clubmakers say it's necessary to do this in order to keep the total balance and feel of the club the same, because graphite shafts are generally lighter than steel.

Manufacturers rarely announce that they're making irons with longer shafts than in the past. If anything, it seems that they conceal this fact. When was the last time you heard a company say you ought to buy its irons, which are really long-hitting because of their longer shafts? No, that would be too simple and undramatic. So they "forget" this fundamental information in favor of more cosmic explanations. It might pay at this point to remind yourself that just as bigger in the clubhead is not necessarily better, so a longer shaft might not necessarily be better. After all, the longer the club, the smaller your margin for error. With an iron shaft ½ to 1 inch longer, you may gain 2 or 4 yards, but the dispersion of your shots will become fractionally more spread out, too.

The club's *lie angle* is the angle at which the clubshaft is inserted into the head. As you'll see, the majority of "standard" lie angles are set at or near 60 degrees for the 5-iron. Everyone should be specifically fitted for accurate lie angle, but generally, taller people tend to need irons with a more upright lie than shorter players. If the club has too upright a lie angle for you, the tendency will

---

If in Doubt, Play Steel

In listening to people who make and sell clubs for a living, the opinions on whether you should invest in graphite shafts in all your irons or stick with steel shafts are surprising. You'd expect them to support the use of graphite. After all, clubmakers can reasonably charge a higher markup on their graphite iron sets, which are always substantially higher priced than their steel offerings (see table).

Yet, there's plenty of resistance to the assumption by many golfers that since graphite shafts cost more, they're better, whether it be in the metalwoods or the irons. "If a golfer definitely needs a lighter, longer club for more clubhead speed, maybe graphite's okay," says Don Wood. "But there's a general perception out there that composites (meaning graphite) are better than steel. Well, they're not! Graphite shafts, as of this date, do not provide the consistency in frequency that steel does. Steel's tolerances are much more tightly controlled.

"Shouldn't the average amateur," he continues, "who lacks tons of ability, at least want his or her clubs to be as consistent throughout the set as possible? They should. For the vast majority, graphite iron shafts will not make golfers play better. All they're doing is going out and spending more money."

---

be for the toe of the club to be off the ground through impact. If the lie is too flat, the heel may be up.

As was mentioned in Chapter 1, lie angle should be measured *dynamically*—while the club is being swung—rather than checking the static lie position at address. The best way to check for the optimum "dynamic" lie is to find a fitter who has a simple device known as a lie board. With it, you hit iron shots off a thin plastic board. This contact between club and board leaves a mark on the club's sole. If the mark is toward the toe, it means the lie is too flat for your swing. If the mark is toward the heel, then the club's lie is too upright for you. A mark in the center, of course, is perfect.

It might be easy to dismiss lie angle as a significant fitting factor, since many models tend to have more radius or "rocker" built into the sole of the club. "When manufacturers do this, it gives the club a kind of 'fits all' quality as far as the lie is concerned," says Don Wood. "I've seen high handicappers on dynamic fitting machines who deliver the club to the ball at wildly differing lie angles. The same person might deliver it 10 degrees 'down' or 'flat' on one swing, then 4 degrees 'up' on the next. He or she would be digging in badly with the toe or the heel on various swings, but if a club has a huge amount of sole rocker, it virtually eliminates the problem."

Goldwin AVDP

There is another, hidden factor to consider concerning playing with an incorrect lie angle, though. Barney Adams of Adams Golf says that clubs within a set can easily be 2 degrees off in their lie angle. And an inaccuracy in the lie angle will also cause the angle of the clubface to be off fractionally in relation to the target. When the iron's lie is too upright for the player's address position (that is, the toe is too high), the clubface points fractionally to the *left* of the target. If the lie angle is too flat for the player (meaning the heel is slightly up), then the clubface will be opened a touch to the right. The greater the loft on the clubface, the more an incorrect lie angle will alter the direction of the face.

How might erratic lie angles hurt your game? "Let's say you have a 7-iron that's got a too-flat lie and a 6-iron whose lie is too upright, but you don't know this," Adams says. "You're out on the course and you have a 7-iron shot. You think you've made a good swing, but the ball hangs out a little to the right. Your subconscious makes a note of this result.

"On the next hole, you have a 6-iron to the green," Adams continues. "You remember from the last hole that you made what felt like a good swing, but your ball stayed right. So you tell yourself, 'I'd better keep this ball a little left of the flag.' Well, since your 6-iron lie is too upright, the face will tend to point a little left to start with. When you hit the shot, aiming slightly left, your shot misses the green entirely, bounces down a bank, and you end up taking a double bogey.

"The information you've gotten from these shots has told you you're swinging poorly. You'll probably be fighting your swing for the rest of the round. However, the fact that you've hit consecutive irons in which the lie angles were off in opposite directions might have really caused the problem," Adams concludes.

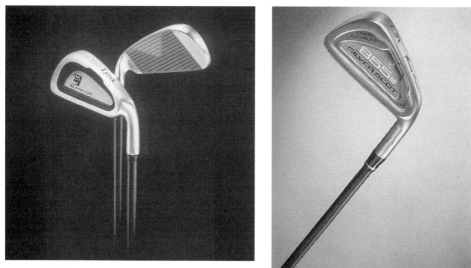

Lynx Black Cat

Tommy Armour Silver Scot

Moral to the story: When you settle on the iron design you like, *have both the lofts and the lies checked* to make sure they are uniformly correct. Moreover, particularly if you play with more bendable, forged-carbon-steel heads, it's wise to measure them again after a year or two of play, since impact with hard ground, rocks, or tree roots may alter them over time.

Games People Play with Lofts

Manufacturers on the whole have been reducing the loft on their irons. And this turns out to be a key reason why golfers are using more metalwoods, fewer irons, and more wedges in their bags.

A bit of explanation is needed here. Again referring to Ralph Maltby's *Golf Club Design, Fitting, Alteration & Repair,* by traditional standards the loft on a 5-iron was 30 degrees. If you look through the lofts of all the 5-irons shown in the table accompanying this chapter, you'll see that the average loft for the 5-iron is now about 27 degrees. All the other irons in the set, of course, have similarly lower lofts in relation to the conventional overall standard.

So, reducing the average loft of a 5-iron from 30 degrees to an average of 27 degrees means the loft is nearly that of one full club *greater* than in the past. Couple this with shafts that are ½ to 1 full inch longer than the old standard, and you have irons that are playing much "longer" than in the past. *This is what*

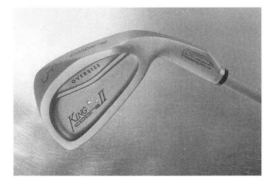

Cobra King Cobra II

manufacturers intended. They want to sell you clubs on the assertion that you will hit the ball "long" with their irons.

Let's stop and think logically for a minute. How much sense does this approach make? Your purpose with all the numbered irons is to hit a shot a specific distance to the hole. You need to know if you hit a certain iron an average of 170 yards, or 150 yards, or 130 yards. Then when you have a shot of that distance, you have a club that will send the ball pin-high if you execute correctly. It does not matter in the slightest whether you hit that 150-yard shot with an 8-iron, a 6-iron, or a 4-iron—as long as you know you have the right club for the shot at hand.

Why in the world, then, have manufacturers artificially "strengthened" the irons? Because they believe that by giving your ego a superficial boost, you'll think their clubs are the greatest! As Barney Adams says, "It's the number on the bottom that makes the golfer feel good. Even if his 6-iron really has a 4-iron's loft, he can hit it into one of the par-3s and then say afterward in the bar, 'Yeah, I smoothed a little 6-iron into number 8.'"

Titleist DCI Oversize + Gold
Titleist DCI Oversize + Black

Now, there's nothing inherently wrong with the irons that are particularly strong-lofted. You can hit great shots with them if the clubs fit you in all other aspects. However, by pandering to the less educated golfers' egos with strong lofts as they do, manufacturers have painted themselves into a corner. They have run out of "loft room," if you will, with the long irons. That's because if a 5-iron has 25 degrees of loft, as some do, then the 1-iron, the 2-iron, and the 3-iron will be unhittable because they have insufficient loft. (Manufacturers also must space these long-iron lofts so tightly together that there's no sense in owning them all, anyway.) On the other side of the set, as we'll see in the next chapter, the loft on the pitching wedge is also way down. So, many golfers will need an extra wedge with a loft greater than the pitching wedge to play short shots in the 80–110-yard range.

In sum, the effect of all this loft manipulation is that when you pull out a 3-iron, you're really hitting a 2-iron; and when you pull out a pitching wedge, you're now hitting at least a 9-iron. It's as simple as that. It's not wrong—it's just silly and confusing. "It's sort of like lying to the golfer," says Wood. "I don't believe for one minute that strong lofts improve the games of average and poorer players in particular. Some, in fact, may find they can actually hit their 5-irons *farther* than they can a 4-, 3-, or 2-. I think it would be helpful if we clubmakers reconfigured our lofts so that the long irons carry *more* loft than in the past, not less."

Don't expect it to happen anytime soon, though. Just be aware that today's iron lofts mean that most golfers will need at least one fewer long iron and one more wedge in the bag. And make sure you know the lofts on the irons you're buying, and make certain that the longest iron you buy is one that you're capable of getting airborne—*easily!*

PowerBilt TPS

A final note regarding loft is that two different designs with the same amount of measured loft may provide slightly differing trajectories and distances. As Don Wood notes, there's a difference between the "mechanical" loft, which is the actual loft reading of the clubface, and what is known as "inertial" loft. Inertial loft refers to the effect of the clubhead's weight distribution on the actual loft as it's delivered to the ball at impact. The lower the clubhead's center of gravity, the higher the inertial or effective loft that is transmitted to the ball. Keep this in mind as you're inspecting irons for possible purchase. Of course, hitting shots with the various models is the best way to tell whether they'll produce the trajectory that's right for you.

Those Other "Game Improvement" Features—and Game Improvement in General

There are several other features to consider in the design of the iron which you should factor into your buying decision. One of these is whether you prefer a club that has a straight versus an "offset" hosel (see the column on hosel offset in the table at the end of this chapter).

Offset means that the clubface's leading edge is set behind the centerline of the shaft to some degree. This by definition means that the clubhead's center of gravity is farther back in relation to the clubshaft. "An offset design adds inertial loft to the clubhead at impact, so the shot will fly a little higher," says Don Wood. "Also, any club that has a high degree of offset will tend to 'turn over' somewhat. This is why better players often have trouble with offset irons: They tend to hit the ball high and to hook it. But for the average golfer who slices and doesn't hit the ball high enough, an offset design will help a lot." An example of substantial offset is shown in Callaway's Big Bertha irons.

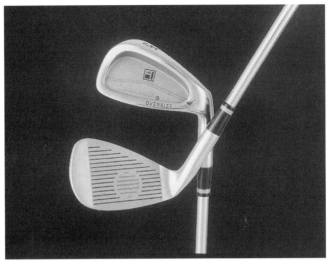

Dynacraft Copperhead

In general, Wood recommends that golfers who slice the ball should look for features such as an offset clubhead, a center of gravity that is more toward the heel than the toe, and the use of a hard metal which would put a lower spin rate on the ball.

However, Wood also states an opinion about the overall approach or attitude toward all these "game improvement" features that have taken over in the marketing of golf clubs. "Really, have all these elements brought about 'game improvement,' or just 'score improvement'?" he asks. "I think today's equipment has made average golfers kind of lethargic about how they play their shots. You used to hear the term 'shotmaking' all the time, but that element of the game is disappearing.

"When you add up all the features that are available now in irons, I think they have numbed golfers' senses to a degree. They've taken away an element of inventiveness in people's golf swings. Meanwhile," Wood adds, "the average golfer has not gotten any better, as we can see from the USGA's handicap reporting.

"Frankly, if a person really and truly wants to improve his or her golf over the long haul, I would suggest using a club that is going to force him or her to improve. The best thing a golfer who really wants improved shotmaking can do would be to go back to playing a standard-size, classic forged blade, to learn to adapt to the demands this will make on his or her shotmaking ability," Wood concludes. "It's sort of like the 'no pain, no gain' theory in physical training. However, golfers must realize they will *not* play better with forged irons if they have no intention of working to develop a repeating swing.

"In the end," Wood concludes, "I believe that whether a person should use a classic design versus a game-improvement iron depends more on his or her level of commitment than it does on level of ability."

Vibration Dampening's Pluses—and Minuses

In the past few years, you may have heard about several ways in which manufacturers have been working to reduce the amount of vibration that the golfer feels when he or she badly mishits a shot. You know—the clanging feel of that proverbial 2-iron hit off the toe of the club on a raw, 40-degree day.

Among these devices are the Sims Shock Relief Insert produced by PowerBilt (an apparatus that is placed partway down the inside of the shaft); True Temper's Stratus shaft, which includes a vibration-dampening core known as Sensicore; and various plastic dowels which companies place on the backs of clubfaces, some ostensibly for the purpose of absorbing unwanted vibration. Indeed, graphite shafts in general are considered to reduce the amount of vibration that eventually reaches the golfer's hands.

The basic idea is that by reducing the amount of vibration the golfer feels, injuries to the joints that accrue over many years of playing and practicing might be eliminated.

On the surface, vibration dampeners would seem like a very positive development, but not all agree. "To reduce vibration, after all, means to reduce 'feel,'" says Don Wood. He points out that better golfers *like* to get feedback, whether it be the smooth feel of perfect impact or the jarring effect of a bad miss. "If vibration-dampening products work well, it means you're depriving the golfer of key information about what is happening between club and ball. I think golfers need to know what kind of shots they're hitting.

"Really, it's the graphite-shaft makers who have promoted this 'need' to reduce the vibration golfers feel after impact," Wood says. "They found that graphite shafts weren't making people play better or even hit farther, so they promote the fact that it dampens vibration." Wood reports, however, that he has found no quantitative, measurable evidence that playing graphite shafts over the course of a lifetime will improve a person's orthopedic health. "I've asked all the major companies for tangible evidence that graphite shafts aid shock reduction, and none of them has yet provided it," Wood reports. "Also, look back to greats such as Hogan, Snead, Nelson, and Palmer, all of whom have played their entire lifetimes using steel shafts, and this 'healthy golfing' trend seems absurd. Golf is a sport, and people should expect some physical demands when playing a sport. Vibration from the club at impact should *not* be considered some terrible hardship. In sum," Wood concludes, "I believe the only real aim of the promotion of vibration-dampening features is to sell more golf clubs."

IRONS PRODUCT INFORMATION

MANUFACTURER	MODEL AND NUMBERS	DESIGN /CLUBHEAD MATERIAL	GROOVE TYPE	CLUBHEAD SIZE	5-IRON	
					LENGTHS (*in.*)	LOFT (*deg.*)
Adams Golf	Assault (1-PW)	Cast, perimeter-weighted, 17-4 ss	U	Midsize	37.75	28
Tommy Armour	Ti 100 (1-Sw)	Cast, perimeter-weighted pure titanium	U	Oversize	37.75 s, 38.25 g	26
	855s Silver Scot (1-PW)	Cast cavity back, 17-4 ss	U	Oversize	37.75 s, 38.25 g	28
	855s Golden Scot (1-PW)	Cast cavity back, 17-4 ss (ceramic-coated)	U	Oversize	38.25	27
	855s Diamond Scot (1-PW)	Cast cavity back, 17-4 ss	U	Oversize	37.25	27
	Comments: Reduced offset available in Diamond Scot; Golden Scot and Diamond Scot have					
Black Ice Golf	Tour Balanced (2-PW)	Cast, perimeter-weighted, 431 ss, ceramic face	V	Midsize	38	27
Bridgestone	Precept Extra (2-PW)	Cast, perimeter-weighted	V	Oversize	38	26
	Precept Tour (2-PW)	Perimeter-weighted, forged steel	V	Midsize	37.5	26
	Precept Power Pack (2-PW)	Cast cavity back, 17-4 ss	V	Oversize	37.5	26

Legend:	g=graphite	R=Men's Regular shaft flex ratings
	s=steel	F=Firm
	ss=stainless steel	S=Men's Stiff shaft flex rating
	L=Ladies' shaft flex rating	X=Men's Extra Stiff shaft flex rating
	A=Seniors' shaft flex ratings	

Lie Angle (deg.)	Degree of Hosel Offset	Shaft Materials and Flexes	Grip Style	Left-Handed	Women's	Suggested Retail (set of 8)
60.5	Moderate	True Temper steel, filament-wound graphite (all flexes custom-fitted)	Royal, Golf Pride, all styles available	Y	Y	$640 steel $800 graphite
60.5	Moderate/ Progressive	Steel R, S, X Aldila graphite A, R, S	Proprietary rubber all-weather	Y	Y	$1200 steel $1500 graphite
60	Progressive	Tour Step II steel, G-Force 2 Tour graphite R, S	Tour Wrap	Y	N	$720 steel $1000 graphite
60.5	Progressive	G-Force 2 Tour graphite (one flex)	Tour Wrap	N	N	$1000
60	Progressive	G-Force 2 Tour graphite (one flex)	Diamond Perf Wrap	N	Y	$1000

wider soles, designed for seniors/women, respectively.

Lie Angle (deg.)	Degree of Hosel Offset	Shaft Materials and Flexes	Grip Style	Left-Handed	Women's	Suggested Retail (set of 8)
60	Progressive	Steel, graphite L, A, R, F, S, X	Griptec Tour Wrap; all others available	Y	Y	$600 steel $920 graphite
60	Progressive	FM Precision steel R, S; graphite R, S	Royal Tour Wrap	N	N	$600 steel $840 graphite
60	Not supplied	High-modulus graphite R, S	Royal Tour Wrap	N	N	$640
60	Not supplied	High-modulus graphite R, S	Royal Tour Wrap	N	N	$640

continued

IRONS PRODUCT INFORMATION (continued)

MANUFACTURER	MODEL AND NUMBERS	DESIGN /CLUBHEAD MATERIAL	GROOVE TYPE	CLUBHEAD SIZE	5-IRON		
					LENGTHS (in.)	LOFT (deg.)	
Bullet Golf	Invincible II (1-PW)	Forged blade, carbon steel	V	Midsize	37.5	27	
	TCB (2-PW)	Forged cavity back, carbon steel	U	Standard	37.5	27	
	444 (1-PW)	Cast, perimeter-weighted, 17-4 ss	V	Oversize	37.5	27	
	444 T (2-PW)	Cast, perimeter-weighted, titanium face	U	Oversize	37.5	27	
	Tour (3-PW)	17-4 ss	V	Oversize	37.5	27	
Callaway Golf	Big Bertha (1-PW)	Cast cavity back, 17-4 ss	U	Oversize	38	26	
	Big Bertha Gold (1-PW)	Cast cavity back, aluminum bronze	U	Oversize	38	26	
Carbite	Viper (2-PW)	Cast cavity back, 431 ss	U	Oversize	38	26	

Legend:	g=graphite	R=Men's Regular shaft flex ratings
	s=steel	F=Firm
	ss=stainless steel	S=Men's Stiff shaft flex rating
	L=Ladies' shaft flex rating	X=Men's Extra Stiff shaft flex rating
	A=Seniors' shaft flex ratings	

LIE ANGLE (deg.)	DEGREE OF HOSEL OFFSET	SHAFT MATERIALS AND FLEXES	GRIP STYLE	LEFT-HANDED	WOMEN'S	SUGGESTED RETAIL (set of 8)
60	Slight	True Temper Dynamic Gold steel R, S	Golf Pride Tour Velvet Wrap	N	N	Not supplied
60	Moderate	True Temper Dynamic Gold steel R, S		N	N	Not supplied
60	Progressive	True Temper Gold Lite steel, ceramic Kevlar (one flex)		Y	Y	$480 steel $640 ceramic Kevlar $800 graphite
60	Progressive	Not supplied		N	Y	Not supplied
60	Progressive	Not supplied		N	Y	$400 steel $560 ceramic Kevlar
61.3	Progressive	RCH graphite L, A, R, F, S; True Temper Memphis 10 steel (single flex)	Proprietary All-Weather	Y	Y	$880 steel $1160 graphite
61.3	Progressive	RCH graphite L, A, R, S, X	Proprietary All-Weather	N	N	$1480
60	Slight	Proprietary lightweight graphite L, A, R, S	Lamkin Lightweight Tour Wrap	N	Y	$790

continued

IRONS PRODUCT INFORMATION *(continued)*

MANUFACTURER	MODEL AND NUMBERS	DESIGN /CLUBHEAD MATERIAL	GROOVE TYPE	CLUBHEAD SIZE	5-IRON	
					LENGTHS *(in.)*	LOFT *(deg.)*
Cleveland Golf	VAS+ (1-PW)	Cast, ss	V 1–7-irons, U 8-PW	Oversize	37.75	27
Cobra Golf	King Cobra Oversize (Driving Iron, 3-PW)	Cast, perimeter-weighted, 17-4 ss	V	Oversize	38	26
	Senior King Cobra (Driving Iron, 3-PW)	Cast, perimeter-weighted, 17-4 ss	V	Oversize	38.5	26
	King Cobra Tour (Driving Iron, 2-PW)	Cast, perimeter-weighted, 15-5 ss	V	Oversize	38	27
	Lady Cobra (3-PW)	Cast, perimeter-weighted, 17-4 ss	V	Oversize	37	26
	Norman Grind (Driving Iron, 3-PW)	Cast muscle back, 15-5 ss	V	Standard	38	28

Legend:	g=graphite	R=Men's Regular shaft flex ratings
	s=steel	F=Firm
	ss=stainless steel	S=Men's Stiff shaft flex rating
	L=Ladies' shaft flex rating	X=Men's Extra Stiff shaft flex rating
	A=Seniors' shaft flex ratings	

Lie Angle (deg.)	Degree of Hosel Offset	Shaft Materials and Flexes	Grip Style	Left-Handed	Women's	Suggested Retail (set of 8)
60.5	Moderate	Lightweight steel A, R, S, X; graphite L, A, R, S, X	Golf Pride Tour Wrap	Y	Y	$745 steel $1115 graphite
61	Progressive	Graphite A, R, S, X; steel A, R, S, X; titanium A, R, S, X	Rubber Tour Wrap	Y	N	$656 steel $1056 graphite $1192 titanium
59.5	Progressive	Graphite A; steel A	Senior Rubber Tour Wrap	Y	N	$656 steel $960 graphite
61	Slight	Tour Weight graphite R, S, X; graphite R, S, X; titanium A, R, S, X; steel L, A, R, S, X	Tour Full Cord, Rubber Tour Wrap	N	N	$720 steel $1056 graphite $1456 Tour graphite $1192 titanium
59.5	Progressive	Graphite, steel L	Ladies Rubber Tour Wrap	Y	Y	$616 steel $912 graphite
61	None	Tour Weight graphite R, S, X; graphite R, S, X; titanium A, R, S, X; steel L, A, R, S, X	Tour Full Cord, Rubber Tour Wrap	N	N	$720 steel $1056 graphite $1456 Tour Weight graphite $1192 titanium

continued

Irons Product Information (continued)

Manufacturer	Model and Numbers	Design /Clubhead Material	Groove Type	Clubhead Size	5-Iron	
					Lengths (in.)	Loft (deg.)
Confidence Golf	Zoom Wide Body (1-PW)	Cast, perimeter-weighted, pure ingot 431 ss	V	Oversize	37.75 s, 38.5 g	26
	Visa (1-PW)	Cast, perimeter-weighted, pure ingot 431 ss	V	Oversize	37.75 s, 38.5 g	26
	Original 73 (1-PW)	Cast blade, pure ingot 431 ss	V	Midsize	37.75	28
Ray Cook	Titanic (1-PW)	Cast, perimeter-weighted, titanium 6AL 4V	V	Oversize	38 s, 38.5 g	28
	Comments: Clubhead has much greater mass in toe and heel—					
Daiwa	G-3 Titan Cavity (4-PW) & Driving Iron	Titanium	V	Oversize	39	25
	Hi-Trac MF-110 (1-10)	Cast, perimeter-weighted, 630 ss	Modified V	Midsize	38	26
	Hi-Trac MF-110 Tour (1-10)	Cast, perimeter-weighted, carbon steel	V	Standard	38	28
	DG-201 Forged (1-11)	Forged blade, carbon steel	V	Standard	38	28

Comments: Hi-Trac MF-110 has Dual Twin Cut sole; DG 201 is a classic muscle-back design.

Legend:	g=graphite	R=Men's Regular shaft flex ratings
	s=steel	F=Firm
	ss=stainless steel	S=Men's Stiff shaft flex rating
	L=Ladies' shaft flex rating	X=Men's Extra Stiff shaft flex rating
	A=Seniors' shaft flex ratings	

Lie Angle (deg.)	Degree of Hosel Offset	Shaft Materials and Flexes	Grip Style	Left-Handed	Women's	Suggested Retail (set of 8)
60	Moderate	Steel, graphite L, R, S	Confidence Soft Wrap, Golf Pride Victory (women)	N	Y	$636 steel $1040 graphite
60	Moderate	Steel, graphite L, R, S	Confidence Soft Wrap, Golf Pride Victory (women)	Y	Y	$536 steel $880 graphite
61	Slight	Steel R, S, X	Golf Pride Velvet Cord	N	N	$640 steel
61	Slight	True Temper Dynamic Gold R, S, X; Fujikara autoclave graphite R, S, X	Griptec Tour Wrap	Y	Y	$1200 steel $1672 graphite

since titanium is 40% lighter than stainless steel.

Lie Angle (deg.)	Degree of Hosel Offset	Shaft Materials and Flexes	Grip Style	Left-Handed	Women's	Suggested Retail (set of 8)
59	Moderate	SVM lightweight graphite R, S	Pebbled Rubber Lightweight	N	N	$3200
60	Progressive	Graphite L, A, R, S	Perforated Wrap Style	Y	Y	$920
60	Slight	Graphite R, S	Perforated Wrap Style	N	N	$1136
60	Slight	Steel R, S	Perforated Wrap Style	N	N	$672

continued

IRONS PRODUCT INFORMATION *(continued)*

MANUFACTURER	MODEL AND NUMBERS	DESIGN /CLUBHEAD MATERIAL	GROOVE TYPE	CLUBHEAD SIZE	5-IRON	
					LENGTHS *(in.)*	LOFT *(deg.)*
Dunlop	Tour DG (1-PW)	304 ss	U	Midsize	38	28
	RMS (1-PW)	431 ss	U	Oversize	38	26
	DDH (3-PW)	431 ss	U	Oversize	38	26
Dynacraft	Copperhead (1-PW)	Cast cavity back, 431 ss	V	Midsize	37.75	28
	Plus Midsize (1-PW)	Cast cavity back, 431 ss	V	Midsize	37.5	28
	Tour Caliber (1-PW)	Forged cavity back, carbon steel	V	Standard to midsize	37.5	28
Comments: Custom-fitting available for all specifications.						
Goldwin Golf	AVDP (1-PW)	Cast cavity back, 17-4 ss	V	Oversize	38	27
Golfsmith	Jetstream (1-PW)	Cast cavity back, 17-4 ss	U	Oversize	38	26
	XPC Plus (1-PW)	Cast cavity back, 431 ss	U	Oversize	38	27
	Harvey Penick Master (1-PW)	Cast cavity back, 431 ss	U	Oversize	38	26

Legend:	g=graphite	R=Men's Regular shaft flex ratings
	s=steel	F=Firm
	ss=stainless steel	S=Men's Stiff shaft flex rating
	L=Ladies' shaft flex rating	X=Men's Extra Stiff shaft flex rating
	A=Seniors' shaft flex ratings	

Lie Angle (deg.)	Degree of Hosel Offset	Shaft Materials and Flexes	Grip Style	Left-Handed	Women's	Suggested Retail (set of 8)
Not supplied	Slight	True Temper Dynamic Gold steel w/ Sensicore R, S	Golf Pride Tour Velvet Wrap	N	N	$480
Not supplied	Moderate	True Temper Status w/ Sensicore A, R, S, Release graphite A, L	Golf Pride Tour Velvet Wrap	N	Y	$520 steel $656 graphite
Not supplied	Moderate	DDH Tour Wide Body graphite L, R, S	Dunlap Perma Wrap	Y	Y	$216 steel $400 graphite
60	Progressive	True Temper Dynamic Gold steel R, S, X	Golf Pride Tour Velvet	Y	Y	$400
60	Progressive			N	N	$375
60	Slight			N	N	$480
60	Moderate/ progressive	AVDP graphite L, L+, A, R, F, S, X	Winn Lightweight Wrap Grip	N	Y	$1040
61	Progressive	Steel, graphite L, A, R, S	Jetstream Wrap	N	Y	$476 steel $680 graphite
60	Moderate	Steel, graphite L, A, R, S	XPC Plus Wrap	Y	Y	$425 steel $630 graphite
59	Moderate	Steel, graphite L, A, R, S	Penick Wrap	Y	Y	$560 steel $736 graphite

continued

IRONS PRODUCT INFORMATION *(continued)*

MANUFACTURER	MODEL AND NUMBERS	DESIGN /CLUBHEAD MATERIAL	GROOVE TYPE	CLUBHEAD SIZE	5-IRON		
					LENGTHS *(in.)*	LOFT *(deg.)*	
The GolfWorks	Tarantula (2-PW)	Cast cavity back, 431 ss	U	Oversize	37.5	26	
	Bio-Mech II (3-PW)	Cast cavity back, 431 ss	U	Oversize	37.5	26	
	Kinetic II (1-PW)	Cast cavity back, 431 ss	U	Oversize	37.5	27	
	Techni-Forge (2-PW)	Forged cavity back, carbon steel	U	Standard	37.5	27	
Comments: Other models are available for left-handed and for women.							
Ben Hogan	Edge GCD (1-PW)	Cast, perimeter-weighted, ss	U	Midsize	37.75 s 38.25 g	28	
	Edge GCD Tour (1-PW)	Forged blade, carbon steel	U	Midsize	37.75 s 38.25 g	28	
	H40 Oversize (Driving Iron, 3-PW)	Cast, perimeter-weighted, ss	V, U	Midsize	37.75 s 38.25 g	26	
	Apex (1-PW)	Forged blade, carbon steel	U	Standard	37.75 s 38.25 g	29	
Izzo	BladZ	Cast cavity back, 431 ss	U	Midsize	37.25 s	28	

Legend:	g=graphite	R=Men's Regular shaft flex ratings
	s=steel	F=Firm
	ss=stainless steel	S=Men's Stiff shaft flex rating
	L=Ladies' shaft flex rating	X=Men's Extra Stiff shaft flex rating
	A=Seniors' shaft flex ratings	

Lie Angle (deg.)	Degree of Hosel Offset	Shaft Materials and Flexes	Grip Style	Left-Handed	Women's	Suggested Retail (set of 8)
57	Progressive	True Temper Dynamic Gold steel R, S	Rubber Wrap Style	N	N	$248 steel $464 graphite
60	Progressive	True Temper Lite steel L, A, R, S		N	Y	$232 steel $392 graphite
60	Progressive	True Temper Rocket steel R, S		N	N	$288 steel $384 graphite
60	Progressive	True Temper Gold Plus steel R, S, X		N	N	Not supplied
60	Not supplied	Apex steel L, A, R, S, X; Apex graphite, L, A, R, S, X	Apex V-Trac Cord	Y	Y	$736 steel $1000 graphite
60	Not supplied	Apex steel A, R, S, X; Apex graphite A, R, S, X	Apex V-Trac Cord	N	N	$920 steel $1160 graphite
60	Not supplied	Apex steel L, A, R, S, X; Apex graphite L, A, R, S, X	Apex V-Trac Cord	N	Y	$640 steel $940 graphite
60	Not supplied	Apex steel A, R, S, X	Apex V-Trac Cord	N	N	$760
60	Slight	FM Precision Rifle steel R, S, X, Izzo LT graphite	Golf Pride Tour Velvet	N	N	$760 steel $1000 graphite

continued

IRONS PRODUCT INFORMATION *(continued)*

MANUFACTURER	MODEL AND NUMBERS	DESIGN /CLUBHEAD MATERIAL	GROOVE TYPE	CLUBHEAD SIZE	5-IRON		
					LENGTHS *(in.)*	LOFT *(deg.)*	
Javelin Blue	Javelin Blue (1-PW)	Cast cavity back, 17-4 ss	V	Midsize	38	28	
Kunnan	EXT Series (EXT International for women) (3-PW)	Cast cavity back	Not supplied	Mid- to oversize	38	26	
	Tribute Series (3-PW)	Cast cavity back, 431 ss w/graphite cavity	Not supplied	Not supplied	38	26	
	Comments: EXT has progressive offset, hosel lengths, and topline width;						
Lynx	Black Cat (1-PW)	Cast cavity back, 17-4 virgin ss	U	Oversize	37.5 s 38 g	27	
	Black Cat Tour (1-PW)	Cast cavity back, feryllium 255	U	Midsize	37.5	28	

Comments: Elastomer-lined cavity dampens sound; beveled topline.

Legend:	g=graphite	R=Men's Regular shaft flex ratings
	s=steel	F=Firm
	ss=stainless steel	S=Men's Stiff shaft flex rating
	L=Ladies' shaft flex rating	X=Men's Extra Stiff shaft flex rating
	A=Seniors' shaft flex ratings	

	Degree of Hosel Offset	Shaft Materials and Flexes	Grip Style	Left-Handed	Women's	Suggested Retail *(set of 8)*
Lie Angle *(deg.)*						
60	Slight	Graphite, 9 flexes available	Tour Wrap, Tour Cord, Ladies Cord	N	Y	$1200
59	Progressive	Graphite L, A, R, S	Golf Pride Tour Wrap	N	Y	$779
60.5	Progressive	Graphite L, A, R, S	Half Cord	Y	Y	$549
Tribute has graphite Vitrotrim back insert which allows more weight around perimeter.						
60	Moderate	True Temper Dynamic Gold steel R, S, X; Lynx Lite steel R, S; Graphite Flare L, A, R, S, X	Golf Pride Tour Wrap	Y	Y	$786 steel $1186 graphite
61	Slight	True Temper Dynamic Gold R300, S300, X300	Golf Pride Tour Velvet	N	N	$736

continued

IRONS PRODUCT INFORMATION (continued)

MANUFACTURER	MODEL AND NUMBERS	DESIGN /CLUBHEAD MATERIAL	GROOVE TYPE	CLUBHEAD SIZE	5-IRON		
					LENGTHS (in.)	LOFT (deg.)	
MacGregor	VIP Oversize Plus	Cast cavity w/ muscle back	Square	Oversize	38 s, 38.25 g	27	
	VIP Oversize	Cast cavity w/muscle back	Square	Midsize	38 s, 38.25 g	27	
	VIP Tour Forged	Forged cavity back, carbon steel	Square	Standard	38	29	

Comments: Elegant designs, nice offerings mix and shaft options to meet all players' needs.

Legend:	g=graphite	R=Men's Regular shaft flex ratings
	s=steel	F=Firm
	ss=stainless steel	S=Men's Stiff shaft flex rating
	L=Ladies' shaft flex rating	X=Men's Extra Stiff shaft flex rating
	A=Seniors' shaft flex ratings	

Lie Angle (deg.)	Degree of Hosel Offset	Shaft Materials and Flexes	Grip Style	Left-Handed	Women's	Suggested Retail (set of 8)
60	Moderate	Apollo Lite steel, midflex; FM Precision Rifle steel R, S; Exel graphite A, R, S	Golf Pride Tour Wrap	N	Y	$560 Lite steel $640 Rifle steel $864 graphite
60	Moderate/ progressive	True Temper Dynamic Gold steel R400, S300; Apollo Lite steel, midflex; Exel graphite L, A, R, S, X	Golf Pride Tour Wrap Cord, Tour Wrap (women)	Y	Y	$560 Lite steel $600 Dynamic steel $864 graphite
60	No offset	True Temper Dynamic Gold steel R400, S300	Golf Pride Tour Wrap Cord	N	N	$600

continued

IRONS PRODUCT INFORMATION *(continued)*

MANUFACTURER	MODEL AND NUMBERS	DESIGN /CLUBHEAD MATERIAL	GROOVE TYPE	CLUBHEAD SIZE	5-IRON		
					LENGTHS *(in.)*	LOFT *(deg.)*	
Maruman Golf	Verity-U (3-PW)	Cast cavity back, 17-4 ss	V	Oversize	37.5	27	
	M301T (3-PW)	Cast cavity back, ss w/titanium	V	Midsize	38	27	
	Titus WA-2 (3-PW)	Cast cavity back, ss w/titanium face	V	Midsize	37.5	27	
	Conductor Pro (1-PW)	Forged cavity back, carbon steel	V	Standard	38	28	
	Conductor 42 CX (1-PW)	Forged cavity back, carbon steel	V	Standard	38	28	
	Comments: M301T has titanium face insert on 3-, 4-, 5-irons;						
Maxfli Golf	VHL Midsize (2-PW)	Cast cavity back, 17-4 ss	U	Midsize	37.75 s, 38 g	27	
	VHL Oversize (2-PW)	Cast cavity back, 17-4 ss	U	Oversize	37.75 s, 38 g	27	

Legend:	g=graphite	R=Men's Regular shaft flex ratings
	s=steel	F=Firm
	ss=stainless steel	S=Men's Stiff shaft flex rating
	L=Ladies' shaft flex rating	X=Men's Extra Stiff shaft flex rating
	A=Seniors' shaft flex ratings	

Lie Angle (deg.)	Degree of Hosel Offset	Shaft Materials and Flexes	Grip Style	Left-Handed	Women's	Suggested Retail (set of 8)
60	Progressive	Carbofit graphite R, S; Dynalite steel R, S	Velvet Tour Wrap	Y	Y	$680 steel $1000 graphite
60	Progressive	Carbofit graphite R, S	Not supplied	N	Y	$1350
60	Not supplied	Carbofit graphite R, S; Parsec GX Kevlar R, S	Proprietary by Maruman	N	Y	$2150 graphite $3000 Kevlar
60	Slight	True Temper Dynamic Gold steel R300, S300	Velvet Tour Wrap	N	N	$760
60	Slight	True Temper Dynamic Gold steel R300, S300	Not supplied	N	N	$760
Titus WA-2 has titanium inserts on full set.						
61	Progressive	Graphite, proprietary steel L, A, R, S	Golf Pride Tour Velvet	Y	Y	$664 steel $1024 graphite
61	Progressive			Y	Y	$664 steel $1024 graphite

continued

IRONS PRODUCT INFORMATION *(continued)*

MANUFACTURER	MODEL AND NUMBERS	DESIGN /CLUBHEAD MATERIAL	GROOVE TYPE	CLUBHEAD SIZE	5-IRON		
					LENGTHS *(in.)*	LOFT *(deg.)*	
Merit Golf	Tour International (1-PW)	Forged blade, carbon steel	V	Standard	38	30	
	Protonic (2-PW)	Cast cavity back, 431 ss	U	Midsize	38	28	
	Prophecy (1-PW)	Cast, 431 ss	U	Midsize	38 s, 38.5 g	28	
Mitsushiba Golf	Curare (2-PW)	Cast cavity back, 431 ss	U	Oversize	38	28	
	Integrity (2-PW)	Cast cavity back, 431 ss	U	Midsize	38	28	
	Verdict (3-PW)	Cast cavity back, zinc alloy	U	Oversize	38	28	

Legend:	g=graphite	R=Men's Regular shaft flex ratings
	s=steel	F=Firm
	ss=stainless steel	S=Men's Stiff shaft flex rating
	L=Ladies' shaft flex rating	X=Men's Extra Stiff shaft flex rating
	A=Seniors' shaft flex ratings	

Lie Angle (deg.)	Degree of Hosel Offset	Shaft Materials and Flexes	Grip Style	Left-Handed	Women's	Suggested Retail (set of 8)
59	None	True Temper Dynamic Gold steel R300, S300	Golf Pride Tour Wrap	N	N	$960
60	None	True Temper Dynalite Gold, Aldila graphite R, S, X	Golf Pride Tour Wrap	N	N	$768 steel $1008 graphite
59.5	Slight	True Temper Dynalite, Aldila graphite L, A, R, S	Golf Pride Tour Wrap	Y	Y	$528 steel $752 graphite
60	Moderate	Steel, graphite L, A, R, X	Lamkin Perma Wrap	Y	Y	$270 steel $456 graphite
60	Substantial		Lamkin Perma Wrap	Y	Y	$250 steel $396 graphite
60	Moderate		Lamkin Tru-Tac	Y	Y	$200 steel $336 graphite

continued

IRONS PRODUCT INFORMATION *(continued)*

MANUFACTURER	MODEL AND NUMBERS	DESIGN /CLUBHEAD MATERIAL	GROOVE TYPE	CLUBHEAD SIZE	5-IRON		
					LENGTHS *(in.)*	LOFT *(deg.)*	
Mizuno USA	Grad MP (1-PW)	Forged cavity back, double-forged carbon steel	V	Standard	37.75 s, 38.25 g	27.5	
	MP-14 (1-PW)	Forged blade, double-forged carbon steel	V	Standard	37.75 s, 38.25 g	29	
	MP-29 (1-PW)	Forged blade, double-forged carbon steel	V	Standard	37.75	29	
	T-Zoid Pro Forged (1-PW)	Forged modified cavity back, carbon steel	V	Midsize	38	27	
	T-Zoid T-3 titanium	Cast cavity back, ss w/ titanium insert	U	Oversize	38.5	27	
	Comments: Outstanding iron line, particularly for those who prefer forged irons.						
Nicklaus Golf	Bear (1-PW)	Cast cavity back, 17-4 ss	U	Progressive sizing	38	27	
	Bear Limited Edition Forging	Forged blade, 431 ss	Modified U	Standard	38	27	
	Comments: Bear irons feature linear dynamics weighting system.						
Arnold Palmer/ Pro Group	Palmer PHD (1-PW)	Cast cavity back, 17-4 ss	U	Oversize	38	26	

Lie Angle (deg.)	Degree of Hosel Offset	Shaft Materials and Flexes	Grip Style	Left-Handed	Women's	Suggested Retail (set of 8)
59.5	Progressive	Exsar V graphite R, S; True Temper Dynamic Gold and Dynalite Gold steel R, S	Golf Pride Tour Wrap	Y	N	$800 steel $1200 graphite
59	Slight	True Temper Dynamic Gold steel R, S; custom graphite available	Golf Pride Tour Wrap	N	N	$800
59	Slight	True Temper Dynamic Gold Steel R, S; custom graphite available	Golf Pride Tour Wrap	N	N	$1200
59	Slight	True Temper Dynamic Gold Sensicore S300	Golf Pride Tour Velvet Wrap	N	N	$960
60.5	Moderate	True Temper Dynalite steel R, Dynamic Gold steel S300, filament wound graphite R, S	Golf Pride Tour Velvet Wrap	N	N	$960 steel $1227 graphite
60	Moderate	Steel, single flex graphite A, R, S, X	Golf Pride or Griptec Tour Wrap	Y	Y	$760 steel $1280 graphite
60	Slight	Steel, single flex graphite A, R, S, X	Golf Pride or Griptec Tour Wrap	N	N	$1000 steel $1680 graphite
60	Substantial/ progressive	Apollo steel (single, medium-stiff flex), Exe 1 co-wound graphite L, A, R, F, S	Golf Pride Tour Velvet	Y	N	$720 steel $1040 graphite

continued

IRONS PRODUCT INFORMATION *(continued)*

MANUFACTURER	MODEL AND NUMBERS	DESIGN /CLUBHEAD MATERIAL	GROOVE TYPE	CLUBHEAD SIZE	5-IRON		
					LENGTHS *(in.)*	LOFT *(deg.)*	
Ping	ISI (1-PW)	Cast cavity back, 17-4 ss, copper, or nickel	U	Midsize (ss head larger than copper or nickel)	Custom-fit in 1/4" increments (all models)	Not supplied	
	Eye 2 (1-PW)	Cast cavity back, 17-4 ss or copper	U	Midsize		Not supplied	
	Zing 2 (1-PW)	17-4 ss	U	Midsize		Not supplied	
	Comments: New ISI offered in softer nickel, has slimmer topline, slightly smaller size;						
Gary Player Golf	Ignitor (3-PW)	Cast, aluminum bronze	U	Midsize	37.5	26	
Players Golf	Prozema (1-PW)	Cast cavity back, 17-4 ss	Not supplied	Oversize	37.5 s, 38 g	27	
	Original (1-PW)	Cast cavity back, ss w/cobalt finish	Not supplied	Oversize	37.5 s, 38 g	28	

Legend:	g=graphite	R=Men's Regular shaft flex ratings
	s=steel	F=Firm
	ss=stainless steel	S=Men's Stiff shaft flex rating
	L=Ladies' shaft flex rating	X=Men's Extra Stiff shaft flex rating
	A=Seniors' shaft flex ratings	

Lie Angle (deg.)	Degree of Hosel Offset	Shaft Materials and Flexes	Grip Style	Left-Handed	Women's	Suggested Retail (set of 8)
Custom 10 lies available for all models	Moderate	JZ steel, ZZ65 steel standard; other steel and graphite options available, all flexes	Proprietary Ping DylaGrip or Textured Spiral standard, with numerous options	Y	Y	$720 ss head $910 copper $1200 nickel
	Moderate	JZ steel standard; other steel and graphite options available, all flexes		Y	Y	$720 ss head $880 copper
	Substantial	KTM steel; other steel and graphite options available		Y	Y	$710

Zing 2 is the most forgiving; Copper Eye-2 (1982) still a classic.

Lie Angle (deg.)	Degree of Hosel Offset	Shaft Materials and Flexes	Grip Style	Left-Handed	Women's	Suggested Retail (set of 8)
60	Slight, progressive	Steel, graphite R, S	Golf Pride All-Weather	N	N	$599 steel $849 graphite
59	Moderate	True Temper Dynamic steel R, S; graphite L, A, R, S	Full Cord	N	Y	$475 steel $650 graphite
60	Slight	True Temper Dynamic steel, low-torque graphite R, S	Rubber Wrap	N	N	$425 steel $600 graphite

continued

IRONS PRODUCT INFORMATION *(continued)*

MANUFACTURER	MODEL AND NUMBERS	DESIGN /CLUBHEAD MATERIAL	GROOVE TYPE	CLUBHEAD SIZE	5-IRON		
					LENGTHS *(in.)*	LOFT *(deg.)*	
PowerBilt	TPS Oversize (1-PW)	Cast cavity back, 17-4 ss	U	Oversize	37.62	27	
	TPS Ladies Oversize (3-PW)	Cast cavity back, 17-4 ss	U	Oversize	37	27	
Pro Select	Prism Tour (2-PW)	Cast, flow-weighted, 431 ss	Not supplied	Oversize	38	26	
	PS-2 (3-PW)	Cast cavity back, 431 ss	Not supplied	Oversize	38	25	
	Power Kick (2-PW)	Cast, flow-weighted, 431 ss	Not supplied	Oversize	38	26	
	NXT Spec (2-PW)	Cast, flow-weighted, 431 ss	Not supplied	Oversize	38	26	
Rainbow Golf	Sealed Power Titanium (1-PW)	Cast cavity back, beryllium copper w/ titanium face	V	Midsize	Not supplied	27	
	Boomer Titanium (1-PW)	Cast cavity back, 431 ss w/ titanium face	V	Midsize	Not supplied	27	

Comments: Company claims titanium faces make irons "one club longer."

Legend:	g=graphite	R=Men's Regular shaft flex ratings
	s=steel	F=Firm
	ss=stainless steel	S=Men's Stiff shaft flex rating
	L=Ladies' shaft flex rating	X=Men's Extra Stiff shaft flex rating
	A=Seniors' shaft flex ratings	

Lie Angle (deg.)	Degree of Hosel Offset	Shaft Materials and Flexes	Grip Style	Left-Handed	Women's	Suggested Retail (*set of 8*)
60.5	Progressive	True Temper Dynamic Gold steel S; UST Dynasty Plus steel R, S; UST Tour Weight graphite S; Dynasty Plus graphite L, A, R, S	Golf Pride Tour Velvet	Y	N	$832 steel $1080–$1320 graphite
60.5	Progressive	UST Dynasty Plus graphite L	Golf Pride Tour Velvet	N	Y	$832 steel $1080–$1320 graphite
59	Slight	True Temper graphite L, A, R, S	Lamkin Black Wrap	N	N	$699
59	Moderate	Steel, Ti-core graphite, UST Gold steel L, R, S	Tour Tech Wrap	N	Y	$375 steel $550 graphite
59	Moderate	Power Kick filament-wound graphite R, S	Tour Tech Black Wrap	N	N	$750
59	Moderate	Steel or graphite L, A, R	Lamkin Black Wrap	Y	Y	$350 steel $650 graphite
Not supplied	Slight	High-modulus graphite/boron R	Golf Pride, Lamkin, Tacki-Mac	N	Y	$1200
Not supplied	Progressive	High-modulus graphite/boron R	Golf Pride, Lamkin, Tacki-Mac	N	Y	$1000

continued

IRONS PRODUCT INFORMATION *(continued)*

MANUFACTURER	MODEL AND NUMBERS	DESIGN /CLUBHEAD MATERIAL	GROOVE TYPE	CLUBHEAD SIZE	5-IRON		
					LENGTHS *(in.)*	LOFT *(deg.)*	
Ram Golf	FX Pro Set Tour Grind (1-PW)	Forged muscle back, nickel-plated carbon steel	U	Standard	37.5 s, 38 g	28	
	FX Pro Set FS (1-PW)	Forged muscle back to cavity back, carbon steel	U	Standard to oversize (short to long)	37.5 s, 38 g	27	
	FX Pro Set CS (1-PW)	Cast cavity back, cobalt steel	Square	Standard to oversize (short to long)	37.5 s, 38 g	26	
	FX Oversize (2-PW)	Cast cavity back, 17-4 ss	Square	Midsize	38	26	
Rawlings	Tour	Cast cavity back, ss w/ cobalt finish	Not supplied	Oversize	37.5 s, 38 g	29	
	MVP	Cast cavity back, 431 ss	Not supplied	Oversize	37.75 s, 38.25 g	29	

Comments: Two-tiered sole, deep cavity, thin hitting surface.

Legend:	g=graphite	R=Men's Regular shaft flex ratings
	s=steel	F=Firm
	ss=stainless steel	S=Men's Stiff shaft flex rating
	L=Ladies' shaft flex rating	X=Men's Extra Stiff shaft flex rating
	A=Seniors' shaft flex ratings	

Lie Angle (deg.)	Degree of Hosel Offset	Shaft Materials and Flexes	Grip Style	Left-Handed	Women's	Suggested Retail (set of 8)
61	Slight	Custom only (steel or graphite)	Custom only	N	N	Custom only, individual pricing
61	Progressive	Ram steel, Ram Speed Weight graphite, Ram Tour Weight graphite R, S, X for all	Ram Wrap	N	N	$760 steel $1000 graphite
61	Progressive	Ram 3-Plexxx steel R, S, X; Ram 3-Plexxx graphite A, R, S, X	Ram X-Grip	Y	N	$760 steel $1000 graphite
61	Moderate	Ram Tempo Weight graphite L, A, R, S	Ram Wrap	Y	Y	$696
60	Moderate	True Temper steel, Aldila graphite L, R, S	Rubber Wrap	N	Y	$280 steel $440 graphite
60	Progressive	True Temper Rocket steel, True Temper Dynamic Lite graphite R, S	Rubber Wrap	N	N	$600 steel $735 graphite

continued

IRONS PRODUCT INFORMATION (continued)

MANUFACTURER	MODEL AND NUMBERS	DESIGN /CLUBHEAD MATERIAL	GROOVE TYPE	CLUBHEAD SIZE	5-IRON		
					LENGTHS (in.)	LOFT (deg.)	
RTS Golf	RTS Midsize (1-PW)	Cast cavity back, 17-4 ss	U	Midsize	38	26	
	RTS Oversize (1-PW)	Cast cavity back, 17-4 ss	U	Oversize	38	26	
	Comments: Patented titanium bent hosel moves shaft axis closer to clubhead's center.						
Slazenger	Crown Limited (1-PW)	Cast cavity back, 431 ss	U	Midsize	38	27	
Kenneth Smith	KS 2000 O/S (2-PW)	Cast cavity back, 431 ss	V	Oversize	37.5	29	
	Royal Signet (1-PW)	Forged blade, ss	V	Standard	37.5	30	
	Comments: All irons are custom-fit for a variety of specifications with personalization included.						
Snake Eyes Golf	New model due early to mid 1997	Modified forged muscle back, carbon steel	V	Standard	38	28	

Legend:	g=graphite	R=Men's Regular shaft flex ratings
	s=steel	F=Firm
	ss=stainless steel	S=Men's Stiff shaft flex rating
	L=Ladies' shaft flex rating	X=Men's Extra Stiff shaft flex rating
	A=Seniors' shaft flex ratings	

Lie Angle (deg.)	Degree of Hosel Offset	Shaft Materials and Flexes	Grip Style	Left-Handed	Women's	Suggested Retail (set of 8)
60	Progressive	Steel A, R, F, S; graphite A, R, F, S, X	Griptec Tour Wrap	N	N	$760 steel $1160 graphite
60	Progressive	Steel A, R, F, S; graphite A, R, F, S, X	Griptec Tour Wrap	N	Y	$760 steel $1160 graphite
61	Progressive offset and zero offset available	FM Precision Rifle steel A, R, S, X; high-modulus and filament-wound graphite A, R, S, X	Golf Pride in various styles	N	N	$720–$800 steel $1120–$1520 graphite
60	Progressive	Steel R, S; ultralight graphite L, A, R, S; boron graphite A, R, S; titanium A, R, S, X	Golf Pride, Royal, Griptec in various styles; Leather Perforated Wrap	N	Y	$920 steel $1200 graphite $1720 titanium
60	Slight	Steel L, A, R, S, X; ultralight graphite L, A, R, S; boron graphite A, R, S; titanium A, R, S, X	Golf Pride, Royal, Griptec in various styles; Leather Perforated Wrap	Y	Y	$1280 steel $1600 graphite $1720 titanium
60	Progressive	Shaft offerings to be announced	Snake Eyes Custom Grip	Y	Y	Prices to be announced

continued

IRONS PRODUCT INFORMATION *(continued)*

MANUFACTURER	MODEL AND NUMBERS	DESIGN /CLUBHEAD MATERIAL	GROOVE TYPE	CLUBHEAD SIZE	5-IRON	
					LENGTHS *(in.)*	LOFT *(deg.)*
Taylor Made	Burner Bubble Tour (1-PW)	Cast cavity back, 431 ss	U	Standard	38	29
	Burner Bubble (2-PW)	Cast cavity back, 17-4 ss	U	Oversize	37.5 s, 38 g	27
	Champagne Burner Bubble (2-PW)	Cast cavity back, 17-4 ss	U	Oversize	37	27
	Comments: Tour model is traditional size with slimmer top line that most low handicappers prefer.					
Titleist	DCI Black (1-PW)	Cast cavity back, 431 ss	U	Standard	37.75	28
	DCI Oversize Black (1-PW)		U	Oversize	37.75	28
	DCI Oversize Gold (1-PW)		U	Oversize	37.75	28
	DCI Oversize Seniors		U	Oversize	38	27
	DCI Oversize Women		U	Oversize	37.25	27

Legend:	g=graphite	R=Men's Regular shaft flex ratings
	s=steel	F=Firm
	ss=stainless steel	S=Men's Stiff shaft flex rating
	L=Ladies' shaft flex rating	X=Men's Extra Stiff shaft flex rating
	A=Seniors' shaft flex ratings	

Lie Angle (deg.)	Degree of Hosel Offset	Shaft Materials and Flexes	Grip Style	Left-Handed	Women's	Suggested Retail (set of 8)
60	Slight	FM Precision Rifle steel R, S, X; Bubble graphite R, S, X	Rubber Tour Wrap	N	N	$856 steel $1200 graphite
61.5	Moderate/ progressive	Bubble graphite A, R, S, X; Brunswick Rifle steel R, S, X	Rubber Tour Wrap	Y	N	$728 steel $1064 graphite
60.5	Moderate/ progressive	Bubble graphite L	Rubber Tour Wrap	N	Y	$1064
62	Slight/ progressive	Tri Spec steel or graphite R, S, X	Golf Pride Buffed Tour Wrap	N	N	$688 steel $1040 graphite
62	Slight/ progressive	Tri Spec steel or graphite R, S, X	Golf Pride Buffed Tour Wrap	N	N	$688 steel $1040 graphite
62	Moderate/ progressive	Tri Spec steel or graphite R, S, X	Golf Pride Buffed Tour Wrap	N	N	$688 steel $1040 graphite
60	Moderate/ progressive	Tri Spec graphite A	Tour Wrap Air Cushion	N	N	$960
60	Moderate/ progressive	Tri Spec steel or graphite L	Golf Pride Air Cushion Victory	N	Y	$616 steel $880 graphite

continued

IRONS PRODUCT INFORMATION *(continued)*

MANUFACTURER	MODEL AND NUMBERS	DESIGN /CLUBHEAD MATERIAL	GROOVE TYPE	CLUBHEAD SIZE	5-IRON		
					LENGTHS *(in.)*	LOFT *(deg.)*	
Top-Flite	Tour Ti	Cast cavity back, ss w/ titanium face insert	V	Midsize	37.5	26	
	Tour Oversize (1-PW)	Cast cavity back, 17-4 ss	V	Oversize	37.5 s, 38 g	26	
	Tour Pro Offset (1-PW)	Cast cavity back, 304 ss	V	Midsize	37.5 s, 38 g	28	
Vulcan	Q-Pointe (1-PW)	Cast cavity back, 17-4 ss	U	Midsize	24 custom lengths	26.5	

Legend:	g=graphite	R=Men's Regular shaft flex ratings
	s=steel	F=Firm
	ss=stainless steel	S=Men's Stiff shaft flex rating
	L=Ladies' shaft flex rating	X=Men's Extra Stiff shaft flex rating
	A=Seniors' shaft flex ratings	

Lie Angle (deg.)	Degree of Hosel Offset	Shaft Materials and Flexes	Grip Style	Left-Handed	Women's	Suggested Retail (set of 8)
60	Progressive	Fenwick muscle graphite L, A, R, S, X; True Temper Dynalite steel R300, S300	Tour Velvet ruffer wrap	N	N	$1100 steel $1400 graphite
60	Progressive	True Temper Dynalite steel R, S; Performance Flex graphite L, A, R, S	Buffed Tour Wrap	Y	Y	$625 steel $850 graphite
60	Progressive	Dynalite steel R, S; Performance Flex graphite R, S	Buffed Tour Wrap	Y	N	$625 steel $850 graphite
Custom	Moderate/ progressive	Jetstream II graphite, 10 custom flexes	Golf Pride Tour Wrap, Lamkin Perma Wrap	Y	Y	$720

continued

IRONS PRODUCT INFORMATION *(continued)*

MANUFACTURER	MODEL AND NUMBERS	DESIGN /CLUBHEAD MATERIAL	GROOVE TYPE	CLUBHEAD SIZE	5-IRON	
					LENGTHS *(in.)*	LOFT *(deg.)*
Wilson	Staff Midsize (1-PW)	Cast cavity back, 17-4 ss	U	Midsize	38	26
	Staff RM (1-PW)	Forged cavity back, carbon steel	U	Midsize	38	27
	Staff FG 51 (1-PW)	Forged blade, carbon steel	U	Standard	38	28
Wood Brothers	Limited Forged Blade (2-PW)	Forged muscle back, carbon steel, brush finish	V	Standard	37.5	28
	Championship Balance Tour Forged (2-PW)	Forged cavity back, carbon steel, brush finish	V	Midsize	37.5	28

Comments: Company believes forged irons provide better shotmaking capability.

Legend:	g=graphite	R=Men's Regular shaft flex ratings
	s=steel	F=Firm
	ss=stainless steel	S=Men's Stiff shaft flex rating
	L=Ladies' shaft flex rating	X=Men's Extra Stiff shaft flex rating
	A=Seniors' shaft flex ratings	

Lie Angle (deg.)	Degree of Hosel Offset	Shaft Materials and Flexes	Grip Style	Left-Handed	Women's	Suggested Retail (set of 8)
62	Progressive	Firestick steel and Firestick graphite LL, AL, A, R, S, X	Golf Pride Tour Wrap	Y	Y	$690 steel $1060 graphite
62	Moderate		Golf Pride Tour Wrap	Y	N	$720 steel $1150 graphite
60	Slight		Golf Pride Tour Wrap	N	N	$640
60.5	Slight	True Temper Dynamic Gold steel R, S, X	Golf Pride Tour Wrap	N	N	$950
60.5	Moderate	True Temper Dynamic Gold steel R, S, X; UST 640 graphite R, S, X	CBTF Tour Wrap	N	N	$505 steel $694 graphite

continued

IRONS PRODUCT INFORMATION *(continued)*

MANUFACTURER	MODEL AND NUMBERS	DESIGN /CLUBHEAD MATERIAL	GROOVE TYPE	CLUBHEAD SIZE	5-IRON		
					LENGTHS *(in.)*	LOFT *(deg.)*	
Yonex	Super ADX Titanium (3-PW)	ss w/titanium face	U	Oversize	Not supplied	Not supplied	
	Super ADX (3-PW)	Cast cavity back, ss	U	Midsize	38	25	
	Super ADX Seniors (4-SW)	Cast cavity back, ss	U	Midsize	38	25	
	Super ADX Ladies (4-SW)	Cast cavity back, ss	U	Midsize	37	25	
	ADX 100 I	Soft cast cavity back	U	Standard	38	26	
	Tour	Forged cavity back, carbon steel	U	Midsize	38	27	
Zevo	Lob (5-PW)	Cast cavity back, ss	U	Oversize	38	25	
	Blade (1-PW)	Forged blade, carbon steel	V	Standard	38	28	
	Oversize (1-PW)	Cast cavity back, ss	U	Oversize	38	28	
	Midsize (1-PW)	Cast cavity back, ss	U	Oversize	38	28	

Comment: Blade irons are available custom-ground for varying toe style and top-line width.

Legend:	g=graphite	R=Men's Regular shaft flex ratings
	s=steel	F=Firm
	ss=stainless steel	S=Men's Stiff shaft flex rating
	L=Ladies' shaft flex rating	X=Men's Extra Stiff shaft flex rating
	A=Seniors' shaft flex ratings	

Lie Angle (deg.)	Degree of Hosel Offset	Shaft Materials and Flexes	Grip Style	Left-Handed	Women's	Suggested Retail (set of 8)
Not supplied	Not supplied	High-modulus, low-torque graphite	Tour Weave Cord	Y	Y	$1600
60	Not supplied	High-modulus, low-torque graphite	Rubber Tour Wrap	Y	N	$1200
60	Not supplied	Ultralight graphite A	Rubber Tour Wrap	Y	N	$1200
60	Not supplied	Ultralight graphite L	Rubber Tour Wrap	N	Y	$1200
59	Not supplied	High-modulus graphite L, R, S	Rubber Tour Wrap	Y	Y	$1080
59	Slight	Graphite/boron	Rubber Tour Wrap	Y	N	$1360
55–67	Slight	5 shafts, 7 flexes	Zevo Pro Wrap	N	Y	$920
55–67	Slight	5 shafts, 7 flexes	Zevo Pro Wrap	N	N	$1200 steel $1600 graphite
55–67	Progressive	5 shafts, 7 flexes	Zevo Pro Wrap	Y	Y	$720 steel $1080 graphite
55–67	Progressive	5 shafts, 7 flexes	Zevo Pro Wrap	N	N	$720 steel $1080 graphite

continued

CHAPTER 6

Building a Better Wedge Arsenal

Recently, many noted teachers, including sport psychologist Bob Rotella in his book *Golf Is Not a Game of Perfect* (Simon & Schuster, 1995), have emphasized that in order to score well, you must do everything possible to improve your play from within 120 yards of the hole. You must learn to hit full wedges, partial wedges, and greenside pitches within one-putt range *without fail* if you intend to shoot anywhere near par.

Let's look at all the good reasons to examine your most-lofted clubs in the bag and consider whether you should beef up your short-shot arsenal.

Lofts on "Standard Set" Pitching Wedges Are Way Down

In the previous chapter we observed how the loft on most manufacturers' iron sets has decreased over the years—either in response to the average golfer's desire to hit all the clubs farther or simply as an approach to selling more irons—however you care to look at it.

This has caused problems on the "high" end of iron sets, which we have demarcated in this book as the pitching wedge (since the most common iron-set purchases have the pitching wedge as the most-lofted club included). Recently, I studied the lofts of major manufacturers' pitching wedges as part of a report for a weekly golf publication. Although I don't claim to have found the loft of every pitching wedge on the market, what I tabulated was certainly a representative sample. Amazingly, I found that the loft on today's pitching wedges averages a little under 47 degrees. And there are some pitching wedges on the market with as little as 43 degrees of loft.

Titleist High Performance

Again referring to clubmaker Ralph Maltby's *Golf Club Design, Fitting, Alteration & Repair,* the "traditional" loft on a pitching wedge is 50 degrees. Over perhaps the last thirty years, the loft on the average pitching wedge has *decreased* by just over 3 degrees.

You can see this for yourself if you ever happen across a $5 bargain bin of old clubs that includes some pitching wedges. Pull out a pitching wedge from the 1950s or 1960s and lay it squarely on the ground. You'll probably be shocked at how much loft you see on the face. In reality, most of today's pitching wedges have become yesterday's 9-irons.

Meanwhile, as you'll see in the table in this chapter, the vast majority of sand wedges carry either 55 or 56 degrees of loft—this has remained fairly constant over time. So, most golfers who carry a pitching wedge and a sand wedge will have, on average, a gap in the lofts between these two clubs of 8 or 9 degrees or greater. And, it's a gap that most amateurs are not even aware of.

Do You Have One Gap or Two?

Among all the clubs you carry, from the driver through the pitching wedge, there should be no more than a 4-degree gap in loft from any one club to the next (a possible exception could be the loft difference between your driver and 3-wood). However, you probably have a gap in loft of 8 to 10 degrees between your pitching and sand wedges. This could mean a difference of 25 to 30 yards between how far you can hit a full pitching wedge versus a full sand wedge. You may hit a nice full pitching wedge, say, 110 yards, but a full sand wedge no more

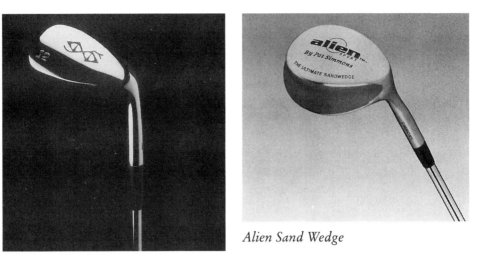

Alien Sand Wedge

Snake Eyes Lob Wedge

than 80 to 85 yards. This obviously creates a problem for you when you have a shot in the 85–100-yard range, because you'll have to hit something less than a normal, full shot.

An 8–10-degree gap between the two wedges also causes you problems in many delicate chipping situations from around the green. You'll encounter shots where the lie, the amount of rough to be carried, and the distance to the hole indicate that the loft you'd play the shot best with is midway between your two current wedges.

Every golfer should be aware of the gaps in loft between each club. It should be no more than 4 degrees between any of the wedges or between all longer clubs, so that you have an equally adequate coverage of distances throughout the bag. Given the trend toward pitching wedges that are much "stronger" in loft than the sand wedge, amateurs would be well served to consider adding an "approach" or "gap" wedge to their sets. This is a club that is designed similarly to a traditional pitching wedge and carries between 50 and 52 degrees of loft.

If you don't know what their lofts are, you should have your current pitching wedge and sand wedge measured. If the gap in loft between the two clubs is 8 degrees or more, an in-between gap or approach wedge, as it's come to be called, is certainly a club to look into. (We'll refer to this club as an approach wedge.)

In addition to the question of whether to add an approach wedge to your set, there's the question of whether you should consider adding a wedge with even higher loft than the average of 55 to 56 on the sand wedge. Such a club, most commonly referred to as a lob wedge, usually has about 60 degrees of loft, although some are available with as much as 64 degrees (see table). Such a club can prove

---

Use an Approach Wedge to "Set Up" the Par-5s

Many amateurs look to the par-5s on a course as a place where they may be able to "get back" some of the strokes that have invariably been lost on the par-3 and par-4 holes. However, their strategy for obtaining that birdie is often counterproductive. They will usually hit two woods as far as they can, in order to get as close as possible to a par-5 green in two. Often, even after two fine shots, this leaves them with a "partial" wedge in the 50–75-yard range, which they must play with a pitching wedge or sand wedge. It's harder for most golfers to gauge a shot that requires less than a full swing, particularly for amateurs who rarely practice them. So, the weekend player often loses the benefit of the two long previous shots with an indifferent pitch that leaves a long putt; or misses the shot entirely and takes an aggravating bogey.

Here's one spot where an approach wedge really helps. Instead of blasting the ball as far as you can on your second to a par-5 that you can't reach anyway, you can set up your second shot on a par-5 efficiently. Try to put your second a distance from the green from which you can hit a nice full shot with an approach wedge. This may mean hitting a 5-wood, or a 3- or 4-iron, instead of banging a 3-wood for your second. (Doing this also increases your chance of placing the second shot in the fairway, which always helps.) Depending on your overall distance, this setup second shot should leave you somewhere in the 90–110-yard range.

Everyone, even the top Tour pros, finds that it's a lot easier to control the distance of a shot that's hit "full" rather than a partial wedge. That's how most of them get their birdies on the par-5s, and it's how you should plan them, too.

---

extremely useful on short greenside shots from rough where there is little green before the hole on which to stop the ball, or on short greenside sand shots from deep bunkers, from where you must pop the ball up quickly and land it softly.

You may wonder whether it's worthwhile to carry a club with even greater loft than that of your sand wedge. Roger Cleveland, formerly president of Cleveland Golf who is now a club designer with Callaway Golf, recalls that for a long time even PGA Tour great Greg Norman felt that a lob wedge wasn't necessary. "Greg used to say, 'Baloney, a sand wedge is all a good player needs,'" Cleveland recalls. "Then at the 1992 British Open, he played with a couple of players who were using a 60-degree wedge and saw what kind of recoveries they were able to make. He finally agreed to put that club in his arsenal. Now," Cleveland concludes, "he's unbelievable with it."

The average amateur golfer might do well to consider the same set addition as Greg Norman did, or to consider adding both an approach and a lob. True, you might argue that if your long game is not up to professional standards, maybe your set should favor more longer clubs than shorter ones. A more pragmatic way of looking at it, especially if you're a middle-to-high-handicap player, might be to realize that you're going to miss far more greens in regulation than you hit; so you'll have far more short-game recovery shots to play than the professional will. And when you miss the green, you're more likely than the pro to miss the green by a lot (as opposed to being on the fringe just off the green). You'll probably face more recovery shots of from 40 to even 100 yards, often from difficult lies. Thus, your need for at least one additional wedge could well be greater than that of the expert player.

A Wealth of Wedge Choices

In the previous chapter I accused manufacturers of arranging their iron-set lofts in ways that do not have the average player's best interests at heart. How-

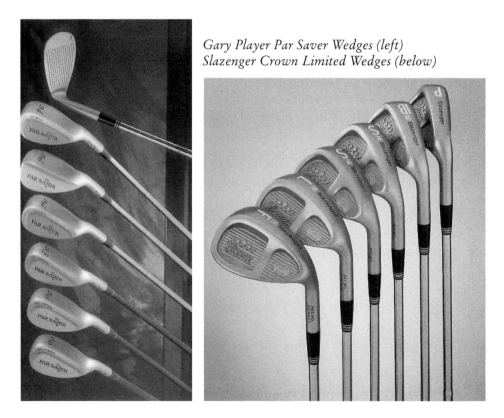

Gary Player Par Saver Wedges (left)
Slazenger Crown Limited Wedges (below)

*Golfsmith Short
Game System*

ever, I'll certainly concede here that in terms of offering wedge alternatives to balance out the lofts in a player's set, the manufacturers have for the most part given you plenty of choices. The majority of companies offer at least one wedge "set," consisting of an approach wedge, a sand wedge, and a lob wedge. And as you inspect the table that follows, you'll notice that a number of companies are offering a large number of wedges that are spaced closely together in terms of loft. Among these are Gary Player, Ping, Slazenger, and Golfsmith. The idea here is not to sell you on every wedge that they offer— the "seven-wedge system" will not become the norm anytime soon! However, the variety of clubs offered allows you to handpick the best additional choice as to both loft and overall design, given the lofts of your current wedges. For example, say your current pitching wedge has 45 degrees of loft, and you have a sand wedge with 55 degrees. If you opted to add an approach wedge, you'd certainly like it to be available with 50 degrees of loft, not 52, so your loft gaps are equal. Or if you decide that a lob wedge is what you need, you might prefer to look at something that has more or less than 60 degrees loft, the most common number for this club.

Many companies offer two separate wedge systems that allow you to choose between different clubhead materials, shapes, and finishes. A few companies, such as Carbite and Ben Hogan, offer three different wedge systems. If you've concluded that your wedge equipment needs shoring up, you'll have plenty of options to look at.

Let's spend some time examining what's important for you to look for, whether you're considering adding an approach wedge, buying a new sand wedge, or adding a lob wedge to your set.

Do Differing Clubface Materials Make for "Softer" Shots?

A substantial number of different materials are used in the clubheads of the many wedge offerings: 17-4 stainless steel, 431 stainless steel, 303 stainless steel (each progressively softer), forged carbon steel, beryllium copper, nickel, bronze, and others. There are also a number of wedge models with various particle-impregnated clubfaces that make for a rougher, abrasive surface. Examples are the Carbite CS and Viper Bite, Taylor Made Tour, and Odyssey Blackspin wedges. The question is, how much difference does the relative hardness, softness, or abrasiveness of the clubface make in getting the ball to land softly and stop quickly?

In speaking to a number of design experts, none could point to definitive proof, gathered in a controlled, nonbiased test situation, that any clubface material puts superior backspin on the ball. Terry Pocklington, president of Hansberger Precision Golf, a major ball manufacturer, does note that some gritty-faced wedges "will tend to abrade a soft-covered balata ball, which *implies* that they may also be putting additional spin on the shot." However, the consensus was that the type of metal (or composite material) that the wedge clubhead/clubface is made of is of relatively minimal importance in whether the ball can be made to stop more quickly or less quickly. The most important factor in how much spin and "stopping power" a ball has off the face of a wedge, or for that matter any club, is the type of ball itself, as we'll see in Chapter 8.

Approach Wedge Considerations

If you've decided to fill the gap between your current pitching wedge and sand wedge, it only makes sense to choose a club with a loft that divides the difference between the two equally.

As to the clubhead's general shape and finish, you would probably prefer a similar look to your other irons. In many cases you'll find that a manufacturer offers an approach wedge that's designed as a direct extension of your iron set. In these cases, and assuming the loft offered is what you need, your choice may be an easy one. If not, and you play a set of irons that is oversize and heavily perimeter-weighted, it may be that you'll need to choose a wedge with the more traditional appearance these clubs often have.

You'll be using an approach wedge much as you use your current pitching wedge—that is, for approach shots from fairway or rough and for chipping

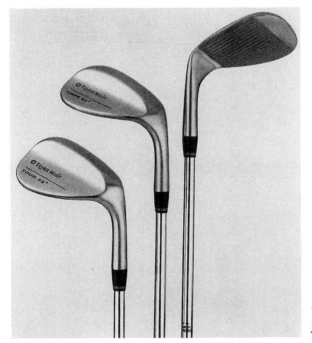

Taylor Made Tour Wedge Series

around the greens. In very few instances will you be playing sand shots with the approach wedge. Thus, the factor known as bounce in the sole of the gap wedge should be relatively slight.

Bounce, as was mentioned in the last chapter, refers to the degree that the leading edge of the sole is above the rear edge when the clubshaft is held perfectly straight up and down. The more the sole's leading edge is above the rear edge when the club is held this way, the greater the amount of sole bounce, which is measured in degrees.

The higher this bounce angle, the more the leading edge of the club will be above ground level as the clubhead is swung through impact. Therefore, a wedge with a high bounce angle would make it more likely that you could skull your pitch shots, with the leading edge meeting the middle of the ball instead of the base of it. For these reasons, the amount of bounce built into most approach wedges is slight—usually an angle of 4 to 6 degrees. (Note: If you happen to play from fairways that are very firm and fast, it will help if your gap has a bounce angle that is lower rather than higher. This will help reduce the risk of a skulled shot, which is greater from hard, tight lies.)

Make sure lengths of wedges are in keeping with the rest of your iron set. As we saw in the last chapter, the lengths of the numbered irons usually decrease by ½ inch with each higher number (also including the pitching wedge); and they have tended to get longer in recent years. Mark Young notes, "Most of the gap,

Teardrop Spinmaster (left)
Wilson Staff Brass Insert Wedges (below)

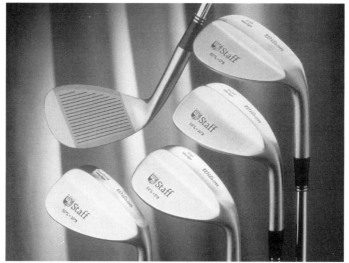

sand, and lob wedges have shafts that are the same length. Some companies make their lob wedge a fraction shorter than the other two, but on the whole, these clubs' length will be consistent, for an easier transition between short shots." The majority of men's approach, sand, and lob wedges measure either 35 or 35.5 inches.

Club Specs to Help You out of the Sand

A strong suggestion here: If you reject the argument for carrying more than two wedges, if you even decide you don't need fourteen clubs, or even if you just want to carry *one* wedge, make sure it's a good *sand wedge!* This is particularly true if you are a golfer who does not get the ball out of sand traps consistently well. To put it another way, in time you could probably learn to play all your greenside pitch shots much more respectably with just a sand wedge than you could learn to get out of bunkers with any one club other than a sand wedge.

Goldwin Blowout Wedge

Most sand wedges will tend to retain a relatively rounded, classic, traditional look. As you heft the sand wedge, you may notice that you feel more weight in the head than in the other clubs, even the other wedges. Barney Adams of Adams Golf notes that many companies do indeed opt to make their sand wedge the heaviest club, the reasoning being that the sand wedge clubface must usually be swung through greater resistance, in the form of either sand or heavy grass.

The most noticeable visual difference between the sand wedge and the other wedges is in the design of the club's sole. The sand wedge sole is designed to glide through sand, rather than dig into it. Manufacturers accomplish this by increasing the degree of bounce in the sand wedge sole. You'll see in the table that for virtually every manufacturer the sand wedge has the highest degree of bounce—between 10 and 13 degrees for the majority of models. With this higher degree of bounce, the rear edge of the sole is substantially lower than the leading edge. When swung correctly, the rear of the flange contacts the sand at least a couple of inches behind the ball. This makes the club glide along the sand with forward rather than downward momentum that helps pop the ball up and out. With a high-bounce sand wedge, it's virtually impossible for the leading edge of the club to dig into the sand, so that the sand's resistance snuffs the club's momentum and the ball stays in the trap.

Ray Cook Precision, Milled Wedges

Bounce angle does vary quite a bit from manufacturer to manufacturer and from model to model. Of course, there are limits to how much bounce in the sole is good. A club with a very high degree of bounce might work well if the

Otey Crisman
Hickory Lob Wedge

sand traps you play from have deep, fluffy, "beach" sand, which is easy to dig deeply into. On the other hand, if the sand at your home course is relatively coarse-grained and/or is shallow instead of deep, you probably would not want too high a degree of bounce on the sole. A high-bounce sand wedge might bounce too much off a firmer surface, so that the high leading edge contacts the ball (instead of the ball "floating" out on a layer of sand), skulling it completely over the green.

In addition, the higher the bounce angle on the sand wedge, the trickier it is to use from lies in the fairway, again because of the higher leading edge which might skull the ball. But as Mark Young points out, "Wedges are becoming more and more specialized—there are different wedges that work well from hard sand, from soft sand, that work well from grass instead of sand, and so on." All these factors should be taken into account when analyzing the sand wedge that will work best for you.

A factor related to the bounce angle is the width of the sole. The wider the sole, the more sand it will displace. If you combine a wide sole with one that has a high degree of bounce, you'll be able to displace a great deal of sand from a bunker, but you'll have a club that is difficult to "nip" the ball with, either off hard sand or from a fairway lie. (Wilson, for one, offers both a regular and a wide-sole sand wedge in its Staff Forged line.) In general, though, most wedge manufacturers create an inversely proportionate balance between the sole's bounce angle and its width. For example, in the Ping ISI or Zing II sand wedges, the very high bounce angle of 20 degrees is balanced by the fact that the sole itself is very narrow—in the ⅜-inch-width range, as opposed to many others which are about twice as wide.

You should match the proportions of your sand wedge clubhead to your current abilities in playing from sand. Generally, from normal lies, expert sand players like to take a fairly small amount of sand from behind the ball, giving it a precise "nip," which pops the ball out with maximum backspin. All things being equal in terms of the type of sand, such a player might want to consider models with relatively compact clubheads and not-too-high bounce angles—for example, the Mizuno Nick Faldo or the Ram Tom Watson Signature sand wedges. If you're more concerned at this point with simply "getting it out" as consistently as possible, a larger-head, higher-bounce design, such as the Carbite Viper Bite or King Cobra Oversize sand wedges, may do the trick for you.

While loft on the sand wedge is generally 55 or 56 degrees, there are some options. Several companies offer more-lofted sand clubs. For example, the Daiwa DG, Taylor Made Wide Flange, and Maruman M301T sand wedges all have 58 degrees of loft. This might help if the bunkers at your course are deep and/or the greens are fast, which puts a premium on getting sand shots to pop up softly and stop quickly.

To Lob or Not to Lob

As was mentioned, most lob wedges have 60 degrees of loft, and some have more. How can you determine whether you should get one?

The best way to decide is simply to think about the results you've been getting on those short "touch" shots around the green, especially from rough. How have you been handling these shots? Do you often hit greenside pitch shots that roll well past the hole no matter how high you try to hit it? Do you tend to hit these shots "fat," by hitting behind the ball in an effort to get the ball up quickly? If so, you may need a lob wedge at the expense of one of the longer clubs.

Sometimes the course you play most of your rounds on really determines your need for a lob wedge. If the greens at your home course are fast and have a substantial amount of slope, the need for a lob wedge increases dramatically because the ball will roll much farther upon landing. The slower and flatter your greens are, the less you're likely to need an extra-high-lofted wedge.

Lob wedges, on average, have more sole bounce than gap wedges, but definitely less than sand wedges. Having a substantial bounce on the sole, say 8 degrees, makes the lob wedge very playable for very short, pop-up sand shots. If you expect to use the lob wedge only from grass, you might want to try a model with a little lower bounce angle.

Ram Tom Watson Signature Wedge Series

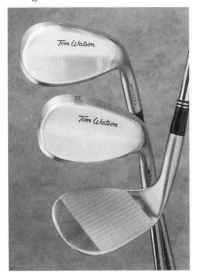

Cleveland 588 Sand Wedge

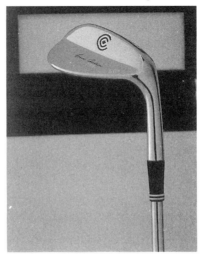

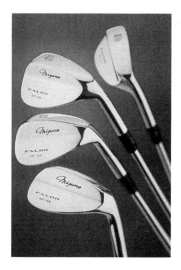

Mizuno Faldo Wedge Series

One last tip regarding your choice of a lob wedge: According to Harry Taylor, director of Tour relations for Mizuno (and who is also a part-time PGA Tour player), as the loft of the club increases, the size of the head probably should, too. "The clubhead should be a little deeper from top to bottom," Taylor says. "At impact, the ball travels up the clubface a lot more on a wedge with 60 degrees loft than one with 47. If you get a very lofty lob wedge but the face is not deep enough, there's a tendency to go right under the ball and pop it straight up."

The Spin on U-Grooves vs. V-Grooves

You'll notice in the table on wedges (as well as in the table on irons in the previous chapter) that the grooves or scoring lines cut into the clubface are marked as one of two types: U- or V-grooves. The letters refer to the actual shape of the grooves. The more traditional type of groove is in the form of a "V," while in recent years grooves in the shape of the letter "U" have become at least equally popular. (U-grooves, incidentally, are also referred to as box grooves.)

The U-groove, as its name implies, has walls that are perpendicular to the surface of the clubface, and a "bottom" that is either cupped or flat as opposed to V-shaped. There was tremendous debate in the late 1980s as to how much effect U-grooves had on the amount of backspin that could be put on the ball, and whether they should be outlawed. Eventually, the United States Golf Association ruled that U-grooves were legal, assuming they met the correct limits regarding their depth and the distance between each groove on the clubface.

Do U-groove wedges help you put more backspin on the ball? According to reports published by the USGA, if you are playing from a clean fairway lie, there does not appear to be any difference between the amount of spin obtained with U-grooves as opposed to V-grooves. However, from grassy or wet lies, the consensus is that U-grooves appear to impart a greater amount of backspin than V-grooves. This seems to make sense in that when the lie is wet, there is more area within the U-grooves in which water can be trapped, so that there is less of it that is actually in contact with the ball as clubface and ball meet.

Keep in mind, however, that the USGA also noted that "differences in spin rates caused by U-grooves in grassy hits occur only when the cover of the ball is relatively soft—when it is made of balata or a similar material." In addition, experts generally agree that any difference in backspin will be noticeable only to the very good player who generates high speed through impact. So, unless you're among the minority who play a ball with a balata cover and you generate high clubhead speed, groove type is a nonissue.

WEDGE PRODUCT INFORMATION

MANUFACTURER	MODEL/TYPES OF WEDGES	DESIGN/CLUBHEAD MATERIAL	GROOVE TYPE	LENGTH (in.)	LOFT (deg.)	
Adams Golf	Pitching	Cast, 17-4 ss classic styling	U	35.25	48, 52	
	Sand		U	35.25	56	
	Lob		U	35.25	60	
Alien	Ultimate Wedge	Cast, 17-4 ss	Dot-Punch scoring	34.5	60	
	Comments: Club features broadest sole flange on the market; nearly impossible to "stick in the sand."					
Tommy Armour	Silver Scot Approach	Cast cavity back, 17-4 ss	U	35.5	52	
	Silver Scot Sand			35.25	56	
	Golden Scot Approach	Cast cavity back, ss (ceramic-coated)	U	36	49	
	Golden Scot Sand			35.75	55	
	Diamond Scot Approach	Cast cavity back, 17-4 ss	U	35	49	
	Diamond Scot Sand			34.75	55	
Black Ice Golf	Pitching	Cast, perimeter-weighted, 431 ss w/ ceramic face	V	35.5	49	
	Sand		V	35	55	
	Lob		V	34.75	60	

Legend:	ss=stainless steel	F=Firm
	L=Ladies' shaft flex rating	S=Men's Stiff shaft flex rating
	A=Seniors' shaft flex rating	X=Men's Extra Stiff shaft flex rating
	R=Men's Regular shaft flex rating	

Lie (deg.)	Bounce Angle (deg.)	Shaft Materials and Flexes	Grip Style	Left-Handed	Women's	Suggested Retail
64	4, 5	Steel, filament-wound graphite L, A, R, S, X	Royal, Golf Pride Tour Wrap; all others available	Y	Y	$80 steel $100 graphite
64	10					
64	6					
60	0	Apollo steel, UST graphite	Lamkin Perma Tac Tour Wrap	Y	Y	$100 steel $130 graphite
63	7	Tour Step steel, G Force 2 Tour graphite R, S	Tour Wrap	Y	N	$90 steel $125 graphite
63	15					
62.75	Not supplied	G Force 2 Tour graphite, single flex	Tour Wrap	N	N	$125
63	Not supplied					
62.25	Not supplied	G Force 2 Tour graphite, single flex	Diamond Perf Wrap	N	Y	$125
62.25	Not supplied					.
63	Not supplied	True Temper Dynamic Gold steel R, S; graphite L, A, R, F, S, X	Griptec Tour Wrap	Y	Y	$75 steel $115 graphite
64	Not supplied			N	Y	$75 steel $115 graphite
64	Not supplied			Y	Y	$78 steel $118 graphite

continued

WEDGE PRODUCT INFORMATION *(continued)*

MANUFACTURER	MODEL/TYPES OF WEDGES	DESIGN/CLUBHEAD MATERIAL	GROOVE TYPE	LENGTH (*in.*)	LOFT (*deg.*)	
Bridgestone	*Ray Floyd Series* Approach	Forged blade, carbon steel, satin finish; or forged cavity back w/cobalt finish	V	35	Blade 53 Cavity 52	
	Sand			35	Blade 58 Cavity 56	
	Lob			35	Blade 62 Cavity 60	
Callaway	*Big Bertha Wedges* Approach	Cast cavity back, 17-4 ss	V	35.5	50.8	
	Sand			35.5	55	
	Lob			35.5	60	
	Big Bertha Tour Series Approach	Cast cavity back, ss, "teardrop" head shape	Modified U	35.25	52	
	Sand			35	56	
	Lob			34.75	60	

Legend:	ss=stainless steel	F=Firm
	L=Ladies' shaft flex rating	S=Men's Stiff shaft flex rating
	A=Seniors' shaft flex rating	X=Men's Extra Stiff shaft flex rating
	R=Men's Regular shaft flex rating	

Lie (deg.)	Bounce Angle (deg.)	Shaft Materials and Flexes	Grip Style	Left-Handed	Women's	Suggested Retail
62	Not supplied	FM Precision steel S	Royal Tour Wrap	N	N	$75 steel $900 cobalt
62	Not supplied					
62	Not supplied					
65	Not supplied	RCH graphite, True Temper Memphis 10 steel	Proprietary All-Weather	Y	Y	$110 steel $145 graphite
65	Not supplied					
65	Not supplied					
Not supplied	Not supplied	RCH graphite, L, R, F, S; True Temper Memphis 10 steel, single flex	Proprietary All-Weather	N	N	$100 steel $140 graphite
Not supplied	Not supplied					
Not supplied	Not supplied					

continued

WEDGE PRODUCT INFORMATION *(continued)*

MANUFACTURER	MODEL/TYPES OF WEDGES	DESIGN/CLUBHEAD MATERIAL	GROOVE TYPE	LENGTH *(in.)*	LOFT *(deg.)*	
Carbite	Viper Bite Approach	Cast, oversize, 431 ss	Modified V	35.5	52	
	Viper Bite Sand			35.5	56	
	Viper Bite Lob			35.5	60	
	CS 200 PW	Cast, 431 ss w/tungsten carbide insert	U	35.5	50	
	CS 200 SW			35.5	55	
	CS 200 LW			35.5	60	
	CS 200 LW			35.5	64	
	Diatanium Face 5204	Cast, 431 ss w/ titanium/diamond insert	U	35.5	52	
	Diatanium Face 5609			35.5	56	
	Diatanium Face 6003			35	60	
	Diatanium Face 6403			34.5	64	

Comments: Viper Bite has high-friction clubface surface.

Legend:	ss=stainless steel	F=Firm
	L=Ladies' shaft flex rating	S=Men's Stiff shaft flex rating
	A=Seniors' shaft flex rating	X=Men's Extra Stiff shaft flex rating
	R=Men's Regular shaft flex rating	

Lie (deg.)	Bounce Angle (deg.)	Shaft Materials and Flexes	Grip Style	Left-Handed	Women's	Suggested Retail
64	4	FM Precision steel S, graphite S	Lamkin Perma Tac Tour Wrap	Y	Y	$105 steel $125 graphite
64	13					
64	8					
64	4	FM Precision steel S, graphite S	Lamkin Perma Tac Tour Wrap	N	Y	$100 steel $125 graphite
64	13					
63	8					
65	3					
64	4	FM Precision steel S, graphite S	Lamkin Perma Tac Tour Wrap	N	Y	$130 steel $155 graphite
64	9					
65	3					
65	0					

continued

WEDGE PRODUCT INFORMATION *(continued)*

MANUFACTURER	MODEL/TYPES OF WEDGES	DESIGN/CLUBHEAD MATERIAL	GROOVE TYPE	LENGTH (*in.*)	LOFT (*deg.*)
Cleveland Golf	485 Sand	Forged, carbon steel	U	35	56
	485 Lob			34.5	60
	691 Pitch	Forged, carbon steel	U	35	52
	691 Sand			35	55
	691 Lob			34.5	58
	588 Pitch	Forged, carbon steel	U	35.25	49
	588 Dual			35	53
	588 Sand			35	56
	588 Lob			34.5	60
	VAS+ Dual	Cast, ss	U	35.25	50
	VAS+ Sand			35	55
	VAS+ Lob			35	60

Comments: One of the most complete and respected wedge lines in the industry.

Lie (deg.)	Bounce Angle (deg.)	Shaft Materials and Flexes	Grip Style	Left-Handed	Women's	Suggested Retail
64	12	Lightweight steel A, R, S, X	Golf Pride Tour Wrap	N	N	$93
64	0					
64	5	Lightweight steel A, R, S, X	Golf Pride Tour Wrap	N	N	$93
64	13					
64	0					
64	5	Lightweight steel A, R, S, X	Golf Pride Tour Wrap	Y	N	$93
64	8					
64	14					
64	3					
64	6	Lightweight steel A, R, S, X; graphite L, A, R, S, X	Golf Pride Tour Wrap	N	Y	$93 steel $139 graphite
64	14					
64	8					

continued

WEDGE PRODUCT INFORMATION *(continued)*

MANUFACTURER	MODEL/TYPES OF WEDGES	DESIGN/CLUBHEAD MATERIAL	GROOVE TYPE	LENGTH (*in.*)	LOFT (*deg.*)
Cobra Golf	*King Cobra Oversize* Approach	Cast, 17-4 ss	V	37.75	50
	Sand			35.75	56
	Lob			35.75	60
	Senior King Cobra Approach	Cast, 17-4 ss	V	36.25	50
	Sand			36.25	56
	King Cobra Tour Approach	Cast, 15-5 ss	V	35.75	50
	Sand			35.75	56
	Norman Signature Sand	Forged blade, 1036 carbon steel	V	35.25	54
	Sand		V	35.25	57
	Lob			35.25	60
	Lady Cobra Approach	Cast, 17-4 ss	V	34.75	50
	Sand			34.75	56
Ray Cook	*Precision Milled Wedges* Gap	Cast, 303 ss	U	35.5	52
	Sand			35.5	56
	Sand			35.5	57
	Lob			35	60

Comments: Clubfaces are milled for absolute flatness. 303 stainless said to provide softer feel.

Legend: ss=stainless steel
L=Ladies' shaft flex rating
A=Seniors' shaft flex rating
R=Men's Regular shaft flex rating

F=Firm
S=Men's Stiff shaft flex rating
X=Men's Extra Stiff shaft flex rating

Lie (deg.)	Bounce Angle (deg.)	Shaft Materials and Flexes	Grip Style	Left-Handed	Women's	Suggested Retail
63	8	Graphite, steel R, S, X; titanium	Rubber Tour Wrap	Y	N	$82–90 steel $132 graphite $149 titanium
63	13					
63	13					
62	8	Graphite, steel R, S, X	Senior Rubber Wrap	Y	N	$77 steel $120 graphite
62	13					
63	8	Graphite, steel R, S, X: FM Precision Rifle; titanium A, R, S, X	Tour Full Cord, Tour Rubber Wrap	N	N	$90 steel $132 graphite $149 titanium $182 Tour graphite
63	13					
64	13	Tour graphite A, R, S, X; graphite R, S, X; steel R, S, X: FM Precision Rifle	Tour Full Cord, Tour Rubber Wrap	N	N	$97 steel $130 graphite $159 Tour graphite
64	12					
64	11					
62	8	Graphite, steel L	Ladies Rubber Wrap	Y	Y	$77 steel $114 graphite
62	13					
64	7	True Temper Dynamic Gold steel S300	Golf Pride Tour Wrap	Y	Y	$92
64	12					
64	4					
64	0					

continued

WEDGE PRODUCT INFORMATION *(continued)*

MANUFACTURER	MODEL/TYPES OF WEDGES	DESIGN/CLUBHEAD MATERIAL	GROOVE TYPE	LENGTH *(in.)*	LOFT *(deg.)*
Otey Crisman	Hickory Lob Wedge	Cast, 17-4 ss	V	35	60
Daiwa	*DG Series Wedges*	Forged, carbon steel	V	35.75	55
				35.5	58
				35.5	60
	Hi-Trac MF-110 Approach	Cast cavity back, SVS steel	Modified V	35.75	52
	Sand			35.5	56
	Lob			35.5	60
Dunlop	*Tour DG* Approach	Cast muscle back, 304 ss	U	35.5	52
	Sand			35.5	56
	Lob			35.5	60
Dynacraft	*Pinmaster* Pitch	Cast, 431 ss	V	35	50, 52
	Sand			35	54, 56
	Utility			35	58, 60, 65
	Pro Wedge Pitch	Cast, 431 ss	V	35	50
	Sand			35	55
	Utility			35	60
	Pro Wedge Beryllium Copper Sand	Cast, beryllium copper	U	35	56
	Utility			35	60

Legend:	ss=stainless steel	F=Firm
	L=Ladies' shaft flex rating	S=Men's Stiff shaft flex rating
	A=Seniors' shaft flex rating	X=Men's Extra Stiff shaft flex rating
	R=Men's Regular shaft flex rating	

LIE (deg.)	BOUNCE ANGLE (deg.)	SHAFT MATERIALS AND FLEXES	GRIP STYLE	LEFT-HANDED	WOMEN'S	SUGGESTED RETAIL
65	8	Hickory shaft (single flex)	Leather Wrap Style	N	Y	$125
63	9	Steel S	Not supplied	N	N	$84
63.5	13					
63.5	13					
62.5	3	Graphite S	Not supplied	Y	Y	$105
63	13					
63	9					
63	4	True Temper Dynamic Gold steel w/sensicore, S300	Golf Pride Tour Velvet Wrap	N	N	$60
63	8					
63	6					
64	4, 7	True Temper Dynamic Gold R, S, X	Golf Pride Tour Velvet; others available	Y	N	$50
64	10, 12					
64	3, 6, 16					
64	3			N	N	$52
64	11					
64	5					
64	11			N	N	$70
64	3					

continued

WEDGE PRODUCT INFORMATION *(continued)*

MANUFACTURER	MODEL/TYPES OF WEDGES	DESIGN/CLUBHEAD MATERIAL	GROOVE TYPE	LENGTH *(in.)*	LOFT *(deg.)*	
Goldwin Golf	Blowout Wedge (SW)	Cast, 431 ss	V	35	55	
Golfsmith	Short Game System (10 wedges with lofts at 2-degree increments and varying bounce angles)	Cast, 431 ss, satin finish	U	36	48	
				36	50	
				36	52	
				36	54	
				36	56	
				36	58	
				36	60	
				36	62	
				36	64	
				36	66	
	Comments: Golfsmith is a "component" company. Components may be purchased individually.					
The GolfWorks	*Bio-Mech II* Approach	Cast cavity back, 431 ss	U	35	52	
	Sand			35	58	
	Lob			35	61	
	Tarantula Pitch	Cast cavity back, 431 ss	U	35	48	
	Sand			35	55	
	Kinetic II Pitch	Cast, perimeter-weighted, 431 ss	U	35	47	
	Sand			35	53	

Legend:	ss=stainless steel	F=Firm
	L=Ladies' shaft flex rating	S=Men's Stiff shaft flex rating
	A=Seniors' shaft flex rating	X=Men's Extra Stiff shaft flex rating
	R=Men's Regular shaft flex rating	

LIE (deg.)	BOUNCE ANGLE (deg.)	SHAFT MATERIALS AND FLEXES	GRIP STYLE	LEFT-HANDED	WOMEN'S	SUGGESTED RETAIL
64	Not supplied	Graphite, steel R, F, S, X	Not supplied	N	N	$105 steel $149 graphite
64	5	Steel R, S	Golfsmith Rubber Custom Wrap	N	N	$37.50 or $99 for 3 wedges
64	3					
65	9					
65	12					
65	15					
65	8					
65	6					
65	4					
65	7					
65	10					

Custom lengths/graphite shafts available.

LIE (deg.)	BOUNCE ANGLE (deg.)	SHAFT MATERIALS AND FLEXES	GRIP STYLE	LEFT-HANDED	WOMEN'S	SUGGESTED RETAIL
63	2	Steel L, A, R, S, X; graphite L, A, R, S, X (all models)	Rubber Wrap	N	Wildfire, Progressive Lady, Accu-Site models	$27 steel $46 graphite
63	10					
63	4					
63	2			N		$27 steel $46 graphite
63	4					
63	4			Y		$27 steel $46 graphite
63	6					

continued

WEDGE PRODUCT INFORMATION (continued)

MANUFACTURER	MODEL/TYPES OF WEDGES	DESIGN/CLUBHEAD MATERIAL	GROOVE TYPE	LENGTH (in.)	LOFT (deg.)	
Ben Hogan	*Tom Kite Personal Grind*	Forged, carbon steel	U			
	Approach			35.25	51	
	Sand			35	56	
	Lob			34.5	62	
	Tour Series II Approach	Forged, carbon steel	U	35.5	53	
	Sand			35	57	
	Lob			34.5	61	
	Beryllium Copper Approach	Forged, beryllium	U	35.5	52	
	Sand			35	56	
	Lob			35	60	
	Pro Grind Sand	Forged, carbon steel	U	35	56	
	Lob			35	60	
	Special SI Sand			35	56	
Izzo	*BeCool WEDGZ* Approach	431 ss and beryllium copper	U	35.5	52	
	Sand			35.25	56	
	Lob			35.25	60	
Lynx	*Tour Wedges* Sand	Cast, high-polish 17-4 ss	U	35.5	56	
	Lob			35.5	60	

Legend: ss=stainless steel	F=Firm	
L=Ladies' shaft flex rating	S=Men's Stiff shaft flex rating	
A=Seniors' shaft flex rating	X=Men's Extra Stiff shaft flex rating	
R=Men's Regular shaft flex rating		

Lie (deg.)	Bounce Angle (deg.)	Shaft Materials and Flexes	Grip Style	Left-Handed	Women's	Suggested Retail
		Apex steel	Hogan Apex V-Trac	N	Y	$95
63	10					
65	12					
66	6					
		Apex steel	Hogan Apex V-Trac	N	Y	$100
64	9					
65	11					
65	3					
		Apex steel	Hogan Apex V-Trac	Y	Y	$110
64	7					
65	13					
65	5					
		Apex steel	Hogan Apex V-Trac	N	Y	$95
65	13					
65	6					
65	11			Y	N	$95
		FM Precision Rifle (single flex), Izzo LT graphite (single flex)	Golf Pride Tour Velvet Wrap	Y	N	$150 steel $150 graphite
64	9					
65	12					
65	8					
		True Temper Dynamic Gold R, S, X; Lynx Lite steel R, S; Lynx lite graphite L, R, S, X	Golf Pride Tour Wrap	Y	Y	$85 steel $125 graphite
64	14					
64	8					

continued

WEDGE PRODUCT INFORMATION (continued)

MANUFACTURER	MODEL/TYPES OF WEDGES	DESIGN/CLUBHEAD MATERIAL	GROOVE TYPE	LENGTH (in.)	LOFT (deg.)	
MacGregor	*VIP Tour Wedges* Approach	Cast, 431 ss, satin finish	U	35.5	52	
	Sand			35.5	54	
	Sand			35.5	56	
	Lob			35.5	60	
Maruman Golf	*Conductor* Approach	Forged, carbon steel	V	35	53	
	Sand			35	56	
	Lob			35	63	
	M301T Approach	Cast, 17-4 ss	V	35	53	
	Sand			35	58	
	Titus WA-2 Approach	Cast, 17-4 ss w/titanium face	V	35	53	
	Sand			35	58	
	Verity Approach	Cast, 17-4 ss	V	35	53	
	Sand			35	58	

Legend: ss=stainless steel F=Firm
L=Ladies' shaft flex rating S=Men's Stiff shaft flex rating
A=Seniors' shaft flex rating X=Men's Extra Stiff shaft flex rating
R=Men's Regular shaft flex rating

Lie (deg.)	Bounce Angle (deg.)	Shaft Materials and Flexes	Grip Style	Left-Handed	Women's	Suggested Retail
63	6	True Temper Dynamic Gold steel R400, S300	Golf Pride Tour Wrap Cord	N	N	$75
63	12					
63	12					
63	6					
63	Not supplied	True Temper Dynamic Gold steel S300	Velvet Tour Wrap	N	Y	$95
63	Not supplied					
63	Not supplied					
63	Not supplied	Carbofit graphite R, S	Velvet Tour Wrap	N	Y	$135
63	Not supplied					
63	Not supplied	Carbofit graphite R, S; Parsec GX Kevlar R, S	Velvet Tour Wrap	N	Y	$245
63	Not supplied					
63	Not supplied	Carbofit graphite R, S; True Temper Dynalite Gold R, S	Velvet Tour Wrap	Y	Y	$125
63	Not supplied					

continued

WEDGE PRODUCT INFORMATION (continued)

MANUFACTURER	MODEL/TYPES OF WEDGES	DESIGN/CLUBHEAD MATERIAL	GROOVE TYPE	LENGTH (in.)	LOFT (deg.)	
Maxfli Golf	*Tad Moore Wedge System*	Cast, 17-4 ss	U			
	TM52 Approach			35.5	52	
	TM55 Sand			35.25	55	
	TM57 Sand			35.25	57	
	TM62 Utility			35	62	
Merit Golf	*Dual Sole Wedges* Approach	Cast, 8620 carbon and 431 ss (chrome, melonite, or satin finish)	U	35.5	52	
	Sand			35.5	56	
	Lob			35.5	60	
Mitsushiba	Tri-Grind Wedges	Cast, 431 ss	V	35	52	
				35	56	
				35	60	
Mizuno USA	*Faldo Wedges* Approach	Forged blade, double-forged carbon steel	U	35.75	52	
	Sand			35.75	56	
	Lob			35.75	60	
	Pro Tour Wedges Approach	Forged blade, double-forged carbon steel	U	35.25	52	
	Sand			35.25	56	
	Lob			35.25	60	

Legend:	ss=stainless steel	F=Firm
	L=Ladies' shaft flex rating	S=Men's Stiff shaft flex rating
	A=Seniors' shaft flex rating	X=Men's Extra Stiff shaft flex rating
	R=Men's Regular shaft flex rating	

Lie (deg.)	Bounce Angle (deg.)	Shaft Materials and Flexes	Grip Style	Left-Handed	Women's	Suggested Retail
		Steel (single flex)	Royal II Textured Wrap	N	N	$81
63.5	7					
63.5	7					
63.5	12					
63.5	7					
63	18/0 split sole	True Temper Dynamic Lite steel S	Golf Pride Tour Wrap	N	N	$84
63	30/0 split sole					
63	25/0 split sole					
64	Not supplied	Brunswick steel R, S	Lamkin Perma Wrap	N	N	$42
65						
66						
64.5	8	True Temper Dynamic Gold S300	Golf Pride Tour Wrap	N	Y	$100
64.5	10					
64.5	5					
64	5	True Temper Dynamic Gold S300	Golf Pride Tour Wrap	N	Y	$100
64	5					
64	5					

continued

WEDGE PRODUCT INFORMATION *(continued)*

MANUFACTURER	MODEL/TYPES OF WEDGES	DESIGN/CLUBHEAD MATERIAL	GROOVE TYPE	LENGTH *(in.)*	LOFT *(deg.)*	
Nicklaus Golf	*I.Q. Wedges* Pitch	Forged blade, 431 ss w/soft metal face insert	U	35	52	
	Sand			35	57	
	Sand			35	57	
	Lob			35	62	
	Comments: Clubfaces are computer-milled. Patented superelastic, vibration-dampening material;					
Odyssey	*Blackspin* Sand	Cast, ss w/Stronomic face insert	U	35.5	56	
	Lob			35.5	61	
	Comments: Patented Stronomic insert provides "gritty" hitting surface.					
Ping	ISI Wedges	Cast cavity back, 17-4 ss, copper, nickel	U	Custom	47 49.5 52 54.5	
	Zing II	Copper			57 61 (both models)	

Comments: Contoured leading edges and soles make for extra playability from any lie.

Legend:	ss=stainless steel	F=Firm
	L=Ladies' shaft flex rating	S=Men's Stiff shaft flex rating
	A=Seniors' shaft flex rating	X=Men's Extra Stiff shaft flex rating
	R=Men's Regular shaft flex rating	

Lie (deg.)	Bounce Angle (deg.)	Shaft Materials and Flexes	Grip Style	Left-Handed	Women's	Suggested Retail
63	6	Steel, single flex	Golf Pride Elongated Grip	N	N	$150
64	12					
64	8					
64	6					

longer grips help on "choke-down" shots.

Lie (deg.)	Bounce Angle (deg.)	Shaft Materials and Flexes	Grip Style	Left-Handed	Women's	Suggested Retail
63.5	9	Steel, "wedge" flex	Proprietary Rubber Wrap Style	N	N	$189
63.5	7					

Said to be highly wear-resistant. Milled clubface.

Lie (deg.)	Bounce Angle (deg.)	Shaft Materials and Flexes	Grip Style	Left-Handed	Women's	Suggested Retail
Custom	12	JZ steel, Z-265 steel	Proprietary Ping DylaGrip or Textured Spiral standard, numerous options	Y	Y	$90 ss $115 copper $150 nickel
	12					
	20					
	20					
	20			Y	Y	$90
	12 (both models)					

Narrow sole on sand wedges counteracts the high bounce angles.

continued

WEDGE PRODUCT INFORMATION (continued)

MANUFACTURER	MODEL/TYPES OF WEDGES	DESIGN/CLUBHEAD MATERIAL	GROOVE TYPE	LENGTH (in.)	LOFT (deg.)	
Gary Player Golf	*Par Saver Wedges* Gap	Cast cavity back, aluminum bronze	U	35.5	52	
	Sand			35.5	54	
	Sand (cavity)			35.5	56	
	Sand (flange)			35.5	56	
	Sand			35.5	58	
	Lob			35.5	60	
	Oversize Par Saver Pitch	Cast cavity back, aluminum bronze		35.5	48	
	Sand			35.5	55	
	Lob			35.5	60	
	Comments: Aluminum bronze said to provide softest impact feel available.					
Players Golf	*Master Wedges* Approach	ss w/cobalt finish	Not supplied	35	52	
	Sand	ss w/cobalt finish		35	56	
	Lob	ss w/cobalt finish		35	62	

Legend:	ss=stainless steel	F=Firm
	L=Ladies' shaft flex rating	S=Men's Stiff shaft flex rating
	A=Seniors' shaft flex rating	X=Men's Extra Stiff shaft flex rating
	R=Men's Regular shaft flex rating	

Lie (deg.)	Bounce Angle (deg.)	Shaft Materials and Flexes	Grip Style	Left-Handed	Women's	Suggested Retail
64	3	Steel, "wedge" flex; graphite, "wedge" flex (higher flex point for slightly lower trajectory)	Proprietary Rubber Grip	N	Y	$100 steel $145 graphite
64	6					
64	9					
64	11					
64	6					
64	11					
64	6	Steel "wedge" flex; graphite "wedge" flex	Proprietary Rubber Grip	N	Y	$115 steel $155 graphite
64	11					
64	2					

Multidimensional sole for easy adaptation to any lie.

Lie (deg.)	Bounce Angle (deg.)	Shaft Materials and Flexes	Grip Style	Left-Handed	Women's	Suggested Retail
65	8	True Temper steel R, S	Lamkin Tour Wrap	N	N	$55
65	11			N	N	$55
65	13			N	N	$55

continued

WEDGE PRODUCT INFORMATION *(continued)*

MANUFACTURER	MODEL/TYPES OF WEDGES	DESIGN/CLUBHEAD MATERIAL	GROOVE TYPE	LENGTH *(in.)*	LOFT *(deg.)*	
PowerBilt	*TPS Oversize* 11	Cast, 17-4 ss	U	35.37	50	
	Sand			35.12	55	
	Sand			35.12	60	
	Comments: Sims Shock Relief insert, heat-treated stainless steel with satin finish.					
Rainbow Golf	Sand Master	Cast, 17-4 ss	V	Not supplied	60	
	Dual Master				58	

Lie (deg.)	Bounce Angle (deg.)	Shaft Materials and Flexes	Grip Style	Left-Handed	Women's	Suggested Retail
64	Not supplied	True Temper Dynamic Gold, Dynasty Plus steel (one flex); UST Tour Weight graphite, UST Dynasty Plus graphite L, A, R, S	Golf Pride Tour Velvet	Y	Y	$105 steel $135–$165 graphite
65	Not supplied					
65	Not supplied					
Not supplied	Not supplied	True Temper Dynamic or Dynamic Gold steel R; Vachelon high-modulus graphite-boron	Golf Pride Victory Half Cord, Lamkin	N	Y	$45

continued

WEDGE PRODUCT INFORMATION *(continued)*

MANUFACTURER	MODEL/TYPES OF WEDGES	DESIGN/CLUBHEAD MATERIAL	GROOVE TYPE	LENGTH *(in.)*	LOFT *(deg.)*	
Ram	*Tom Watson Signature Series*	Forged muscle back, carbon steel	U	35.75	50	
				35.75	55	
				35.75	60	
				35.75	64	
	FX Oversize Approach	Cast cavity back, ss	U	35.5	50	
	Sand			35.5	53	
	Lob			35.5	58	
	FX Pro Set FS/CS Approach	Cast muscle back, forged steel (FS); cast shallow muscle back, cobalt steel (CS)	U	35.5	FS 51	CS 50
	Sand			35.5	54	53
	Lob			35.5	59	58
	Troon Series	Forged muscle back, carbon steel	U	35.75	52	
				35.75	55	
				35.75	58	
	Comments: One of largest wedge offerings on the market.					
Slazenger	*Crown Limited* Approach	Cast cavity back, 431 ss	U	35.5	50	
	Sand			35.25	54	
	Sand			35.25	58	
	Lob			35	60	
	FW			35	64	
	Comments: Standard lengths and lies shown; wide variations in lengths and lies available					

> **Legend:** ss=stainless steel
> L=Ladies' shaft flex rating
> A=Seniors' shaft flex rating
> R=Men's Regular shaft flex rating
>
> F=Firm
> S=Men's Stiff shaft flex rating
> X=Men's Extra Stiff shaft flex rating

Lie (deg.)	Bounce Angle (deg.)	Shaft Materials and Flexes	Grip Style	Left-Handed	Women's	Suggested Retail
64	2	Steel, graphite, single flex	Ram Reverse Wrap	Y	N	$87 steel $125 graphite
64.5	10					
64.5	4					
64.5	2					
64.5	3	Graphite A, R, S	Ram Wrap	Y	Y	$87
64.5	10					
64.5	4					
64.5	3	Steel, graphite A, R, S (FS); steel, graphite A, R, S, X(CS)	Ram Wrap (FS), Ram X-Grip (CS)	Y (CS)	N	$95 steel $125 graphite
64.5	10					
64.5	2, 3					
64.5	3	Not supplied	Not supplied	Y	N	Not supplied
64.5	6					
64.5	2					
63.5	4	FM Precision or Rifle steel L, A, R, S, X; high-modulus graphite, filament-wound graphite A, R, S, X	Golf Pride, all styles	N	Y	Not supplied
64	9					
64	9					
64.5	4					
64.5	4					

to suit all golfers.

continued

WEDGE PRODUCT INFORMATION *(continued)*

MANUFACTURER	MODEL/TYPES OF WEDGES	DESIGN/CLUBHEAD MATERIAL	GROOVE TYPE	LENGTH *(in.)*	LOFT *(deg.)*	
Kenneth Smith	*KS 2000 O/S* Pitch	Cast cavity back, 431 ss	V	Custom	50	
	Sand				55	
	Lob				60	
	Royal Signet Pitch	Forged, 416 ss	V		47–51	
	Approach				51–54	
	Sand				55–58	
	Lob				58–64	
	Comments: Full customized fitting for all specifications.					
Snake Eyes	*Snake Eyes* #10 Pitch	Forged, 10-30 carbon steel	V	35.75	50	
	#11 Sand			35.5	56	
	#12 Lob			35.5	60	
	Comments: Optional lofts and lies offered at no extra charge.					
Taylor Made	*Tour Wedge Series* Fairway Wedge	Cast, 431 ss w/copper-tungsten face insert	V	35	50	
	Sand Wedge			35	55	
	Wide Flange Sand Wedge			35	58	
	Lob Wedge			34.5	61	

Comments: Constant friction insert said to produce soft feel, better spin.

Legend:	ss=stainless steel	F=Firm
	L=Ladies' shaft flex rating	S=Men's Stiff shaft flex rating
	A=Seniors' shaft flex rating	X=Men's Extra Stiff shaft flex rating
	R=Men's Regular shaft flex rating	

LIE (deg.)	BOUNCE ANGLE (deg.)	SHAFT MATERIALS AND FLEXES	GRIP STYLE	LEFT-HANDED	WOMEN'S	SUGGESTED RETAIL
Custom	5	Steel R, S; ultralight graphite L, A, R, S; boron-graphite A, R, S; titanium A, R, S, X	Golf Pride, Royal, Griptec in various styles; Leather Perforated Wrap	N	Y	$115 steel $150 graphite $170 titanium
	8					
	12					
Y	Y	Steel L, A, R, S, X; Ultralight graphite L, A, R, S; boron-graphite A, R, S; titanium A, R, S, X				$160 steel
	0–8					
	0–8					$200 graphite $215 titanium
	8–15					
	0–10					
Custom	5–7	True Temper Dynamic Gold steel S200; graphite available by special order	Synthetic Custom Grip	Y	N	$225 steel
	8.5–12.5					
	3–10.5					

Preworn sole; slightly higher center of gravity.

LIE (deg.)	BOUNCE ANGLE (deg.)	SHAFT MATERIALS AND FLEXES	GRIP STYLE	LEFT-HANDED	WOMEN'S	SUGGESTED RETAIL
64	6	True Temper Dynalite steel S	Rubber Tour Wrap	N	N	$119
64	8					
64	12					
64	3					

continued

WEDGE PRODUCT INFORMATION *(continued)*

MANUFACTURER	MODEL/TYPES OF WEDGES	DESIGN/CLUBHEAD MATERIAL	GROOVE TYPE	LENGTH *(in.)*	LOFT *(deg.)*	
Teardrop Golf	*Spinmaster* Pitch	Cast, 431 ss w/titanium-treated "friction" clubface	U	35.5	52	
	Sand			35.5	56	
	Lob			35	61	
Titleist	High Performance Tri Sole, High Performance Tri Sole Beryllium Copper	Cast cavity back, soft 304 ss or beryllium copper	Modified U	35.25	App 52	
				35.25	54	
				35.25	Sand 56	
				35.25	58	
				35.25	Lob 60	
	Comments: 52-, 56-, and 60-degree clubs are classic approach, sand, and lob wedges.					
Top Flite	*Top Flite Tour Oversize* Approach	Cast, oversize, 17-4 ss	V	35	51	
	Sand			35	56	
	Lob			35	60	
	Top Flite Tour Pro Offset Approach	Cast, 304 ss	V	35	52	
	Sand			35	56	
	Lob			35	60	

LIE (deg.)	BOUNCE ANGLE (deg.)	SHAFT MATERIALS AND FLEXES	GRIP STYLE	LEFT-HANDED	WOMEN'S	SUGGESTED RETAIL
Not supplied	0	FM Precision Rifle steel, medium-stiff	Golf Pride Tour Velvet or Velvet Cord	N	N	$125
Not supplied	10					
Not supplied	0					
64	10	Tri-Spec steel, single flex	Golf Pride Buffed Tour Wrap	Y	N	$93 steel $129 beryllium copper
64	20					
64	14					
64	24					
64	18					

54- and 58-degree wedges feature high bounce for "aggressive" shots from difficult lies. Custom-fitting available.

LIE (deg.)	BOUNCE ANGLE (deg.)	SHAFT MATERIALS AND FLEXES	GRIP STYLE	LEFT-HANDED	WOMEN'S	SUGGESTED RETAIL
		True Temper Dynalite steel R, S; Performance Flex graphite R, S	Buffed Tour Wrap	Y	Y	$78 steel $106 graphite
63	6					
63	10					
63	8					
				Y	Y	$78 steel $106 graphite
63	7					
63	12					
63	8					

continued

WEDGE PRODUCT INFORMATION *(continued)*

MANUFACTURER	MODEL/TYPES OF WEDGES	DESIGN/CLUBHEAD MATERIAL	GROOVE TYPE	LENGTH *(in.)*	LOFT *(deg.)*
Vulcan	Pitch	Cast, midsize, 17-4 ss	U	Custom	46.5
	Sand				53
	Lob				58
Wilson	*Staff Brass Insert* Pitch	Cast, 17-4 ss w/brass face insert	U	35.5	50
	Gap			35.5	54
	Sand			35.5	56
	Lob			35.5	60
	Staff Forged Gap	Forged, carbon steel	U	35.5	53
	Sand			35.5	56
	Sand Wide Sole			35.5	56
	Lob			35.5	59
	Staff 58 Sand	Forged, carbon steel	U	35.5	55
	R-90 Sand	Forged, carbon steel	U	35.5	55

LIE (deg.)	BOUNCE ANGLE (deg.)	SHAFT MATERIALS AND FLEXES	GRIP STYLE	LEFT-HANDED	WOMEN'S	SUGGESTED RETAIL
Custom	Not supplied	UST high-modulus graphite	Golf Pride Tour Wrap, Lamkin Perma Wrap, Royal	Y	Y	$90
	Not supplied					$90
	Not supplied					$90
62	10	Firestick steel, single flex	Golf Pride Tour Wrap	N	N	$100
63	5					
63	10					
64	0					
64	8	Firestick steel, single flex	Golf Pride Tour Wrap	Y (staff forged sand wedge)	N	$80
64	10					
64	10					
64	5					
64	10	Firestick steel, single flex	Golf Pride Tour Wrap	N	N	$80
64	10	Firestick steel, single flex	Golf Pride Tour Wrap	N	N	$80

continued

WEDGE PRODUCT INFORMATION (continued)

MANUFACTURER	MODEL/TYPES OF WEDGES	DESIGN/CLUBHEAD MATERIAL	GROOVE TYPE	LENGTH (in.)	LOFT (deg.)	
Wood Brothers	*Championship Balance Tour Forged* Approach	Forged, carbon steel, chrome finish	V	35	51	
	Sand			35	55	
	Lob			35	60	
Yonex	*Phil Mickelson Signature* Sand	Forged cavity back, carbon steel	U	35.5	56	
	Lob			35.5	60	
Zevo	*Attack Zone Series 1* Gap	Cast traditional blade styler, 431 ss chrome finish	U	35.5	50	
	Sand			35.5	55	
	Lob			35	61	
	Attack Zone Series 2 Gap 2	Cast traditional blade style, 431 ss, chrome finish	U	35.5	52	
	Sand 2			35.5	56	
	Lob 2			35	60	

Legend: ss=stainless steel
L=Ladies' shaft flex rating
A=Seniors' shaft flex rating
R=Men's Regular shaft flex rating

F=Firm
S=Men's Stiff shaft flex rating
X=Men's Extra Stiff shaft flex rating

Lie (deg.)	Bounce Angle (deg.)	Shaft Materials and Flexes	Grip Style	Left-Handed	Women's	Suggested Retail
63	4	True Temper Dynamic Gold steel R, S, X; UST 640 graphite A, R, S, X	Tour Wrap	N	Y (SW only)	$63 steel $87 graphite
63	6					
63	8					
64	6	Graphite/boron, single flex	Rubber Tour Wrap	Y	N	$215
64	0					
59–71	6	5 shafts, 7 flexes	Zevo Pro Wrap	Y	Y	$90 steel $135 graphite
59–71	14	5 shafts, 7 flexes	Zevo Pro Wrap	Y	Y	$90 steel $135 graphite
59–71	6	5 shafts, 7 flexes	Zevo Pro Wrap	Y	Y	$90 steel $135 graphite
59–71	4	5 shafts, 7 flexes	Zevo Pro Wrap	N	Y	$90 steel $135 graphite
59–71	12	5 shafts, 7 flexes	Zevo Pro Wrap	N	Y	$90 steel $135 graphite
59–71	2	5 shafts, 7 flexes	Zevo Pro Wrap	N	Y	$90 steel $135 graphite

CHAPTER 7

Putters: Finding a "Flatstick" to Count On Through Thick and Thin

If you asked Ben Hogan what are the most important clubs in the bag, he would have told you, in this order, the driver, the putter, and the wedge. Hogan, of course, will go down in history as one of the greatest strikers of the golf ball who ever lived. In the late stages of his career, though, Hogan ranked as one of the poorest putters among championship-caliber golfers. So, his placement of the driver ahead of the putter is understandable, and many other great players and teachers might agree.

Others would argue, however, that without question the putter is the most important club in the bag. This argument would be upheld by putting guru Dave Pelz, who points out in his instruction book, *Putt Like the Pros,* (Harper-Perennial, 1989, 1991), that for the average golfer, a full 43 percent of the strokes made during the round are putts!

Now, it could be argued that this statistic is misleading. It's true that while 43 percent of the average player's strokes are indeed putts, we should also take into account that a certain number of these putts, perhaps ten or twelve per round, are virtual tap-ins or "gimmes" that come after the previous putt just misses. Moreover, in terms of the club itself, there is not nearly as much need for concern with its dynamics as with the driver or other long clubs, since with the putter the stroke usually requires very little force. So, factors such as shaft flex and torque do not really enter into the equation.

Still, the argument that the putter is the most important club deserves plenty of support. The old adage that a putt missed is a stroke lost forever is absolutely true. You can hit a mediocre drive into the rough and still recover with a good

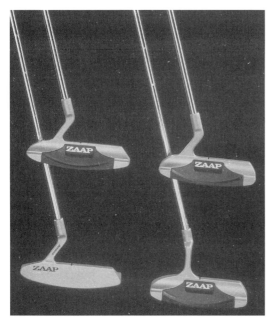

Tommy Armour ZAAP Putters

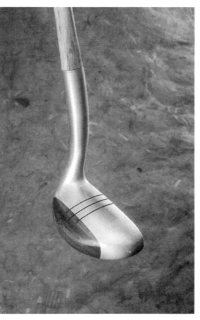

Otey Crisman 18HBW Wood-Shafted Mallet

iron shot or a fine chip. But miss a putt of six feet or less and there's no recourse: you've lost one full stroke.

Obviously, you've got to find a putter you like. I mean one you *really* like. You probably know a lot of golfers who own a garageful of putters, who are trying different ones constantly, hoping someday to "strike gold" with one of them. This grab-bag method never works for very long. Let's look at the key factors in selecting a putter that you can start a long-lasting relationship with, one you can have complete confidence in—whether in a "fairly friendly" match, a $5 Nassau, or a prestigious tournament that's on the line with the next putt you stroke.

Looks Aren't Everything

The first thing that you're going to scrutinize with any putter is the overall shape and look of the clubhead. With putters, you're exerting only a fraction of the force used in the full swing to roll a ball a short distance along a smooth, closely cut green. So, there are fewer geometric or aerodynamic rules than there are with any of the longer clubs, and you'll see a far greater variance in "looks" in the putter than with any other club.

*Ping Scottsdale Anser
(Nickel)*

How important is this "look" of the putter? Some players or instructors will advise that if a putter looks truly bizarre to you, you shouldn't waste any time trying to get used to it. However, what looks weird to one golfer may be appealing to the next. And sometimes a style may grow on you: What you hated last year may somehow give you a different impression now. (This usually happens after you've seen this particular style of putter wielded by another member of your weekend foursome for a while, and you've watched a surprising number of his or her putts fall in—and you've also handed a dismaying number of your hard-earned dollars over to that player.)

Speaking briefly from my own experience (and not to specifically recommend these models to anybody), I can tell you that in the last ten years I've consistently used only two putters, and the first time I saw each of them I disliked them. In the late 1960s, as a youngster really getting into golf, I remember seeing a number of golfers on the putting green using the then-revolutionary, heel-toe-weighted Ping Anser putter. "How can anybody possibly putt with that? It looks like a piece of plumbing," I thought. After nearly twenty years of watching golfers use Ping models, often very well, I finally joined the Ping club myself. The only other putter I've used in the last decade is the Odyssey Rossie I, a large mallet model that I thought would make an excellent potato masher at first inspection. I did give it a try on the putting green, quickly concluded that it was very easy to align on short putts, and have had good luck with it.

The point is that you might be unwise to eliminate a particular putter simply because of the way it looks. Sure, if you're shopping for a putter and you don't know what you want, it's fine to first pick out a few models that appeal to your eye. You might like a design that has very square, hard-looking lines. Or you might think you prefer a softer, more rounded look. But a number of factors that we will discuss must be right for you, and it could turn out that that "odd-looking" model has those specifications. So, keep an open mind.

Five Basic Putter Styles

Here are the five basic models of putters as described by putter designer Don Wood of Zevo Golf:

1. *Heel-Shafted Blade.* "This is a basic, flat type of blade with the clubshaft entering the head at its rear or heel. In original blade styles such as Bobby Jones's famous Calamity Jane, there was no specific weight distribution toward the clubhead's toe, heel, or sole. It was just a flat blade. In more recent years, many blade putter models have had flanges attached to the rear-sole area, and also, many of these putters now feature on offset hosel, with the

clubface behind the centerline of the shaft." A good example of this style is the MacGregor VIP Classic line.

2. *Center-Shafted Blade.* "This is also a relatively basic, uncluttered blade club-head, with the difference from the previous style being that the clubshaft enters the head closer to (although not precisely at) the center of the clubhead." The best examples of a center-shafted blade are the various models within the classic Titleist Bull's Eye line.

3. *Heel-Shafted Skirted Blade.* "This is a heel-shafted putter in which weight is added to the back of the blade; however, instead of a flange at the base of the blade, this weight is more slanted or 'skirted' over the entire rear of the blade. This style usually has some offset in the hosel and for whatever reason, it often has a black or deep metallic finish to it."

4. *Mallet Style.* "This is a putter with a large, rounded head style. There is often an inertial difference between most mallets and other styles of putters in that many mallets are 'face-balanced' [a term to be discussed shortly]. This face-balancing helps the putter to travel along a very straight line throughout the stroke. Mallets are often made of soft metals which usually provide a good sense of 'feel.'" Mallets have enjoyed a resurgence in recent years, and popular examples are Titleist's Scotty Cameron Caliente Bolero, Daiwa's Disc, Otey Crisman's wood-shafted 18HBW, and Cobra's King Cobra mallet.

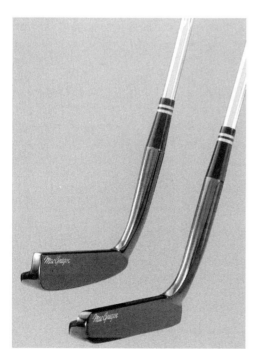

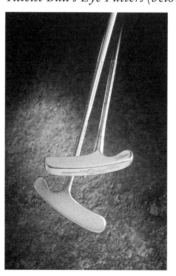

MacGregor VIP Classic Ironmaster IMG5
MacGregor VIP Classic 600 (left)
Titleist Bull's Eye Putters (below)

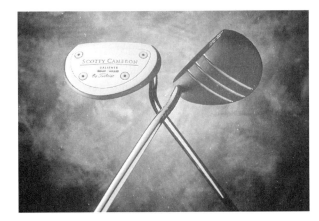

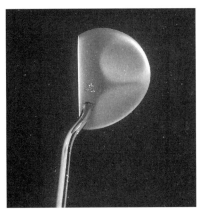

Titleist Scotty Cameron Mallets (above left);
Bullet Rimfire Series (above right); Cobra
King Cobra Mallet (left)

5. *Heel-Toe-Weighted.* "Basically, the heel-toe-weighted putter is a very forgiving design for those times when you don't strike the putt solidly. The design is intended to stabilize the clubhead, so the greatest amounts of weight
are placed at the heel and toe. The end result is that you don't get a great difference in the roll whether you hit the putt perfectly squarely or not. These
putters usually carry some degree of offset in the hosel as well." There are a
great many heel-toe-weighted putters on the market, exemplified well by the
Ping Scottsdale Anser and the Bullet Rimfire series.

Length, Lie, and Loft for Your Putter

Putting is the most individual stroke in golf. There are few rules in terms of the
width of the stance, how far to bend from the waist, how to grip the club, and

so on. Therefore, it's important to make sure the putter fits your own personal size and address style.

First, make sure that the putter's length is correct for you. Zevo's Wood advises that the player get into his or her natural posture for putting, with this cautionary note: "One thing I advise golfers when they assume their stance is that they try to get their eyes directly over the ball. If your eyes are either inside or outside a line directly over the ball and running to the target, it could distort your read of the putt's line. This in turn leads to inconsistent putting. Many golfers who have a putter that's too short will have their eyes inside a line down to the ball," Wood adds. So, once you've assumed your posture with this caveat in mind, grip the putter you're trying out at the point where the arms hang naturally. If the point at which your hands grasp the club is just below the end of the grip, this length putter should be just right for you. If you find yourself choking down the handle more than 1 inch, or if your top hand is partly off the butt of the grip, you need a different length. Most "regular"-style putters as listed in the table that follows will range between 33 and 36 inches in length, with 34 and 35 inches being the most popular lengths.

Ideally, the lie of the putter will be such that the sole of the club rests perfectly flat on the green's surface. If either the heel or the toe makes contact with the ground as the putter meets the ball, the clubface may twist enough to cause a miss (to the left if the heel hits, to the right if the toe makes contact, for a right-handed player). However, as we noted with the irons in Chapter 5, a great many putters have a degree of "radius" built into the sole to keep the heel or toe from catching, even if the club's lie is fractionally off.

One other point to keep in mind is that a lie that is too upright or too flat could have a slight effect on the alignment of the face, just as we discussed with the irons. However, Wood notes, "There's so little loft on the face of the putter that a slight imperfection in the club's lie is really not going to make much dif-

PowerBilt MD2 (top)
PowerBilt MD4 (bottom)

ference in the ball's line of roll. In addition, the human being is an amazing animal. The golfer can intuitively adjust to any face alignment flaws caused by a putter that's not lying flat. Isao Aoki and Payne Stewart both address the ball with the toe of the putter off the ground, yet they are both fabulous putters." So, unless you notice that the lie is quite a bit off given your address posture, don't worry about this factor too much.

Loft on the putter, though, is another matter and one that many golfers have very little awareness of. Some golfers may think the putter has no loft at all, but almost all models will have between 2 and 7 degrees loft. What determines the right loft for you? Much of it depends on the type of surface you putt on most frequently. Basically, *the faster and smoother the greens, the lower the loft you should choose; and the slower and bumpier they are, the more a higher loft on the putter can help you.*

If you putt on fast, smooth greens, which most often will be of the bent-grass variety, you want to get the ball rolling end over end as quickly as possible. Thus, 2 degrees loft might be fine. However, if the greens you putt on are customarily very slow, shaggy, and bumpy, Wood says, "You actually want to get the ball up in the air a bit at the start—not a lot, but enough to get it off the surface so that it can roll immediately." Golfers who customarily play on municipal courses, which usually cannot keep their greens cut low because of constant heavy play (which also leaves them bumpy), should consider putters that have a minimum of 4 to 5 degrees loft. "A putter with a higher loft angle can also help golfers who like to use a forward press to start the stroke, since doing so serves to deloft the putter a bit," Wood adds.

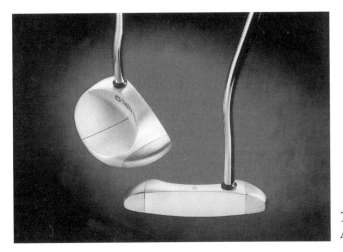

Taylor Made Roho Mallet

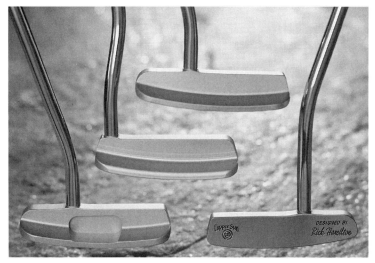

Rawlings Copper Sun Putters

Choose a Helpful Alignment Aid

Most amateurs, when they miss a relatively makable putt, immediately look to the stroke itself to figure out what went wrong. They often fail to realize that the stroke may have been perfect but their *alignment of the putter prior to the stroke* did not match the perfect line to the hole. In fact, if your alignment is always off and your stroke is perfect, you'll never sink anything! By contrast, if your alignment is poor and your stroke is erratic, you may occasionally create a "two wrongs make a right" situation in which you end up sinking a putt here and there. However, your chances of holing your fair share are much, much greater if you start with a perfectly aligned blade.

There are many ways that putter designers can help you to align well. Perhaps the simplest they use is to draw an alignment line across the putter from front to back, which is perfectly perpendicular to the face of the club. A high percentage of putters will have such an alignment line. Keep in mind that the longer this line is, the better. Putters that are very deep from front to back, which include mallets and many flanged-blade styles, have an advantage in that a longer line can be drawn across the head to sight with.

One thing to keep in mind regarding alignment lines: They are usually drawn across the center of the head. This does not necessarily mean that they are drawn precisely at the putter's *center of percussion* (see sidebar on page 250). You may find that the right point at which to contact the middle of the ball on your putts is *not* at the alignment line.

In addition to the alignment line feature, Don Wood also points out, "The entire design of the putterhead can also be an alignment feature in itself. A put-

Finding That Center of Percussion

If the "sweet spot," or center of percussion, of the putter is not exactly in the middle of the blade, right where an alignment line is likely to be drawn perpendicular to the clubface, then how can you find out where the heck it is?

Actually it's quite simple. Take your putter and hold the grip between your thumb and forefinger so that the shaft is hanging straight down. Hold it high enough so that the clubface is close to eye level.

Next take either a wooden golf tee or a quarter in your free hand. With the tip of the tee or the side of the quarter, tap the face of the putter sharply near its center. Observe the putterface. Did it rebound directly backward, or did it twist a little in one direction or the other? If you noticed any twist at all, it means you made contact either to the heel side or to the toe side of the center of percussion.

More often than not, you will find that the putter's center of percussion, the spot at which the putterface rebounds straight back from the point of impact, will be slightly toward the *heel* side of the putter. This may be a bit more noticeable with a heel-shafted putter than with a putter whose shaft is connected to the head closer to its center. At any rate, for most consistent results, once you've found the center of percussion, that's the spot you should try to contact the center of the ball with.

ter that has very square features will generally be easy to line up. That's one of the reasons that the Ping Anser has been so popular over the years—the entire head is like a little rectangular box down there. A putter like this is inherently easy to line up."

Offset vs. Straight Hosels

A straight hosel on the putter is simply one in which there are no angles, the result being that the putterface is parallel to or level with the centerline of the shaft. An offset putter design, meanwhile, is one in which the leading edge of the blade is set behind the centerline of the shaft. Either the shaft can be curved to effect this offset, or there can be a rearward crook in the hosel itself. As you'll see by looking in the column on hosel offset in the table that follows, for most companies that have listed a specific degree of offset, this range is usually between ¼ and ½ inch. Probably the majority of putters designed today have some degree of offset in the hosel.

As Zevo's Wood points out, while putting styles are very individualistic, one

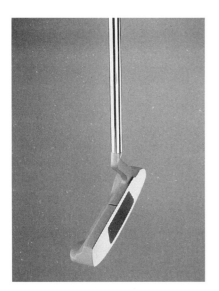

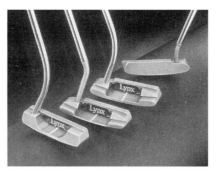

Odyssey DF 665 (left)
Lynx Copper Milled Putters (above)

axiom you'll hear most often is to "keep the hands ahead of the ball through impact." And a putter with an offset hosel puts your hands ahead of the blade right from the start. This in turn makes it easier to keep them there throughout the stroke. If you have had the habit of "scuffing" your putts and/or allowing your lead wrist to break down through the impact zone, a putter with more hosel offset may help you to execute a firmer stroke.

An additional advantage of offset is that if you do indeed keep your hands slightly ahead of the ball throughout the stroke, you'll contact the ball with pretty much the same loft that was built into the clubface. Some players who use a nonoffset design get their hands ahead of the ball, which serves to deloft the clubface. This may cause the ball to get off to a more bouncy start than is desirable. Finally, "An offset head provides a look that's very desirable to most players," Wood adds.

The Mystery of Face-Balancing

Here's an experiment that may interest you. Take any iron club from your bag and balance the clubshaft horizontally across your extended index finger, about 6 inches up from the hosel. Now look at the clubhead. The toe will be pointing straight down to the ground. For this reason, the iron club is said to be "toe-balanced."

The majority of putters, and almost every putter that is of the heel-shafted-

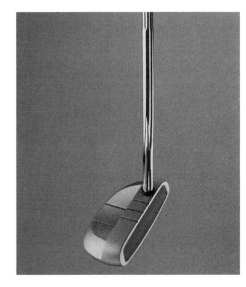

Odyssey Rossie II

blade variety, are also toe-balanced. This should not be surprising; in fact, you'd probably be surprised to see anything else. However, an increasing number of putters today are balanced much differently. If you were to balance the shaft of some of these putters across your finger, you'd find that instead of the toe pointing down, the clubface, seemingly in defiance of gravity, *will point straight up*. Such a putter would be termed a *face-balanced* putter. Odyssey's Rossie mallet-style putters are examples of face-balanced models.

What's the reasoning behind weighting that makes a putter face-balanced? According to Don Wood, "If a putter's toe points straight down, this means that during the stroke, it will also have a tendency toward opening a bit on the backstroke, then squaring at impact and closing beyond it, very similar to the movement of the clubhead through the full swing." Meanwhile, a putter that's face-balanced tends to be extremely stable, with the face remaining squarer to the target line throughout the stroke. You can open and close the face of a face-balanced putter if you want to, of course. It would just take a bit more manipulation on your part to make this happen. "A face-balanced putter would be desirable for a person who wants to make a straight-back, straight-through kind of stroke, with the path of the putter never moving off the target line," Wood says.

It would seem that a putter that's face-balanced will automatically be a more consistent putter, a definite technological improvement. Not necessarily so. "A face-balanced putter will work well for that certain type of straight-back, straight-through stroke," notes Wood, "but it would *not* work as well for a putter like Ben Crenshaw or John Daly, or anyone who rotates the putter a little to the inside both on the backswing and on the follow-through. In fact, I'd

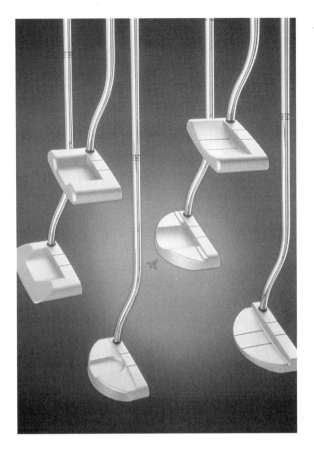

Mizuno GT Putter Series

guess that a fully face-balanced putter would *not* be the best type for 75 percent of the players on the PGA Tour.

"Unless you have a very 'vertical' stroke," Wood continues, "I'd suggest you use a putter that has the shaft back in the heel, and one that is *not* face-balanced. Face-balanced putters are not necessarily superior in design to toe-balanced putters—they're simply a newer, optional form of balancing."

There are a number of putters today that are on the middle ground between being toe-balanced and face-balanced. For example, if you were to take many Ping models, which are almost all in the heel-toe-weighted category, and try the balance test described, you'd find that the toe will often angle slightly downward, but it will be far from straight down. This in-between balancing can work effectively with either a more rounded or a "straight-back, straight-through" type of stroke.

Choose a "Feels Good" Putter

Observe the column on clubhead materials in the following table, and you'll find that the list of materials is almost endless. Putterheads can be made of various forms of stainless steel, carbon steel, bronze, brass, aluminum, zinc, copper, nickel, graphite, tungsten, and other materials. In addition, many putters on the market today include face inserts of various types, all in the name of providing a feel that's just right when you stroke the ball.

Of course, feel in putting is highly individual. Some golfers may prefer a firm feel and a sharp "click" when putterhead meets ball. This preference might suggest the selection of a stainless-steel-headed model. For those for whom a soft feel at impact is preferable, an aluminum-faced model such as those in the Bobby Grace line or one of the putters with a rubberized face insert would be preferable.

In general, the majority of golfers would probably both appreciate and benefit from a softer feel. "What softer does is allow the ball to stay on the clubface a little bit longer—it gives a little more information to the golfer's hands, if you will. I'm a big believer in soft material for the putter clubface," says Don Wood.

There's another reason that softer putterfaces seem to have become the wave of the present. If anything, as we'll see in the next chapter, golf balls have somewhat harder covers today than the balls made with natural balata in years past. The result, in some cases, has been that impact with the putter can feel somewhat rocky.

There is probably very little difference in the distance the ball actually rolls when putted with a "hard" versus "soft" putter. "The clubhead is not moving fast enough on most putts to actually compress the ball," notes Wood. "There's not enough measurable restitution in either the clubface or the ball to conclude that there's a discernible difference in the distance the ball will roll."

Bobby Grace Pip Squeak

Still, that intangible feel factor is tremendously important to the results you get on the greens. "If impact feels so hard that you hardly felt the ball on the face, it stands to reason that you'll have a harder time controlling the distance you roll your putts," Wood, formerly a top amateur player, points out. "And golfers should remember that in putting, 'distance is line.' What I mean by that is that you not only have to pick out the ideal line to roll the ball into the hole—you must then stroke the putt so it carries the perfect amount of speed to make it follow that line. Too much force with the correct line means the putt will not break as much as you thought, so it misses on the 'high' side. A putt that's hit too softly will break more and miss on the 'low' side, if it even reaches the hole." Of course, the most important thing you need with regard to distance control in putting is lots of practice. But you should certainly experiment with several models and try to observe, on medium- and longer-length putts, which putter seems to let you roll the ball the most consistently in terms of distance.

Don't Forget the Right Grip!

Teardrop Original

Chances are that if you pick out a putter that seems to suit you and you don't take much notice of the grip, then it's likely that it's fine for you. We'll talk about the club grip in Chapter 9. However, some points that are specific to putter grips that do not apply to the long clubs should be noted here.

You may notice that most putter grips have a "flat top," if you will—the top or front portion of the grip, on which you would rest your thumbs if you use a conventional putting grip. Some putter grips may have a wider "flat top" than others—these are referred to as a paddle grip and may offer an advantage if you like to make a stroke in which the hands stay inactive. There is also a grip that is referred to as a pistol grip. Here, the rear side of the grip extends outward somewhat, so it feels as though your top hand is gripping a pistol.

At any rate, whichever overall style you choose, the flat top on the grip is actually an important aid to aligning the putter correctly. This flat top is (or should be) perfectly perpendicular to the putterface, and parallel to the target line. This in turn helps you to automatically get your hands "square" to the line on which you wish to roll the ball.

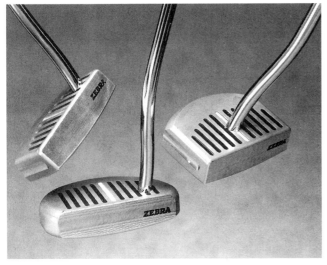

Ram Zebra Tour Milled Flat Top
Ram Zebra LZ1
Ram Zebra LZ2

What About Trying a "Long" Putter?

You're probably aware of putters that, instead of being 34 or 35 inches in length, instead are 50 or more inches long (an example in the table is Bobby Grace's Heavyweight Champion). These long putters by design must be used with a split-handed grip in which the right hand is much higher than the left (for a right-handed player). They have gained some popularity—mainly with older golfers whose back problems cause them grief when bending over to putt, or with those who simply have putted poorly for an extended time using a conventional-length club.

Should you ever consider a long putter? And if so, what should you look for? "Obviously, the design parameters for these clubs are completely different," says Don Wood. "Both the clubhead and the shaft must be much heavier than for a normal putter.

"One reason I'm not a fan of the long putter is that you obviously must make the putting stroke with the hands completely separated on the club. This alone can cause a lot of inconsistencies in the stroke. It's a completely different action, like learning to play golf all over again.

"Some people swear by these things, but I have not seen anyone putt consistently well with a long putter," Wood concludes. "I believe anyone who is under the impression that just because a putter is 50-plus inches long, it will help them putt better is grasping at straws."

You should take advantage of a flat top on the grip, which incidentally is within the Rules of Golf for use only on the putter. A putter whose grip is perfectly round will make it much harder to get your hands set into position while assuring that the clubface is setting perfectly square. Finally, check to make sure your potential new putter's grip has been aligned perfectly. If that flat top is not squarely on top, it's a factor that can quickly and mysteriously throw your putting game off. Also make sure that if and when you change your putter grip, the flat top is replaced perfectly perpendicular to the clubface.

Some Final Notes on Putter Pricing

As you pore over the table, you may note (possibly with some dismay) that there are a lot of pricey putters out there. Although few reach the stratosphere of $500 models such as Maruman's Tungsten or its TAP series (and there are also putters listed retailing for as little as $24), there are almost as many putters on the market that cost $100 or more as there are those that retail for less than that figure.

Sure, we'd all like to get a putter that we love for $40 or so. Zevo's Wood points out, though, that putters have become a more complex animal, particularly in the past five years. "It's not the materials that may make a putter expensive, it's the manufacturing techniques used," he says. "This is especially true for putters that have a cavity in the clubface, into which a soft-feeling material is inserted. There are more steps to complete, and at each step there may be manufacturing incongruities that cause more rejects. Another example of more complex manufacturing," he continues, "is with putters where the entire clubhead is fully computer-milled. By definition, these are simply much more precise instruments to putt with. The faces are always dead flat and the lofts are just right.

"I'd like to ask the readers a question. Would they rather pay $50 for a putter and wind up putting just mediocre with it, or would they rather pay $100 and make, say, even one more putt, every round they play, for as long as they own it?"

Well, since you put it that way, perhaps we'd better not make too big an issue of the price of putters. However, *do* make sure you pay attention to all the factors we've discussed that will go into your final selection. Then you'll feel no need whatsoever to go through the process again anytime soon.

PUTTER PRODUCT INFORMATION

MANUFACTURER	MODEL/DESIGN STYLE	CLUBHEAD MATERIAL/ SHAFT MATERIAL	PUTTER WEIGHT (oz.)
Adams Golf	VM14, VM17—heel-shafted, heel-toe-weighted	Carbon steel/steel	16 men 15.5 women
Alien	TUTCH mallet	Alium (heat-treated alloy)/graphite	19.9
Tommy Armour	ZAAP Putters Kappa Series—4 center-shafted, heel-toe-weighted models	17-4 ss/parallel tip Sensi-Feel steel	Not supplied
	Alpha Series—4 center-shafted, heel-toe-weighted models		
	Comments: Black polymeric insert behind face allows increased perimeter weighting.		
Black Ice Golf	Black Ice—heel-shafted, heel-toe-weighted	431 ss, ceramic face/steel, alloy, or graphite	App. 14–17.6, depending on head, shaft type, and length
	Aquila LX—heel-shafted, heel-toe-weighted	Brass w/balata or graphite insert/steel, alloy, or graphite	
	Aquila MXP mallet	Wood/steel, alloy, or graphite	
	Aquila 4.0—center-shafted "dual axis" weighted	17-4 ss/steel, alloy, or graphite	
	Aquila CZ—center-shafted "dual axis" weighted	17.4 ss or bronze w/composite insert/steel, alloy, or graphite	

Legend: ss=stainless steel

Hosel Offset (in.)	Grip Style	Clubface Loft (deg.)	Lengths (in.)	Left-Handed	Suggested Retail
.350 or none	Synthetic Rubber or Leather	VMI4 2.5, VMI7 5	34, 35	N	$90
Slight	Oversize Custom Wrap	4	34, 35	Y	$140
None, slight, or moderate	Golf Pride Rubber Pistol	3	33, 34, 35, 36	N	$100
None, slight, or moderate	Golf Pride Rubber Pistol	2	33, 34, 35, 36	Y	$100
Not supplied	Rubber Tour Wrap	0	Custom from 30 to 52	Not supplied	$99
		2			$69
		2			$89
		2			$69
		2			$69

continued

PUTTER PRODUCT INFORMATION *(continued)*

MANUFACTURER	MODEL/DESIGN STYLE	CLUBHEAD MATERIAL/ SHAFT MATERIAL	PUTTER WEIGHT (oz.)
Bridgestone	Ray Floyd KC Series mallet	Aluminum alloy/steel	Not supplied
	Precept KC Series Extra Feel—mallet	Steel alloy/steel	Not supplied
	Classic Blade	Steel alloy/steel	Not supplied
	Full Square	Steel alloy/steel	Not supplied
	Mini-Square	Steel alloy/steel	Not supplied
Bullet Golf	Rimfire I, II, III—heel-toe-weighted	ss/steel	15
	Invincible—mallet	Aluminum/bent steel	15
Callaway Golf	Big Bertha Blade	ss/steel	Not supplied
	Bobby Jones—heel-toe weighted flanged blade (3 models)	ss/steel	Not supplied
	Tuttle—mallet	Aluminum/steel	Not supplied
	Comments: Tuttle has rounded sole plate, allows adjustment to various green contours.		
Cleveland Golf	"Designed By" Blade	Carbon steel/steel	Not supplied
	VAS #1 heel-toe	ss/steel	Not supplied
	VAS #2 mallet	ss/steel	Not supplied
	VAS #3 mallet	ss/steel	Not supplied
	VAS #4 heel-toe	ss/steel	Not supplied
	VAS #5 heel-toe	ss/steel	Not supplied
	VAS #6 heel-toe	ss/steel	Not supplied
	VAS #7 semi-mallet	ss/steel	Not supplied
	VAS #8 mallet	ss/steel	Not supplied
	VAS #9 mallet	ss/steel	Not supplied

Legend: ss=stainless steel

Hosel Offset (in.)	Grip Style	Clubface Loft (deg.)	Lengths (in.)	Left-Handed	Suggested Retail
Not supplied	Royal Fine Textured	6	35	N	$125
Not supplied		6	35	N	$125
Not supplied		6	35	N	$110
Not supplied		6	35	N	$110
Not supplied		6	35	Y	$110
.25	Rubber Paddle	4	33, 35	Y	$50
.50	Rubber Paddle	4	33, 35	Y	$50
.25	Rubber Flat Top	Not supplied	33, 34, 35	Y	$125
Slight	Serrated rubber	Not supplied	33, 34, 35	Y	$110
None	Rubber Flat Top	Not supplied	33, 34, 35	Y	$125
Not supplied	Rubber or Leather	Not supplied	34, 35	Y	$93
Moderate			34, 35	N	$75
Slight			34, 35	N	$89
Moderate			34, 35	N	$89
Slight			34, 35	N	$75
Moderate			34, 35	N	$75
Moderate			34, 35	Y	$75
Moderate			34, 35	N	$75
Slight			34, 35	N	$89
Moderate			34, 35	Y	$89

continued

PUTTER PRODUCT INFORMATION *(continued)*

MANUFACTURER	MODEL/DESIGN STYLE	CLUBHEAD MATERIAL/ SHAFT MATERIAL	PUTTER WEIGHT (oz.)
Cobra Golf	King Cobra mallet (original, medium, small)	Cast aluminum/steel	Not supplied
	King Cobra Tricep	Cast aluminum/steel	Not supplied
Ray Cook	Sofstroke—heel-toe weighted, copper or black finish	Forged aluminum w/brass heel-toe inlays/steel	Not supplied
	Blue Goose—5 heel-toe-weighted blades, 1 heel-toe-weighted mallet	Carbon steel and brass/steel	18
	Mallets—2 heel-shafted, 2 face-balanced	Forged aluminum/steel	18
	Billy Baroo—3 heel-toe-weighted blades, 1 heel-toe-weighted mallet	303 ss/steel	18
	Silver Ray—3 heel-toe-weighted blades, 1 heel-toe-weighted mallet	303 ss/steel	18
	Classic Plus—3 heel-shafted blades, 1 heel-toe-weighted blade, 1 mallet	Zinc and brass/ss	17.1
	Comments: Most diverse putter offerings on the market.		
Otey Crisman	18HB, 18HBW, 16HB, 320 mallets; MS1, MS1D mallets; MS2, 3HW semi-mallets; Golden Touch 30H, 38H, 42H blades	All putters have aluminum heads w/brass insert; hickory shafts for all except steel shaft in MS1, MS1D, MS2	Not supplied (hickory-shafted models slightly lighter than steel)
Daiwa	Disc mallet	Rust-resistant alloy/steel	18
	DG Series milled—heel-toe-weighted	Rust-resistant copper and ss/steel	18
	Comments: Disc is face-balanced and circular shape;		

Legend: ss=stainless steel

Hosel Offset (in.)	Grip Style	Clubface Loft (deg.)	Lengths (in.)	Left-Handed	Suggested Retail
Not supplied	Rubber Flat Top	5	35	N	$109
Not supplied	Rubber Flat Top	7	52	N	$125
Not supplied	Graphic Tour Wrap, slight oversize	4	34, 35, 36	Y	$87
.125–.375	Griptec Tour Wrap, slight oversize	4	34, 35, 36	Y	$105
0–.375	Griptec Tour Wrap, slight oversize	4	34, 35, 36	Y	$82
.125–.250	Griptec Tour Wrap, slight oversize	4	34, 35, 36	Y	$67
.125–250	Griptec Tour Wrap, slight oversize	4	34, 35, 36	Y	$57
0–.250	Pro Grip Synthetic Rubber, slight oversize	4	34, 35, 36	Y	$34
.25–.50	Leather Wrap for hickory models; EPDM Synthetic Rubber Wrap on MS1, MS1D, MS2	3	35	Y (18HBW, 38H, MS1, MS1D Golden Touch)	$120 (all models)
None	Rubber Pistol	5	34, 35	N	$100
None	Rubber Pistol	5	34, 35	N	$100

DG Series has special sight notch to aid alignment.   continued

PUTTER PRODUCT INFORMATION *(continued)*

MANUFACTURER	MODEL/DESIGN STYLE	CLUBHEAD MATERIAL/ SHAFT MATERIAL	PUTTER WEIGHT *(oz.)*
Dunlop	Collector's Series Blade	ss, fluted steel shaft	Medium-light
	Tour DG Milled Brass	Brass/steel	Medium
	DDH Tour Milled Mallet	Aluminum w/brass insert, steel	Medium
Dynacraft	PFD—oversize mallet	Aluminum/steel	17.5
	STS—heel-toe-weighted	Brass w/rubber face insert/steel	17.5
	Dyna Tech Monster mallet— oversize mallet	Aluminum/steel	17.5
Goldwin Golf	Crazy Jane—mallet	Soft aluminum	Not supplied
	Bonnie Blue—standard or long blade	431 ss/steel	Not supplied
Golfsmith	Soft Stroke—heel-toe	Brass w/rubber face insert/steel	18
	XPC Plus—heel-toe	431 ss/steel	18
	Harvey Penick Lake Austin mallet	431 ss/steel	18
The GolfWorks	Bio Mech II—tunnel-sole mallet	17-4 ss/steel	17.5
	Tarantula—scalloped blade	17-4 ss/steel	17.5
	Back Of The Cup Two-way blade	Zinc/steel	16.6
	Midsize mallet	Zinc/steel	18.1
	Mallet	Zinc/steel	17.8
	Heel-toe-weighted	Zinc/steel	16.9
	T-Bar model	Zinc/steel	17.8

Legend: ss=stainless steel

Hosel Offset (in.)	Grip Style	Clubface Loft (deg.)	Lengths (in.)	Left-Handed	Suggested Retail
None	Royal Oversize flat top	2.5	33, 35	N	$90
Slight	Royal Oversize flat top	2.5	33, 35	N	$100
Slight	Lamkin Perma Wrap flat top	2.5	33, 35	N	$50
.375	Rubber Paddle; others available	3	34, 35, 36	N	$60
.25		3	34, 35, 36	N	$55
.375		5	34, 35, 36	N	$60
Very slight	Golf Pride Rubber Flat Top	6	33, 34, 35, 36	Y	$100
Very slight		6	33, 34, 35, 36	N	$100
.875	Rubber Pistol	3	35	N	$45
.375	Rubber Pistol	3	35	Y	$45
None	Rubber Pistol	2.5	35	Y	$60
Moderate	Rubber Flat Top	3	35	N	$36
		3	35	N	$36
		3	35	Y	$24
		3	35	N	$24
		3	35	N	$24
		3	35	N	$24
		3	35	N	$24

continued

PUTTER PRODUCT INFORMATION *(continued)*

MANUFACTURER	MODEL/DESIGN STYLE	CLUBHEAD MATERIAL/ SHAFT MATERIAL	PUTTER WEIGHT *(oz.)*
Bobby Grace	Fat Lady Swings—mallet	Milled aluminum or sand-cast aluminum/steel	18.5 all models
	Fat Man—mallet	Milled aluminum/steel	
	Little Lady—mallet	Milled aluminum/steel	
	Cute Kid—mallet	Milled aluminum/steel	
	Pip-Squeak—mallet	Milled aluminum/steel	
	KBI Scottsdale	Cast blade in manganese bronze, beryllium copper, or beryllium nickel/steel	Not supplied
	Heavyweight Champion—mallet	Milled aluminum/steel	Not supplied
Kunnan	*IGI Series* IP1—mallet	Graphite and ss/graphite	17.5
	IP3—Heel-toe-weighted	Graphite and ss/graphite	17.5
	IPS	Graphite and brass/graphite	18.3
	EXT Series Heel-toe-weighted	Graphite and ss/steel or graphite	18.6
	Mallet	Graphite and ss/steel or graphite shaft	18.6

Comments: IPI models have computer-milled face; IGI and IXT are face-balanced.

Legend: ss=stainless steel

Hosel Offset (in.)	Grip Style	Clubface Loft (deg.)	Lengths (in.)	Left-Handed	Suggested Retail
.375	Golf Pride Tour Arch (perforated modified pistol) or Golf Pride Special II (smooth flat top)	5	33, 33.5, 34, 34.5, 35, 35.5 36, all models except Heavyweight Champion	Y	$185 milled $150 sand-cast
		5		Y	$185
		5		Y	$185
		5		Y	$185
		5		Y	$185
		5		N	$100 manganese bronze $185 beryllium copper $275 beryllium nickel
		5	48–52	N	$185
.05	Rubber Pistol	3	35	N	$125
.42	Rubber Pistol	3	35	N	$125
Not supplied	Rubber Pistol	3	35	N	$125
.32	Rubber Pistol	3	36	N	$110 steel $125 graphite
.32	Rubber Pistol	3	36	N	$110 steel $125 graphite

continued

PUTTER PRODUCT INFORMATION *(continued)*

MANUFACTURER	MODEL/DESIGN STYLE	CLUBHEAD MATERIAL/ SHAFT MATERIAL	PUTTER WEIGHT (oz.)
Lynx	Lynx Tour Putter—offset long hosel	17-4 ss/steel	Not supplied
	Copper Mill series (four heel-toe weighted models)	Computer milled 100% copper/steel	Not supplied
MacGregor	Ironmaster IMG 5—milled classic flanged blade	Carbon steel/steel	Not supplied
	VIP Model 600—milled classic flanged blade	Carbon steel/steel	Not supplied
Maruman Golf	TAP Series—heel-toe-weighted	Phosphorous bronze w/ceramic face/steel	Not supplied
	MP Series—perimeter-weighted	18-8 ss/steel	Not supplied
	ML Series—heel-shafted blade	Carbon steel/steel	Not supplied
	Tungsten MT	Tungsten/graphite	Not supplied
Maxfli Golf	Tad Moore milled putters—6 styles	Mild carbon steel/steel	18.0
	Tad Moore cast putters—6 styles	Cast 17-4 ss/steel	18.0
	Tad Moore Yipstick	17-4 ss/steel	24.0
	Tad Moore T-Bone mallet—2 styles	Aluminum and brass/steel	17.0
	Tad Moore Tad Pole	17-4 ss/steel	31.0

Comments: Yipstick has heavy head, large round grip to encourage slow pendulum stroke;

Legend: ss=stainless steel

Hosel Offset (in.)	Grip Style	Clubface Loft (deg.)	Lengths (in.)	Left-Handed	Suggested Retail
Substantial	Golf Pride Tour Wrap Pistol	4	33, 34, 35, 36, 37	Y	$60
Models vary from zero to substantial offset	Lamkin flat top	4	34, 35, 36	N	$130
Moderate	Golf Pride Tour Wrap	3	35	N	$175
Moderate	Golf Pride Tour Wrap	3	35	N	$175
Not supplied	Not supplied	Not supplied	34, 35	N	$500
Not supplied	Not supplied	Not supplied	33, 34, or 35 in various models	Y	$150–$175
Not supplied	Not supplied	Not supplied	35	N	$125
Not supplied	Not supplied	Not supplied	35	N	$500
.157–.394	Sanded rubber, flat top/oval back	4	35	Y (one model)	$148
.236–.550	Sanded rubber, flat top/oval back	4	35	Y (one model)	$70
.079	Oversize round sanded rubber, flat top/oval back	3	32	N	$91
.157, .315	Oversize round sanded rubber, flat top/oval back	3	35	Y (one model)	$81
.079	Sanded rubber, flat top/oval back	4	48	N	$125

Tad Pole is long putter model.

continued

PUTTER PRODUCT INFORMATION (continued)

MANUFACTURER	MODEL/DESIGN STYLE	CLUBHEAD MATERIAL/ SHAFT MATERIAL	PUTTER WEIGHT (oz.)
Merit Golf	Prophecy—blade, midsize, mallet styles	431 ss/steel	Not supplied
	Fusion—milled flanged blade	"Powdered" ss, carbon steel, or brass/steel	Not supplied
Mitsushiba Golf	Merlin Putters I, II, III—center-shafted mallets	Zinc alloy heads, titanium/magnesium shafts	Not supplied
	Performance Series—5 center-shafted, heel-toe-weighted, 1 rear-shafted blade		
Mizuno USA	TC putters—5 models, mainly heel-toe-weighted styles	17-4 ss w/milled clubface/steel	Not supplied
	GT putters—7 models, all mallet styles	Computer-milled aluminum/steel	Not supplied
	Comments: GT putters are made of aluminum for soft feel;		
Nicklaus Golf	I.Q.—oversize heel-toe-weighted	17-4 ss/steel	17.3
	Bear—oversize heel-toe-weighted	17-4 ss/steel	16.9
	Bear Track—mallet	Aluminum/steel	18.2
	Limited Edition—heel-shafted blade	431 ss/steel	17.9

Legend: ss=stainless steel

Hosel Offset (in.)	Grip Style	Clubface Loft (deg.)	Lengths (in.)	Left-Handed	Suggested Retail
.125	Golf Pride Pro Score	4	34, 35, 36	N	$78
.200	Golf Pride Pro Score	4	34, 35, 36	N	$150
.40	Synthetic Rubber Pistol	2	32, 33, 34, 35, 36	Not supplied	$50
.40		2	32, 33, 34, 35, 36	Not supplied	$27
Not supplied	Golf Pride Tour Wrap Putter Grip	4	34, 35	Y (TC140)	$75
.114	Royal Sand Wrap Putter Grip	4	34, 35	Y (GT102L)	$125

lead-weighted sole for expanded sweet spot.

Hosel Offset (in.)	Grip Style	Clubface Loft (deg.)	Lengths (in.)	Left-Handed	Suggested Retail
Not supplied	Golf Pride	3	33, 34, 35, 36	N	$150
Not supplied	Golf Pride	3	33, 34, 35, 36	N	$70
Not supplied	Griptec Oversize Wrap Paddle	2	33, 34, 35, 36	N	$110
Not supplied	Griptec Tour Size Wrap Paddle	4	33, 34, 35, 36	N	$190

continued

PUTTER PRODUCT INFORMATION *(continued)*

MANUFACTURER	MODEL/DESIGN STYLE	CLUBHEAD MATERIAL/ SHAFT MATERIAL	PUTTER WEIGHT (oz.)
Odyssey	*Dual Force Models* 220—flanged blade	220, 440, 552, 660, 662, and 665 bronze alloy head w/ Stronomic face insert/steel shaft; 550, 880, 990, 992, Rossie, ss head w/Stronomic face insert/steel shaft	17.2 (with 35" shaft)
	440—flanged blade		
	550—heel-toe-weighted		
	552—heel-toe-weighted		
	660—heel-toe-weighted		
	662—heel-toe-weighted		
	665—face-balanced		
	882—heel-shafted		
	990—heel-toe-weighted		
	992—heel-toe-weighted		
	Rossie I—large mallet		
	Rossie II—small mallet		
	Comments: Lightweight Stronomic insert provides super-soft impact		
Ping	Anser Series—7 models	Various models in ss, copper, manganese, bronze, nickel/steel	Not supplied
	Zing B Series—7 models		
	BZ Series—9 models		
	KS Series—7 models		
	Pal & Cushin Series—7 models		
	Original, Blade and Long Putters— 8 models		

Comments: Huge putter line; top 7 models have been used for over 400 pro tour victories; KS Series features extra-long hosels; great "alignability" for most models.

Legend: ss=stainless steel

Hosel Offset (in.)	Grip Style	Clubface Loft (deg.)	Lengths (in.)	Left-Handed	Suggested Retail
.185	Synthetic rubber pistol	4	33, 34, 35, 36	N	$98
.185		4		N	$98
.185		4		N	$98
.37		4		N	$98
.37		4		Y	$98
.37		4		N	$98
None		4		N	$98
.185		4		N	$98
.37		4		N	$98
.0925		4		N	$98
.37		4		N	$115
.185		4		Y	$115

feel, even with harder-covered two-piece balls.

Wide variety with moderate to substantial offset in majority of designs	Ping Rubber Flat Top is standard; GLI, Textured Spiral, Cord Spiral optional	Standard lofts are 3, 4, or 5; custom available	35 is standard; custom length in ¼" increments	Y	$75 ss or manganese bronze (most models) $95 copper (most models) $155 nickel (most models)
				Y	
				Y	
				Y	
				Y	
				Y	

most models have high degree of heel-toe-weighting; BZ Series models are face-balanced;

continued

PUTTER PRODUCT INFORMATION (continued)

MANUFACTURER	MODEL/DESIGN STYLE	CLUBHEAD MATERIAL/ SHAFT MATERIAL	PUTTER WEIGHT (oz.)
Gary Player Golf	*Precision Putting Instruments* PP1 heel-toe-weighted	Soft metal aluminum bronze alloy/steel or graphite shaft, all models	15–17 for all depending on shaft material and length
	PP2 heel-toe-weighted flange		
	PP3 mallet		
	PP4 heel-toe-weighted		
	PP5 oversize heel-toe-weighted		
	PP6 mallet		
	Comments: Soft metal absorbs contact shock 20% faster than stainless steel,		
Players Golf	Oversize mallet	Milled ss w/cobalt finish/steel	Not supplied
	Cad-Cam milled, forged— 4 heel-toe-weighted models	Brass/steel	
PowerBilt	*TPS MD Series* MD1, MD3, MD3N semi-mallets MD2 two-way blade MD4, MD4N, MD5, MD6 flanged blades MD8 mallet	431 ss/Apollo steel (MD2 and MD8 models feature aluminum face inserts)	Not supplied
Pro Select	*Polymer milled* Heel-toe-weighted cavity back	ss/steel	Not supplied
	Heel-toe-weighted mallet	ss/steel	
	Spectra—heel-toe-weighted	ss/steel	
	NXT Two—oversize mallet	Aluminum/steel	
	NXT	ss/steel	

Legend: ss=stainless steel

Hosel Offset (in.)	Grip Style	Clubface Loft (deg.)	Lengths (in.)	Left-Handed	Suggested Retail
Moderate	Synthetic Rubber; custom oversize	2	34, 35, 36	N	$95 steel $120 graphite
Moderate		2	34, 35, 36	N	$95 steel $120 graphite
None		2	34, 35, 36	N	$100 steel $120 graphite
Slight		2	34, 35, 36	N	$95 steel $120 graphite
Slight		2	34, 35, 36	N	$95 steel $120 graphite
Moderate		2	34, 35, 36	N	$95 steel $120 graphite

said to provide superior feel.

Hosel Offset (in.)	Grip Style	Clubface Loft (deg.)	Lengths (in.)	Left-Handed	Suggested Retail
None	Jumbo Putter Grip	Not supplied	34, 35	N	$65
Moderate to substantial	Jumbo Putter Grip	Not supplied	34, 35	N	$85
Slight to moderate	PowerBilt Full Cord Jumbo Pistol Grip	4	34, 35, 36	Y (MD2 only)	$75
Not supplied	Tour Tech Wrap	4	35	N	$39
	Tour Tech Wrap	4	35	N	$45
	Pro Select Wrap	4	33, 35	Y	$25
	Tour Tech Wrap	4	33, 35	N	$49
	Tour Tech Wrap	4	33, 35	N	$45

continued

PUTTER PRODUCT INFORMATION *(continued)*

MANUFACTURER	MODEL/DESIGN STYLE	CLUBHEAD MATERIAL/ SHAFT MATERIAL	PUTTER WEIGHT (oz.)
Rainbow Golf	Original Series—12 models	17-4 ss/steel or graphite	16.5
	All milled—heel-shafted blade	1018 carbon steel/steel or graphite	16.5
Ram Golf	Zebra Traditional—3 weight-adjustable mallets	Zinc, aluminum/steel or graphite	Not supplied
	Zebra Standard—4 models	ss/steel	
	Zebra Tour milled—6 models	Soft block aluminum or carbon steel/steel	
	Zebra EMP Insert—2 mallets	Zinc or aluminum w/ EMP insert/steel	
	Comments: Tour milled putters said to offer ultimate precision for squareness, weighting,		
Rawlings	Copper Sun Series—3 milled flanged blade models	110 copper/steel	Not supplied
	Revenge—square mallet	Aluminum w/brass insert/steel	Not supplied
	One Piece milled—heel-toe-weighted	Carbon steel/steel	Not supplied
Kenneth Smith	KS2000—3 milled flanged blades, 3 milled heel-toe-weighted	4 carbon steel, either melonite or nickel-composite finish/steel; 2 brass/steel	16.8–18
	FB 10—flanged blade	Forged ss/steel, graphite, hickory, or titanium	15–17 depending on shaft type
	Roll-In—mallet	Wood/steel, graphite, hickory, titanium	15–17 depending on shaft type

Legend: ss=stainless steel

Hosel Offset (in.)	Grip Style	Clubface Loft (deg.)	Lengths (in.)	Left-Handed	Suggested Retail
Not supplied	Composition Pistol Shape	2	32, 33, 34, 35, 36	Not supplied	$45
Not supplied	Composition Pistol Shape	2	32, 33, 34, 35, 36	Not supplied	$75
All mallet models have Z-Bend shaft, .25 offset	Zebra Full Cord Pistol	3	33, 34, 35, 36, 37, 38	Y	$86 steel $139 graphite
	Zebra Full Cord Pistol	3	33, 34, 35, 36, 37, 38	Y	$57
	Zebra Rubber Pistol	3	33, 34, 35, 36, 37, 38	Y	$185
	Zebra Rubber Pistol	3	34, 35	Y	$120
metal densities.					
None	Griptec Flat-Top Wrap	4	34, 35	N	$150
None		4	34, 35	Y	$85
Moderate		4	34, 35	N	$210
.325–.380	Leather Perforated Wrap w/Flat Top, or Synthetic Rubber Modified Pistol or Paddle	4	Custom	N	$105–$115
.350		4 (custom available)		N	$160 steel $200 graphite $205 hickory $215 titanium (both FB 10 and Roll-In)
None		4 (custom available)		Y	

continued

PUTTER PRODUCT INFORMATION *(continued)*

MANUFACTURER	MODEL/DESIGN STYLE	CLUBHEAD MATERIAL/ SHAFT MATERIAL	PUTTER WEIGHT *(oz.)*
Snake Eyes	Medinah	Proprietary metal	Not supplied
	Pinehurst	Proprietary metal	Not supplied
	#88	Carbon metal	Not supplied
	#14	Proprietary metal	Not supplied
	Prestwick	Aircraft aluminum	Not supplied
	Carnoustic	Aircraft aluminum	Not supplied
	Brookline	Aircraft aluminum	Not supplied
	Comments: All putters have precision-milled faces. Black nickel finish.		
STX Golf	Sync Tour—center-shafted blade	Silicon bronze/steel	17.5–18.5
	Switch Blade—heel-shafted flange w/changeable face inserts	431 ss/steel	
	9610—center-shafted flange	Silicon brass/steel	
	9620—heel-toe-weighted	431 ss/steel	
	9630—mallet	Aluminum/ss	
	Comments: With Du Pont elastomer face inserts, company claims "softest legal face" in golf.		

Legend: ss=stainless steel

Hosel Offset (in.)	Grip Style	Clubface Loft (deg.)	Lengths (in.)	Left-Handed	Suggested Retail
None	Golf Pride Paddle	3.5	34, 35	N	$165
Substantial		3.5		N	$165
Slight		3.5		N	$165
None		3.5		N	$165
Moderate		3.5	34, 35	N	$165
Substantial		3.5		N	$165
Slight		3.5		N	$165
None	Synthetic Rubber Diamond Wrap Pistol Grip	3	34, 35 standard (custom available)	Y	$89
.160		3		Y	$129
.125		3		Y	$89
.160		3		Y	$89
None		3		Y	$99

continued

PUTTER PRODUCT INFORMATION *(continued)*

MANUFACTURER	MODEL/DESIGN STYLE	CLUBHEAD MATERIAL/ SHAFT MATERIAL	PUTTER WEIGHT (oz.)
Taylor Made	Roho I—full mallet	Forged copper and aluminum/steel	15.9
	Roho II—half mallet		15.9
	Roho III—quarter mallet		15.9
	Comments: Ultrasuede putter cover included.		
Teardrop Golf	Original—modified mallet	Titanium aluminum alloy/steel	16.3
	Lady—modified mallet	Titanium aluminum alloy/steel	13.3
	Mallet	Titanium aluminum alloy/steel	17.0
	Tour II—modified mallet	Titanium aluminum alloy/steel	16.5
	Classic I & II—heel-toe-weighted	ss/steel	16.2
Titleist	Caliente Mallet Series—4 models, Caliente and Bolero	Aluminum/steel	Not supplied
	Scotty Cameron by Titleist— 7 models	Carbon steel/steel	Not supplied
	Bull's Eye Putters—5 models	Brass alloy/steel	Not supplied

Comments: Caliente, Bolero putters feature removable brass sole plate, "horseshoe" designs. Bull's Eye line includes 5 variations on classic center-shafted blade design.

Legend: ss=stainless steel

Hosel Offset (in.)	Grip Style	Clubface Loft (deg.)	Lengths (in.)	Left-Handed	Suggested Retail
.370	Rubber Pistol	4	34, 35	Y	$130
.370	Rubber Pistol	4	34, 35	Y	$130
.370	Rubber Pistol	4	34, 35	Y	$130
None	Griptec Tour Wrap Pistol Grip	Radiused or "rolled" clubface (lofts not measurable)	34, 35, 36	Y	$99
None			33, 34	N	$99
Slight			34, 35, 36	N	$99
Slight			34, 35, 36	N	$99
Substantial			34, 35, 36	N	$99
Slight (double bend shaft)	Golf Pride Tour Arch	4	33, 34, 35	N	$95 (Caliente) $135 (Bolero)
Varies from slight to moderate	Royal Pistol Paddle Wrap	4	35	N	$199
Variety of offsets	Golf Pride Bull's Eye Cord	4	33 (women's model), 35	Y	$60

weighting system. Scotty Cameron by Titleist models include heel-toe-weighted flanged blade and modified mallet

continued

PUTTER PRODUCT INFORMATION *(continued)*

MANUFACTURER	MODEL/DESIGN STYLE	CLUBHEAD MATERIAL/ SHAFT MATERIAL	PUTTER WEIGHT (oz.)
Top Flite	TF-01 flanged blade	17-4 ss/steel	17.4
	TF-02 flanged blade		17.4
	TF-03 semi-mallet		17.4
	TF-04 mallet		17.8
	TF-05 mallet		17.8
	TF-06 flanged blade		17.4
	TF-07 mallet		17.8
	Comments: Welded sole plates (as on metalwoods); milled clubfaces.		
Wilson	8802—heel-shafted blade	Carbon steel/steel	Not supplied
	8802 Milled—flanged blade	Soft carbon steel/steel	Not supplied
	8813—heel-shafted blade	Carbon steel/steel	Not supplied
	Invex	ss/steel	Not supplied
	Milled brass—heel-toe-weighted	Brass/steel	17.6
	Alignment Design Series AD mallet	Aluminum/steel	Not supplied
	Small mallet	ss/steel	
	Heel-toe blade	ss/steel	
	Comments: 8802 is longtime Wilson classic and a much-copied design.		

Legend: ss=stainless steel

Hosel Offset (in.)	Grip Style	Clubface Loft (deg.)	Lengths (in.)	Left-Handed	Suggested Retail
.30	Tour Wrap Pistol Grip	2	33, 34, 35, 36	N	$75
.30		2	33, 34, 35, 36	N	$75
.30		2	33, 34, 35, 36	N	$75
.40		2	33, 34, 35, 36	N	$75
.40		2	33, 34, 35, 36	N	$75
.30		2	33, 34, 35, 36	Y	$75
.30		2	33, 34, 35, 36	Y	$75
Not supplied	Leather Paddle Grip	Not supplied	34, 35	Y	$100
Very slight	Rubber flat top	Not supplied	34, 35	N	$169
Not supplied	Leather Paddle Grip	Not supplied	34, 35	N	$100
Slight	Rubber flat top	Not supplied	34, 35	N	$99
.50	Leather Paddle Grip	4	34, 35	N	$75
.50	Golf Pride Pro Score Cord Paddle Grip	3	33, 34, 35, 36	N	$90
.50		3	33, 34, 35, 36	N	$90
.50		3	33, 34, 35, 36	N	$90

continued

PUTTER PRODUCT INFORMATION *(continued)*

MANUFACTURER	MODEL/DESIGN STYLE	CLUBHEAD MATERIAL/ SHAFT MATERIAL	PUTTER WEIGHT *(oz.)*
Wood Brothers	*Switch Mallets* Eye of Ra	Ceramic head/steel	18+/- (varies with interchange-able weights in grip and clubhead)
	Mosaic	Ceramic head/steel	
	Trinity	Ceramic head/steel	
	DaVinci	Ceramic head/steel	
	Techno	Ceramic head/steel	
	Comments: Mallets are oversize with ornate mosaic head designs.		
Yonex	ADX 30—heel-toe-weighted	ss w/graphite face	Not supplied
	ADX 50—heel-toe-weighted	graphite	Not supplied

Legend: ss=stainless steel

Hosel Offset (in.)	Grip Style	Clubface Loft (deg.)	Lengths (in.)	Left-Handed	Suggested Retail
.50	Weight-adjustable cork grip or cork grip with leather wrap	3.5	34, 35	Y	$149
.50		3.5	34, 35	Y	$149
.50		3.5	34, 35	Y	$149
.50		3.5	34, 35	Y	$165
.50		3.5	34, 35	Y	$49

Weight movement system can move more weight into head for slower greens, more weight to top of grip for faster surfaces.

Not supplied	Not supplied	3.5	33, 35	N	$125
Not supplied	Not supplied	3.5	33, 35	N	$170

CHAPTER 8

Spheres of Influence:
The Golf Ball

No book on golf equipment would be complete without reporting on what is the most fundamental piece of equipment in the game—the golf ball that you'll strike somewhere between 70 and 110 times during an 18-hole round, depending on your skill level.

This chapter will dispel some myths you've seen or heard in too many advertisements by various ball manufacturers that have proclaimed, or at least implied, that their model is without question the "longest" ball. You'll see why there is really no such animal. And, just as we questioned in earlier chapters the value of owning the "longest" clubs, you may also think twice about this type of mind-set in selecting what golf ball to play.

As in the previous chapters, you'll find in table form a list of offerings of the top golf ball manufacturers in the United States today, with information on the most significant construction and performance characteristics of each of the various models.

A Legal Ball Can Only Be So Long

If there actually were a golf ball that you could hit as far as a ball travels in just about every ad you're forced to endure as you watch the week's top televised Tour event, remember this: You couldn't win any matches or tournaments with it, because you'd be playing an illegal ball. There are specific limitations that the United States Golf Association places on the distance that a golf ball can travel (as well as other factors regarding its design). So before we get into the issue of what being the "longest" ball really means, let's make sure you understand what the limits for a legal golf ball are.

There are five basic criteria that a golf ball must meet in order to be approved for competition by the USGA (which, incidentally, publishes a list of conforming golf balls twice annually):

1. *Weight.* The ball must weigh no more than 1.62 ounces. Note that the ball need not necessarily weigh *exactly* 1.62 ounces. It can weigh less—in the table you'll see that there are a few companies that offer "lightweight" golf balls—but it must not exceed 1.62 ounces. For this test, the USGA weighs twenty-four balls of a given model. Any balls out of the twenty-four that are overweight will count toward a total number of "failures" the USGA will allow among the twenty-four balls, for all of its test categories combined.

2. *Size.* The ball must measure not less than 1.68 inches in diameter. (The ball can be larger than 1.68 inches in diameter and be approved by the USGA; a few balls, such as the Top Flite Magna line, are slightly oversize.) The USGA places the test golf balls in a ring gauge exactly 1.68 inches in diameter, then jiggles them. If a ball falls through the ring more than 25 percent of the time, it is too small and will be counted toward the ball's overall failure rate.

3. *Initial Velocity.* The USGA tests twenty-four samples of every ball model, using a mechanical striking arm which contacts each ball while moving at 143.8 feet per second. Any ball that takes off at a speed higher than 250 feet per second (plus a 2 percent tolerance) fails the velocity test.

   For these first three criteria (weight, size, and initial velocity) if more than three out of the twenty-four balls tested fail in any category, the ball will be ruled "nonconforming."

4. *Overall Distance Standard.* Without providing all the intricate details, the USGA measures the carry and roll of twenty-four balls after they've been struck by a clubhead traveling at 109 mph, which is about the clubhead speed of the average PGA Tour pro. The Overall Distance Standard requires that the total carry and roll must not exceed 280 yards (plus a 6 percent tolerance, which actually increases the "outer limit" distance in the test to 296.8 yards). A ball that averages a total distance of more than 296.8 yards will be considered illegal. (In addition, if the average exceeds 291.2 yards, the USGA

Top Flite Magna EX

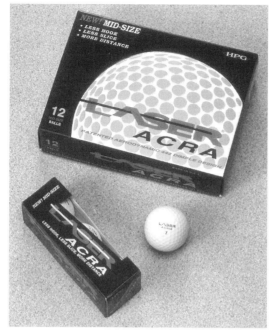

Ram Tour Laser Acra

will warn the manufacturer that the model in question is "on the red line," close to the limit.)

5. *Symmetry.* Again without going into detail, the balls are tested to make sure they are symmetric, so that they will perform consistently when placed in any given orientation and then struck.

The key measurements with regard to the question of overall distance are initial velocity and Overall Distance Standard. All of the models listed in the table are on the USGA's conforming list; thus you know that they all have managed to stay below the top line of the Overall Distance Standard. (The balls listed in the table *do not* constitute the USGA's entire list of conforming balls; there are numerous others.) Frank Thomas, technical director for the USGA, has commented that today's ball manufacturers are so good that they can get right to the edge of the tolerances for size, weight, initial velocity, and overall distance, which indicates that differences in distance from one major manufacturer or one model to the next are very slight.

Do Today's Golf Balls Go Farther?

Today's PGA Tour pros hit the ball for enormous distances—325 to 350 yards is not uncommon when a Tour pro needs to "let it out" on a par-5. Tour statistics show that many PGA Senior Tour players, past age fifty, really are hitting it farther than ever. Even among amateurs, many of you who have been playing for twenty years or more may sense you're hitting the ball farther than you used to.

Is there a fountain of youth for golfers, or have golf balls really gotten longer?

Terry Pocklington of Ram Tour insists that, club technology aside (which has certainly added to distance possibilities, as we've seen), most golf balls today are longer than their brethren of, say, 1970. Pocklington estimates that the balls that strain the USGA's current Overall Distance Standard would average approximately 10 yards longer off the driver than a three-piece wound ball from the 1970 era. More significant, the ball is even longer off the irons than it is off the driver—Pocklington estimates a 12-yard gain off the average 5-iron.

Put these together on a medium-length par-4 hole, and you've just picked up 22 yards. No wonder you can play such a hole with the same (or shorter) clubs than you once did!

Manufacturers Are "Selective" Regarding Distance Data

How can anyone (and everyone) claim that their ball is the longest? Easily: by selecting one specific measurement for which their particular ball happens to outdistance others. For instance, a company might test its ball against the competition for the amount of carry it gets with a driver; for the amount of carry and roll it gets with a driver; for the amount of carry obtained with a 5-iron; for the amount of carry and roll obtained with a 5-iron; for the combined carries of the driver *and* the 5-iron; or for the combined carry and roll of the driver *and* the 5-iron. That's six categories for which a company has an opportunity to claim its ball was the longest; and doubtless they can conjure up others. (All this says nothing about taking advantage of conditions that assure the company's ball comes out on top, such as testing it when there's a nice little tailwind to give it a boost.)

Beyond claiming a long-distance "title" through selective reporting on actual test results, companies can also advertise that their ball is the longest without actually reporting any specific test figures. So, suffice it to say that any manufacturer can find a way to say that its ball comes out on top in the distance race.

Don't Play Illegal Balls!

There are many, many golf balls that are specifically designed *not* to conform to the rigid specifications of the United States Golf Association. You've probably seen the newspaper-style ads that "announce" that the golf ball being promoted has been found to travel much too far.

Several points here: First, golf has long been considered one of the most honorably played sports in the world. It's a reputation that is flouted by anyone who opts to play with equipment, such as "hot" golf balls, that does not provide a level playing field.

Second, it's stupid to play with an illegal ball. Not only will you be disqualified when found that you play a nonconforming ball in any formal competition, but your opponents in your regular weekly foursome can renege on any bets you may think you have won, and could even rightfully demand that *you* pay *them* instead. It's not worth having arguments with your golfing friends.

Third, you're outsmarting yourself by thinking you'll play better with an illegal ball. You'll probably play worse. Where golf balls are concerned, the more you gain in distance, the more you'll give up in "scorability" when playing to and around the greens.

Lastly, it's doubtful that illegal balls are made to the same stringent standards of consistency as balls that must pass the tests required by the USGA. You'll probably get less consistent performance from any such products.

What should these claims mean to you? Next to nothing. Meanwhile, factors in the way a ball is constructed and how it performs should mean a lot.

Cover Material Options Abound

Until the late 1960s there was a single material from which virtually all golf balls were made; and through the 1970s there were basically two. Today, there are numerous variations in the cover material used in golf balls. Terry Pocklington, president of Ram Tour, provides the following information on some of the cover types you will see listed in the table.

Balata: Golf balls were originally made from pure balata, a natural rubber product. The balata used for balls today is actually a synthetic balata known as transpolyisoprene—a highly crystalline, opaque, hard substance with a

Bullet USA Balata (left)
Maxfli XF, XS, XD Series (below)

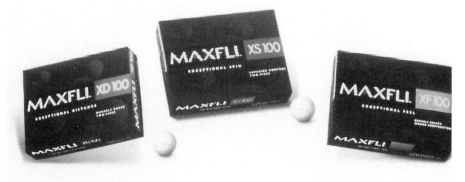

relatively low softening point (its molding temperature is about 210 degrees F.). Transpolyisoprene has the same chemical compound as natural balata, minus impurities that come with natural rubber.

Elastomer: a synthetic rubberlike product with properties that can be enhanced and stabilized by chemical reaction

Ionomer: an electrically charged thermoplastic material that behaves more like a vulcanized rubber

Lithium balata: a low-modulus (soft and flexible) resin with a percentage of lithium ionomer (a version of Surlyn) for added toughness

Lithium Surlyn: a high-modulus (stiff and rigid) resin with a percentage of lithium ionomer (a version of Surlyn) for added toughness

Surlyn: the ionomer resin manufactured by the Du Pont corporation. Surlyn joined balata as a popular material as a golf ball cover around 1970. Pockling-ton defines it as "a thermoplastic elastomer exhibiting excellent durability and shape retention, with molding temperatures between 310 and 450 degrees F."

Tri-blend: a combination of ionomer resins manufactured by blending them with various metal salts such as zinc, sodium, or lithium

VLMI: a very low modulus (soft and flexible) ionomer

Top Flite Z-Balata

There are other cover materials that are proprietary to particular companies. One such is Zylin™, used for all balls made by Top Flite.

How Different Cover Materials and Thicknesses Perform

The synthetic balata used in golf balls today is the softest material used on the cover of a golf ball. The softer the cover material, the greater the backspin that will be applied to the ball, but its velocity off the clubface will be slightly lower. Among the other various materials used in covers, Pocklington says, "Low-modulus ionomers will also tend to have lower velocity with higher spin rates. High-modulus ionomer resins promote higher velocities and lower spin rates. Predictably, the higher-modulus resins will also be more durable."

You've often heard the terms "high performance" and "durability" attributed to various ball brands and models. A "high performance" label usually refers to a ball with a soft cover that responds to the demands of the fine player, the shotmaker who hits draws and fades, and wants to make the ball stop quickly when it lands. The Titleist Tour Balata and Maxfli's RM and HT meet this definition. "Durability" usually connotes the antithesis of "high performance": It refers to a ball with a hard, tough cover that comes off the clubface as fast as USGA limits allow, and it will take a pounding and come back for more. However, it's not a "workable" ball. Examples might be the Top Flite Hot XL and the Wilson TC3.

Ram Tour's Pocklington, though, suggests that such categorizations are too limiting. "Performance is in the eye of the beholder. Performance to the low handicapper means soft feel, maneuverability, and ultimate control around the green. This dictates the choice of a low-modulus-ionomer-covered ball. However," he continues, "performance to a high handicapper means greater distance and reduced hooks and slices. These needs dictate a high-modulus-ionomer, two-piece ball."

Most of the companies' models listed show the thickness of the cover mate-

Ping Karsten CT-374

rial used, in hundredths of inches. This is also a significant factor in how the ball will play. All cover thicknesses are between .04 and .095 inches, which is quite a substantial spread. Pocklington says that as with the variations in type of cover material, "Thickness of the cover reduces the contact time between club and ball at impact and therefore reduces the amount of backspin. Less spin equates to greater distance with less hook and slice." Among the Ram Tour models listed, then, if your top priority is to keep the ball in play on your full shots, the Laser Acra would be worth a try. It has a thick (.095 inch), high-modulus-ionomer cover that would help it move more forward and less sideways.

Two-Piece Balls Now Dominate the Market

Until about 1970, golf balls were usually of a three-piece construction. A small rubber core, sometimes with liquid injected into its center, would be surrounded by hundreds of yards of very thin, taut rubber thread. Usually the third piece was a cover of natural balata.

Gradually, in conjunction with the growing use of Surlyn and other synthetic cover materials, a solid one-piece core began to replace the previous thread-wound interior. Today, the simpler and easier-to-manufacture two-piece designs dominate. Of the sixty-eight ball models shown in the table that follows, fifty-three are of two-piece construction. And of the fourteen models listed as three-piece, four are actually not wound, but instead have a two-layer core that does not include thread windings. Even the longtime champion of top performance balls, Titleist, now offers a line of six different models, three of which are two-piece construction.

It's doubtful that thread-wound three-piece golf balls will ever disappear

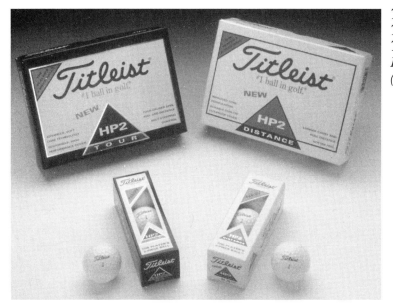

*Titleist HP2
Tour (left)
Titleist HP2
Distance
(right)*

totally from the marketplace, just as forged-carbon-steel irons stubbornly hold on to a small market share. Despite the fact that a number of PGA Tour stars such as Nick Price (Bridgestone Precept Extra Spin) and Corey Pavin (Titleist HP2 Tour) have switched to a two-piece construction ball, many top players, both professional and amateur, are sold on the soft feel, backspin, and control of the short shots around the green that a balata three-piece ball offers.

There is a difference in the total distance that most players can obtain with the harder two-piece balls and the top performance balls such as the Titleist Tour Balata and the Maxfli HT. According to Pocklington, "The longest two-piece balls will tend to carry, on average, approximately 7 yards farther than the top three-piece balata balls. Total carry and roll favors the longest two-piece balls by 10 yards with the driver." Most pros will gladly give up this yardage for several reasons: (1) They are almost all mighty long anyway; (2) they play to firm, fast tournament greens, with pins in difficult positions that require maximum backspin on most iron shots to stop the ball close to the pin; (3) they need to be able to put controlled draw and fade spin on tee shots and especially approach shots, again to set up birdie opportunities; and (4) they need to be able to stop their pitch and sand shot recoveries "on a dime" in order to save par.

Remember that if you're playing one of the "longest" balls off the tee, you will also be playing one of the longest balls around the greens. In this regard there's something to be said for a ball that has some stopping power, even for the middle or high handicapper.

The Golf Ball's "Birthing" Process

How long does it actually take to produce a completed golf ball? Without explaining the arduous steps that go into creating a golf ball or the various processes from one company to the next, Titleist, given the variety of types of construction that it uses and the number of steps required (which includes substantial cooling times for heated materials), reports the following start-to-finish construction times for its model types:

Thread-wound three-piece Balata	24 days
Thread-wound three-piece Surlyn	5 days
Two-piece Surlyn	3 days

This might help explain why you'll find that the three-piece balata balls are almost always the most expensive.

Compression: Mostly a Matter of Preference

Some of the models shown in the table are offered in more than one compression (these are the models that have the numbers "90 & 100" listed after their names). Compression is simply a measurement of the hardness of the ball. It is measured in a compression gauge, a viselike device that compresses the ball on its opposite sides and provides a reading of its hardness. A 100-compression ball is slightly harder than a 90-compression.

The numbers 90 and 100 are generalizations of each ball's actual hardness. A tour of the Titleist golf ball plant in Fairhaven, Massachusetts, showed that three-piece balls go through the construction process and are sorted afterward for their compression rating. A ball that measures 92 on the compression gauge, for example, will eventually be labeled as a 90-compression version of the particular model. A ball that reads out at 98 will eventually reach the marketplace as a 100. For two-piece balls, Titleist points out, the compression level (if a ball comes in multiple compressions) is developed within the specifics of the manufacturing process.

More than anything, choosing a ball in a 90 versus a 100 compression is mostly a matter of personal feel. Generally, the harder-swinging player may prefer the feel of the higher (100) compression ball. But there's certainly no rule that says a power hitter can't use a 90-compression ball, or a short hitter can't use a 100. For example, Davis Love, one of the longest hitters on the PGA Tour,

---

A New "Spin": Multilayered Balls

As this manuscript went to press, some new-model balls were just reaching the U.S. consumer market. They are neither two-piece balls nor traditional wound three-piece construction. These "multilayer" balls are the Bridgestone Precept Tour Double Cover and Bridgestone Dynawing, and Top Flite's Strata Tour.

The Precept Tour Double Cover actually has four "parts": a relatively soft outer, dimpled cover, a second, interior layer or cover, and a layer of windings surrounding a solid center. Top Flite's latest ball has three layers: the dimpled cover (also with relatively soft feel), a harder interior layer (of the same material as on the cover of its Hot XL model), and a solid center.

What's the reasoning behind these design changes? Top Flite claimed (at press time) that their multilayer ball actually had *lower*-than-average spin rates when struck with the driver, while having *higher*-than-average spin rates off short irons and pitch shots. Sounds terrific, doesn't it? However, there are no money-back guarantees that you'll shoot your lowest score by playing any of these multicover balls. You'll still have to make quite a few good swings to accomplish that, no matter what you play.

---

has used a 90-compression Titleist (previously the Tour Balata, more recently the Professional) for a number of years.

Some golfers find that it helps their feel to adjust compression depending on the temperature. You may like the feel of a 100-compression ball when it's, say, 70 degrees or above, but when the temperature is in the sixties or lower, impact feels a little "rocky." If that's the case, going to a 90-compression model when it's cooler might help.

Interestingly, there is some difference of opinion regarding the generally held notion that 100-compression balls go farther than those with a 90 compression. Ram Tour's Pocklington says, "The higher the compression, the lower the duration of impact between ball and clubface. This means the softer ball, which stays on the face infinitesimally longer, can be maneuvered and controlled to a greater degree. The ball's spin rate will be greater with the lower-compression model. Meanwhile, higher-compression balls will travel slightly greater distances." He adds that the variations mentioned will be most noticeable when you compare a hard, two-piece ionomer-covered ball to a soft, thread-wound three-piece ball.

However, Jerry Bellis, director of sales for Titleist U.S., says that compression actually has no effect on a ball's distance or performance. "The only point of concern about compression should be how the ball feels to you," he says.

Titleist Professional

Best advice: If it's a decision between a 90- or 100-compression Titleist Professional, or between a 90- or 100-compression Ram Tour Balata LB, don't worry about whether you'll get an extra yard out of the higher-compression ball—go with what feels best.

What About Those Dimples?

The table includes a column listing the number of dimples that are placed on the various ball models. The number of dimples and the dimple pattern are other factors that, along with cover material, core material, and spin rate, give a ball what the company's engineers believe is optimum performance. The 422 dimples set up in the particular pattern for a Top Flite Tour SD would probably not provide the optimum performance if applied to the cover of a Wilson Ultra Tour Balata.

Generally, the number of dimples appearing on most golf balls has increased steadily over the years, having crested (to date) with the 500 appearing on the three Wilson Ultra 500 models. There are several main patterns of dimples used by manufacturers (known as octahedral, icosahedral, and dodecahedral) as well as myriad offshoots of these three patterns. You'll probably be glad to hear that you'll not be burdened with a mind-numbing classification of these polysyllabic formations. It's not really necessary because, as Terry Pocklington points out,

---

What Happens to a Ball with No Dimples?

Did you ever wonder how a golf ball would perform if it was designed with no dimples at all, so that it simply had a smooth white surface?

A demonstration performed by Titleist shows that the aerodynamic properties imbued in a golf ball as a result of its dimple structure—something we more or less take for granted—are quite remarkable. Titleist makes up golf balls for demo purposes that are constructed identically to its three-piece wound ball, the Titleist DT—except that the demo ball has no dimples. This ball is then struck by its "Iron Byron" ball-hitting machine.

For an instant after impact, the viewer gets the impression that the ball is taking off normally and that it will fly like a normal drive. Then suddenly, the dimpleless ball wavers wildly in flight and dives quickly to the ground. Titleist reports that the total flight and roll of the undimpled ball is only about 120 yards. This is less than half the distance the exact same golf ball would have traveled if it had a dimple pattern.

"The pattern itself is not as significant as is the number, depth, and diameter of the dimples within the pattern. The rule of thumb," he says, "is that *larger, shallower dimples will yield higher trajectories than smaller, deeper ones.*"

Spin Rate: A Key Determinant of Which Ball to Play

The ball's spin rate is probably the most important by-product of the total construction of the golf ball. Spin rate, which is measured on a device called a launch monitor, is measured in rpm (revolutions per minute), usually on shots hit with a driver and a shorter iron.

If you know the ball's spin rate, you have key information as to how the ball will perform. Of the balls for which spin rates are listed here, the Titleist Tour Balata has the highest spin rate when hit with a driver, which is 4,100 rpm. Its spin rate of 9,000 rpm with an 8-iron is also high. What does this tell you? It says that off the tee, you had better hit this ball squarely and solidly: If you hit a shot with substantial hook or slice spin, it's going to "show" more than it would with most other balls. If the wind's blowing against you, a ball that takes on substantial backspin with the driver will have more tendency to be lifted by a headwind. This "upshooting" effect can cost you yardage. On the plus side, when hitting to the greens, you can expect to hold them as well as or better than with any other ball. Moreover, it's easier to fade or draw your approach shots, another plus in getting the ball close to well-guarded flag positions. Lastly, you can expect the ball to "check" very well on short pitches or sand shots around the green.

By comparison, Titleist's DT 2-Piece, introduced in 1995, is a low-spin ball.

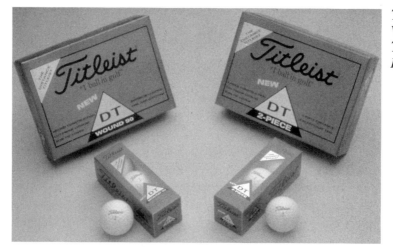

Titleist DT Wound (left) Titleist DT 2-Piece (right)

Its playability characteristics are toward the opposite end of the spectrum. That is, it will be easier to drive relatively straight, since it takes on about 25 percent less spin than the Tour Balata. On the other hand, you'll have more trouble "working" your iron shots, and in keeping the ball from running instead of "biting" on short greenside wedge and sand shots.

Ultimately, you must measure your game and decide which playability features are most important to you. The pros almost unanimously favor high-spin golf balls. High handicappers generally gravitate to low-spin models, which not only simplify long shots but will generally prove more durable. However, there are many in-between choices available to you. Perhaps if you've been playing a hard-cover, low-spin model, it would be instructive to try a sleeve of high-spin balls and observe the differences in feel and performance. Perhaps there's a middle-ground spin rate that would help you score better.

Unfortunately, of the companies whose models are listed in the table that follows, only Titleist, Ram Tour, Wilson, and Ben Hogan list spin rates for any of their models. Where spin rates are not available, companies were asked to provide an estimate of the trajectory type (low, medium, or high) that each model provides. While this information is not as precise, it can still help. For example,

Wilson Ultra 500 Tour Balata (left)
Ben Hogan 428 Series (below)

say you are a low-ball hitter, and one of your problems is that even your well-struck shots have trouble holding the greens, particularly if the greens are elevated or well guarded in front. If you like a Top Flite XL, you might want to try it in the High Trajectory model, since the XL is offered with variations that result in three slightly varying trajectories.

Incidentally, Pocklington clarifies a point regarding the relationship of the ball's spin rate to the type of trajectory it supplies. "Many golfers assume that if a ball has a high spin rate, its trajectory will automatically be a high one. This is usually not the case. The softer the cover, the longer the ball stays on the clubface at impact, the more backspin it acquires, and it also leaves the face at a lower angle. This ball will tend to stay somewhat lower in its entire trajectory than a harder-covered ball.

"The harder-covered ball will tend to skid up the clubface at impact, with less backspin being applied," Pocklington continues. "The relatively hard, low-spin ball will actually take off at a higher launch angle and stay higher than the soft-covered high-spin ball throughout its flight."

Size and Weight Variables

As was mentioned earlier, the maximum allowable weight for a ball conforming to USGA specifications is 1.62 ounces, and the minimum size allowance is 1.68 inches in diameter. Companies are free to market balls with lighter weights than 1.62 ounces, or diameters larger than 1.68 inches. A few have put lighter or larger balls on the market, most notably Top Flite with its Magna series. These models are 1.717 inches in diameter, or less than 4/100 of an inch over standard size. So it's not a great difference.

On this area of design, Ram Tour's Pocklington (whose company also markets a slightly oversize model, the Laser Acra) comments, "A larger ball has a greater radius of gyration, which inhibits the ball's spin rate. And lower spin rate equates to less hook or slice." This sounds all well and good, except for the fact that as we've seen, companies can develop different materials and construction for a golf ball in order to produce virtually any spin rate they want. "Oversizing" the ball is another method of producing a ball with low-spin characteristics.

It would seem logical that a ball larger than 1.68 inches, since its center of gravity is higher in relation to the clubface, would be easier to hit higher than the 1.68-inch ball, and likewise it would land softer. There's nothing wrong with this if it suits your needs. However, it's also interesting to note that there has been no stampede by other companies to market an oversize golf ball.

Titleist Pinnacle

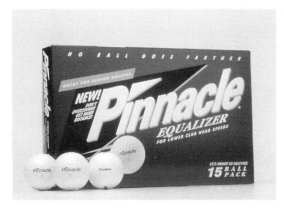

As to weight, Cayman makes the lightest "legal" ball, with its Spectra model weighing in at 1.48 ounces (Ram Tour's Laser Lite weighs 1.54 ounces). Pocklington notes, "Lighter-than-standard balls are beneficial to some golfers, since they're easier to launch and tend to carry for more of their total distance than standard-weight models."

Again, it seems logical that the lighter a ball is, the more likely it will be affected by the wind. Will a shot played into a strong headwind with a lighter ball get knocked down much faster than with a 1.62-ounce ball? Will a downwind shot be carried by the wind much farther than you'd think? Again, weight adjustments seem like just another way to adjust a ball's performance that could have been done through other means in designing the ball, while keeping its size and weight standard.

Some Recommendations

If you are hitting solid shots with the clubs you have tested and determined to be the best for your physique and swing, you've taken care of the most important part of the equipment puzzle. However, you can certainly augment your ability to shoot lower scores by playing the right ball.

I would recommend that any amateur spend a little time in casual rounds experimenting with golf balls with different playing characteristics—high-, medium-, and low-spin balls, balls with varying cover materials and thicknesses—to get a feel for how they perform for you in all the situations you'll meet on the golf course. This is likely to take some time, since it's wise to test out the same ball in varying conditions. Say you want to try out a higher-spin ball than you've played in the past. The first day you try it may be perfectly

---

Will Playing "X-Outs" Hurt Your Game?

When shopping for balls in a pro shop or retail outlet, you may find that various models are available at heavily discounted prices in "reject" or "X-out" form. They'll commonly be available for between 35 and 50 percent off the retail price of a perfect ball.

Should you consider playing X-outs if you need to save money? Or is there a risk that you'll get an inferior-performing product? The answers are yes, you should; and no, the product will play just as well as the "perfect" balls.

Both Titleist and Ram Tour report that rejected balls are defective only in some minor cosmetic fashion, such as a label that was not stamped onto the ball in the perfect position. *There is nothing wrong with the playability of an X-out ball!* In fact, both Titleist and Ram Tour actually destroy all the balls that inspections show to have any physical defects, however minor. They never get to the market. (Titleist, incidentally, reports that its rejection rate for cosmetic defects in balls is about 6 percent.)

So, if you really like to play a ball that retails for $40 or more per dozen, can't afford them but can find them in X-outs for half the price, there's no reason not to take advantage of them.

---

calm, and you appreciate the great feel it gives you around the greens. The next time out, if a firm wind is blowing, you might have the sensation that it's harder to control your tee shots with the high-spin ball.

Gradually, you'll determine which ball gives you the best combination of distance, feel at impact, and both full-swing and short-game control—the ball that, in short, best enhances your chance to shoot a good score. Once you draw that conclusion, *stick with that model of ball.* The consistency you'll get from the ball in all phases of play will help your scores over time.

So once you've found the ball that has the best mix of qualities for your game, stick with it. You might find that this ball is one of the more expensive ones on the market (see suggested retail prices in the last column of the table). I suggest you resist the tendency to buy balls based on price, because consistency in what to expect from a ball, day in and day out, will make your shotmaking more successful. Shop around, and you'll find good buys are often available on even the highest-priced balls.

Bridgestone Precept Tour

If You Can Find It, You Can Keep Playing It

You've probably heard of how PGA Tour stars use six golf balls per round, alternating the six so they're always fresh and totally unmarked. Should you take this to mean that your game will improve if you do the same? And will you need to take out a loan equal to your car payment to play six balls per round?

Rest easy. You can actually play most golf balls for a lot longer than it will take for you to lose them in the water or the woods.

According to Ram Tour's Terry Pocklington, "If the golfer is playing a two-piece ball, it will almost surely remain playable for many rounds. I think a golfer can play one ball for four to five rounds without worrying about it.

"After many rounds of play, performance can be affected," Pocklington notes. "The paint cover will begin to abrade, as will the edges of the ball's dimples so that they begin to get shallower. When this happens, the ball will begin to fly higher than it did originally, and it will also begin to fly erratically."

If you choose to play a balata-covered three-piece ball, Pocklington concedes that the cover will become abraded more quickly and that it's more likely to get slightly out of round sooner than a ball with a solid core. Still, Pocklington concludes, as long as you don't hit any extremely poor shots that badly mark or dent the softer cover, there's no reason that you couldn't play a balata ball with confidence for two full 18-hole rounds.

GOLF BALL PRODUCT INFORMATION

MANUFACTURER	MODEL	COVER MATERIAL	COVER THICKNESS (*in.*)	CONSTRUCTION TYPE
Bridgestone	Precept Tour Double Cover	Not supplied	Not supplied	Four-piece (double cover, wound layer, solid center)
	Dynawing	Not supplied	Not supplied	Three-piece double cover
	Precept Extra Spin	Surlyn	Not supplied	Two-piece
	Precept Extra Distance	Surlyn	Not supplied	Two-piece
	Precept EV Senior	Surlyn	Not supplied	Two-piece
	Precept EV Lady	Surlyn	Not supplied	Two-piece
	Comments: Precept Double Cover released late '96;			
Bullet Golf	Bullet USA Balata	Balata	Not supplied	Three-piece, wound
	Bullet 444	Lithium Surlyn	Not supplied	Two-piece
	Bullet Lady 444	Lithium Surlyn	Not supplied	Two-piece
Cayman	Grand Tour	Elastomer	.085	Three-piece, nonwound
	Spectra	Surlyn	.085	Two-piece
	Galaxy	Surlyn	.085	Two-piece

Comments: Spectra is a "lightweight" ball designed to aid slower-swinging seniors and women

No. of Dimples	Spin Rate (Driver, 8-Iron)	Trajectory Type	Standard Size/Weight	Suggested Retail (*doz.*)
Not supplied	Not supplied	High	Y	$54
Not supplied	Not supplied	Medium	Y	$44
392	Very high	Medium	Y	$38
432	Medium	Medium	Y	$38
432	Low	Medium	Y	$38
432	Very low	Medium	Y	$32
company claims design adds more spin to shorter shots.				
432	Not supplied	Not supplied	Y	$45
444	Not supplied	Not supplied	Y	$13/16-pack
444	Not supplied	Not supplied	Y	$35/16-pack
492	Not supplied	Medium	Y	$32.95
442	Not supplied	High	Standard size, 1.48 oz. wt.	$26.95
450	Not supplied	Medium	Y	$26.95

(same specs, different-colored label for senior ball and women's ball).   continued

GOLF BALL PRODUCT INFORMATION *(continued)*

MANUFACTURER	MODEL	COVER MATERIAL	COVER THICKNESS *(in.)*	CONSTRUCTION TYPE
Ben Hogan	428 Balata	Balata	.065	Three-piece, wound, liquid center
	428 Distance	Zinc/lithium/sodium Surlyn	.070	Two-piece
	428 Hi-Spin	VLMI Surlyn	.070	Two-piece
MacGregor	VIP (90 & 100)	Soft Surlyn	Not supplied	Two-piece
Maxfli Golf	Maxfli RM (90 & 100)	Balata	Not supplied	Three piece, wound, liquid center
	Maxfli HT (90 & 100)	Balata	.05	Three-piece, wound, liquid center
	Maxfli XF (90 & 100)	Double Balata	.05	Three-piece, wound
	Maxfli XS (90 & 100)	Ionomer blend	.085	Two-piece
	Maxfli XD (90 & 100)	Surlyn	.085	Two-piece
	Maxfli MD	Surlyn	.085	Two-piece
	Dunlop DDH Distance	Surlyn	.085	Two-piece
	Dunlop DDH Accuracy	Surlyn	.085	Two-piece
	Dunlop DDH for Women	Surlyn	.085	Two-piece
Ping	Karsten CT-374	Polymer blend	Not supplied	Two-piece
	Ping Eye 2 (2-colored)	Surlyn	Not supplied	Two-piece
Players Golf	Tournament 80, 90, 100	Lithium Surlyn	.0625	Two-piece
	Edition 90	Lithium Surlyn	.0625	Two-piece

No. of Dimples	Spin Rate (Driver, 8-Iron)	Trajectory Type	Standard Size/Weight	Suggested Retail (*doz.*)
428 TDK	Not supplied, 9300 (5-iron)	Not supplied	Y	$42.50
428 TDK	4665, 9037 (9-iron)	Not supplied	Y	$36
428 TDK	4227, 8181 (9-iron)	Not supplied	Y	$36
432	Not supplied	Medium	Y	$36
432	Not supplied	High	Y	$56
432		Low	Y	$48
432		Medium	Y	$42
432		Medium-high	Y	$36
432		Not supplied	Y	$34
432		Not supplied	Y	$28/15-pack
350		Not supplied	Y	$20/15-pack
350		Not supplied	Y	$20/15-pack
350		Not supplied	Y	$20/15-pack
374	Not supplied	Not supplied	Y	$36
392	Not supplied	Not supplied	Y	$32
518	2800, 8000	High	Y	$23/15-pack
462	2800, 6000	High	Y	$22/16-pack

continued

GOLF BALL PRODUCT INFORMATION *(continued)*

MANUFACTURER	MODEL	COVER MATERIAL	COVER THICKNESS (*in.*)	CONSTRUCTION TYPE
Ram Tour	Laser Acra	High-modulus ionomer	.095	Two-piece
	Laser Tour	Balata blend	.090	Two-piece
	Laser TDX 150	High-modulus ionomer	.0625	Two-piece
	Laser Lite	High-modulus ionomer	.0625	Two-piece
	Ram Tour Balata LB 90 & 100	Lithium balata	.0625	Two-piece
	Ram Tour Pro Balata 90 & 100	Balata blend	.090	Two-piece
	Ram Tour XDC	Lithium Surlyn	.0625	Two-piece
	Golden Girl	Tri-blend	.0625	Two-piece
	Comments: Acra reduces hooks and slices; TDX "double dimples" increase total distance through			
Slazenger	420i Raw Distance	Stiff Surlyn	Not supplied	Two-piece
	420p Power Spin	Mid-soft Surlyn	Not supplied	Two-piece
	420+ Touch Spin	Soft Surlyn	Not supplied	Two-piece
	420 Interlok	Balata	Not supplied	Three-piece, wound

No. of Dimples	Spin Rate (Driver, 8-Iron)	Trajectory Type	Standard Size/Weight	Suggested Retail (*doz.*)
442	1950, 7200	Medium	Standard weight, 1.69" dia.	$26
442	2700, 8800	Medium	Y	$34
380	2400, 7500	Medium-high	Y	$26
380	2400, 7500	Medium-high	Standard size, 1.54 oz. wt.	$26
442	2700, 8800	Medium	Y	$34
442	2700, 8800	Medium	Y	$40
442	2400, 7500	Medium-high	Y	$24
442	2400, 7500	Medium	Y	$24

the air. Laser Lite aids slow-swing speed players.

No. of Dimples	Spin Rate (Driver, 8-Iron)	Trajectory Type	Standard Size/Weight	Suggested Retail (*doz.*)
420	Not supplied	Medium	Y	$34
420	Not supplied	High	Y	$34
420	Not supplied	High	Y	$34
420	Not supplied	High	Y	$44

continued

GOLF BALL PRODUCT INFORMATION *(continued)*

MANUFACTURER	MODEL	COVER MATERIAL	COVER THICKNESS *(in.)*	CONSTRUCTION TYPE
Titleist	Titleist Tour Balata 90 & 100	Balata	.040	Three-piece, wound
	Titleist Professional 90 & 100	Elastomer	.050	Three-piece, wound
	Titleist DT 90 & 100	Lithium Surlyn	.080	Three-piece, wound
	Titleist DT 2-Piece	Lithium Surlyn	.050	Two-piece
	Titleist HP2 Tour	VLMI/lithium Surlyn	.050	Two-piece
	Titleist HP2 Distance	VLMI/lithium Surlyn	.050	Two-piece
	Pinnacle Distance Extreme	Lithium/sodium Surlyn	.085	Two-piece
	Pinnacle Distance Oversized	Lithium/sodium Surlyn	.070	Two-piece
	Pinnacle Gold	Lithium/sodium Surlyn	.085	Two-piece
	Pinnacle Equalizer	Lithium Surlyn/VLMI	.065	Two-piece
	Pinnacle For Women	Lithium Surlyn/VLMI	.065	Two-piece

Comments: Titleist brand name, with six offerings that are notably different from one another in performance and feel, tries to capture the entire market instead of concentration on "good players." Professional may be worth stiff price, providing amazing durability for such a high-performance product.

No. of Dimples	Spin Rate (Driver, 8-Iron)	Trajectory Type	Standard Size/Weight	Suggested Retail (*doz.*)
392	4100, 9000	Not supplied	Y	$40
392	3800, 8200		Y	$50
392	3700, 8300		Y	$34
392	3000, 7600		Y	$28
440	3400, 8200		Y	$34
440	3000, 7500		Y	$34
392	Not supplied		Y	$25/15-pack
392	Not supplied		Standard weight 1.72" dia.	$25/15-pack
392	Not supplied		Y	$18.95/15-pack
392	Not supplied		Standard size, 1.55 oz.	$18.95/15-pack
332	Not supplied		Y	$18.95/15-pack

continued

GOLF BALL PRODUCT INFORMATION *(continued)*

MANUFACTURER	MODEL	COVER MATERIAL	COVER THICKNESS *(in.)*	CONSTRUCTION TYPE
Top Flite	Strata Tour	ZS Balata (TM)	Not supplied	Multilayer (three-piece, nonwound)
	Z Balata (90 & 100)	Softest Zylin	.069 (90), .056 (100)	Two-piece
	Tour SD (90 & 100)	Soft Zylin	.069	Two-piece
	Magna	Zylin	.086	Two-piece
	Magna EX	Thinner Zylin	.074	Two-piece
	Magna EX-W	Thinner Zylin	.074	Two-piece
	XL Performance	Zylin	.069	Two-piece
	XL	Zylin	.069	Two-piece
	XL-W	Zylin	.069	Two-piece
	Hot XL (Regular, Tour, High trajectories)	Thinner Zylin	.069	Two-piece

No. of Dimples	Spin Rate (Driver, 8-Iron)	Trajectory Type	Standard Size/Weight	Suggested Retail (*doz.*)
422	Not supplied	Medium-low	Y	$52
422 Hex		Medium-low	Y	$40
422 Tri		"Tour"	Y	$34
422 Tri		Not supplied	Standard weight, 1.717" dia.	$29/15-pack
422 Tri		Not supplied	Standard weight, 1.717" dia.	$30
422 Tri		Not supplied	Standard weight, 1.717" dia.	$30
422 Tri		Not supplied	Y	$27/15-pack
Differing dimple counts and configurations		Regular, Tour, High	Y	$26/18-pack
422 Tri		Not supplied	Y	$26/18-pack
Differing dimple counts and configurations		Regular, Tour, High	Y	$28/15-pack

continued

GOLF BALL PRODUCT INFORMATION *(continued)*

MANUFACTURER	MODEL	COVER MATERIAL	COVER THICKNESS *(in.)*	CONSTRUCTION TYPE
Wilson	Titanium Spin	Magnesium Surlyn	Not supplied	Two-piece w/ titanium core
	Titanium Distance	Magnesium Surlyn	Not supplied	Two-piece w/ titanium core
	Titanium Balata	Balata	Not supplied	Two-piece w/ titanium core
	Ultra 500 Tour Balata (90 & 100)	Balata	.053	Three-piece, nonwound
	Ultra 500 Competition (90 & 100)	Soft Surlyn	.070	Two-piece
	Ultra 500 Distance (90 & 100	Surlyn	.087	Two-piece
	Ultra DPS (90 & 100)	Surlyn	Not supplied	Two-piece
	Ultra DPS Tour Spin (90 & 100)	Softer Surlyn	Not supplied	Two-piece
	Ultra DPS Classic Wound (90 & 100)	Surlyn	Not supplied	Three-piece, wound
	TC^2	Surlyn	Not supplied	Two-piece

Comments: Company says new titanium compound allows for better bonding of core,

NO. OF DIMPLES	SPIN RATE (DRIVER, 8-IRON)	TRAJECTORY TYPE	STANDARD SIZE/WEIGHT	SUGGESTED RETAIL (*doz.*)
500	Not supplied	Not supplied	Y	$37
500	Not supplied		Y	$35
500	Not supplied		Y	$43
500	3620, 8050		Y	$42
500	3515, 7880		Y	$36
500	3211, 6140		Y	$34
432	Not supplied		Y	$29/15-pack
432	Not supplied		Y	$29/15-pack
432	Not supplied		Y	$29/15-pack
392	Not supplied		Y	$25/15-pack

thus greater energy.

continued

CHAPTER 9

Getting the Right Grip on Your Game

A golf club is made up of only three basic parts: a head, a shaft, and a grip. The grip is most definitely the least glamorous, least appreciated, most taken-for-granted element of the three. How often do you hear somebody say, "These grips are just fabulous, they're the only kind I'd ever use"? Probably never. In fact, the humble grip only seems to get noticed when something is wrong with it. If it is of a certain diameter that's either too large or too small for your hands, you'll notice it. If the grip is old and slick, you may notice it. If its material configuration is such that it feels hard or soft in comparison with what you're used to, you'll notice it. And if your grips get wet when you're caught in a heavy rainstorm, you'll *really* notice it.

However, if a grip is performing perfectly for you, providing a comfortable, tacky feel and a secure hold throughout the swing, you probably won't take note of it at all. A grip that you take no particular notice of is usually the best grip of all.

While the grip is easily overlooked, it can play a large part in the quality and consistency of your shotmaking. And there's a wide assortment of grip models for you to choose from, either on new equipment or as replacements when your current grips get worn. For all of the club models listed in the previous chapters, there is a column that mentions the standard grips that the manufacturer makes available. Let's examine the golf grip so that you'll know the pluses and minuses of the various grips you'll see as you shop for your next set of clubs.

Grip Material Types

There are four types of materials used in the manufacture of golf grips today. Two are natural materials and two are synthetics.

Standard Grip Sizes

As you look through the listings of grip models, you'll see some grips listed as "oversize." Or you may have heard golfing friends who like their grips "½ of an inch oversize." Well, it might be helpful to you to know how grip diameters are measured and what is standard in the first place.

Unlike with other elements of the golf club, such as club length or clubface loft, grip experts (thankfully!) agree on what is a standard grip diameter for both men's and women's grips. The measurement is actually made at four points along the grip, which tapers from top to bottom, as follows:

	MEN'S STANDARD (inches)	WOMEN'S STANDARD (inches)
1 inch below grip cap	0.960	0.925
2 inches below grip cap	0.900	0.870
3 inches below grip cap	0.860	0.840
6 inches below grip cap	0.780	0.775

Oversize or undersize grips are usually measured in terms of being either $\frac{1}{64}$, $\frac{1}{32}$, $\frac{1}{16}$, or $\frac{1}{8}$ inch over or under the standard diameters.

Leather. Prior to about 1960, virtually all top-line clubs were outfitted with natural leather grips. Leather grips consisted of long calfskin or leather strips which were wrapped at a diagonal angle over the clubshaft. More recently, slip-on style leather grips became popular, as they are much less time-consuming to install.

Without question, real leather grips give an unmatched, tacky feel and a rich look to the golf club. However, as you look through the listing of clubs in the previous chapters under the column on grips, you'll note that virtually no one offers them as a standard feature on their clubs. And of the major gripmakers, only one, Lamkin, still offers leather grips as a featured item. Why has such a high-performance element of the golf club gone by the wayside? Three reasons:

1. Leather grips are very expensive. The cost of a spiral-wrap leather grip, including an installation process that requires an underlisting as well as a separate grip cap and collar, has been estimated at about $22 *per club.*
2. Leather grips are a high-maintenance item. Leather grips do feel great, as long as they're constantly treated with leather conditioners to keep them soft and supple. Otherwise they can become dry and hard quickly, and thus can become a deficit to good shotmaking.

3. Leather grips can be bad news in bad weather. If you get caught in a rainstorm with leather grips, you need a great caddie to keep the grips dry—leather grips definitely do not provide playability in wet weather that the other grip materials do.

Natural Rubber. When less expensive and more easily maintained alternatives to leather were being sought, natural rubber became the most popular material for the grip. It is still very much in evidence. Eaton Corporation, makers of Golf Pride grips, which have for many years been the top-selling line of grips in golf, makes its very popular Victory line from natural rubber and its Tour Velvet line with a blend that includes it.

Natural rubber grips are often extended with filler material, usually cork (if you were to look at a Golf Pride standard Victory grip, for example, you'd notice the brown flecks that course through the black rubber). Natural rubber grips offer outstanding frictional gripping characteristics. It's still considered by many as the best "base" material for a grip that will perform well in wet weather. The possible deficit to natural rubber is that its ability to retain a tacky feel is somewhat limited. According to Ed Van Alst, engineering manager for Avon Golf Grips, "Poor grip life of natural rubber is directly related to its chemical structure . . . it is susceptible to degradation from light, heat, oxygen, and ozone." These factors can cause the surface of the grip to harden and become shiny and slippery if the grips aren't cleaned regularly, so natural rubber grips may have to be replaced slightly more often than grips made of synthetic materials.

EPDM. This is the abbreviated version of the technical name for a synthetic

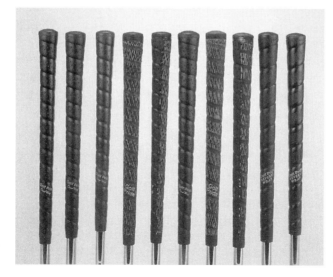

Golf Pride Collection

rubber compound that is probably the most often used grip material today. (This EPDM compound may differ slightly from one company to the next.) It is used, for example, in Golf Pride's Tour Wrap grip series and in nearly all of the grips produced by Avon, Lamkin, Royal Grip, and Mint Grip, among others.

According to Avon's Van Alst, "EPDM has exceptional heat, oxygen, and ozone resistance, resulting in superior performance and grip life. A well-engineered synthetic compound will match or exceed the frictional gripping properties of the current range of natural rubber grip compounds in wet and dry conditions." It should be added that grips made of EPDM will generally be a little more expensive than those of natural rubber.

Thermoplastic elastomers (TPE). This is another type of synthetic grip material, with Tacki-Mac being a company that uses this material exclusively. (Griptec offers its grips in both TPE and EPDM formulations.) According to Avon's Van Alst, TPE possesses above-average resistance to ozone degradations. It is a very tacky-feeling compound, but it is also one that is sensitive to temperature changes and tends to perform best in warm weather.

One commonly used type of thermoplastic elastomer, known as kraton, is white in color. It therefore lends itself well to grips offered in a wide variety of colors, as exemplified by the Tacki-Mac line.

Rating the Materials

Information from Avon Grips (which it should again be noted uses EPDM rubber compounds exclusively in its grip line) ranks the four materials discussed in terms of their performance in both dry and wet conditions, as well as for overall grip life. You should keep in mind that these are general guidelines—both the gripping property and the life of the grip are also dependent on how well you maintain your grips by cleaning and conditioning them.

	DRY CONDITIONS	WET CONDITIONS	GRIP LIFE
Natural rubber compounds	Very good	Average	Average
EPDM rubber compounds	Very good	Good	Very good
Thermoplastic elastomers	Very good	Average	Good
Leather	Very good	Poor	Average

Taken from *In Search of the Perfect Grip: Analysis of Golf Grip Materials*, 1995, by Edward Van Alst, Engineering Manager, Avon Golf Grips.

Caring for Your Grips

It's safe to say that the majority of amateurs don't take sufficient care of their grips. This not only causes your grips to wear out prematurely, it also can cost you strokes when you lose control of a slippery grip on a drive or approach shot.

This is particularly wasteful because with the predominance of today's rubber and synthetic rubber and thermoplastic materials, keeping your grips nice and tacky is a breeze. Unlike leather, which requires frequent use of specific conditioners to keep the grips from becoming hard and slick, all you need to wash your grips is a mixture of warm water and a mild detergent soap, applied with either a coarse towel or a soft scrub brush.

Some gripmakers recommend that you clean your grips after every round you play. That may be a bit excessive, since there will be rounds where you don't even touch, say, your 4-iron or your 7-iron. However, it's a good rule of thumb to clean your grips after every three to four rounds—more frequently if you practice a lot or if the weather's hot, so that hand perspiration builds up. You'll find that frequent cleaning will make the grips feel consistently secure and add confidence to your shotmaking.

What's Your Favorite Grip Style?

As you look through the listings of the various clubs, you'll see that the majority of companies have listed the type of grip that they use as "standard" on their metalwoods, irons, and wedges. In many cases the grip manufacturer's name is "proprietary"—that is, it is not specified. However, the style of the grip is listed by most companies.

Keep in mind that in almost all cases, club manufacturers will equip your clubs with a different type of grip than their standard grip if you make such a request. If, for example, you've decided to buy a Lynx Black Cat Titanium driver but think you'd prefer it with a Golf Pride Victory Velvet Cord grip, it should be no problem getting it.

That said, let's briefly review the basic styles or patterns of rubber or synthetic rubber grips that are on the market today. (In some cases the features of one style may overlap with another style; for example, a grip including cordlike material might also be used in certain "wrap"-style grips.)

Rubber "wrap" grips. The style you'll see most frequently on the club listings is a "wrap"-style grip (almost always a synthetic compound as opposed to natural rubber), which is offered in some form by every major gripmaker. Actually, this grip is not "wrapped" at all. It is a one-piece, slip-on grip that is manufac-

Avon Collection

tured with a look that simulates the old wrapped-leather grips. Many of these wrap styles actually come close to the rich feel of real leather, and with reasonable care they retain this feel while being far more durable than leather.

The majority of rubber wrap grips are "unbuffed," that is, not sanded, so that they have a somewhat glossy finish. Because of this, they do not absorb any moisture. So, make sure you always have a completely dry towel handy for when you get caught in a shower, or even if your hands perspire a lot.

Rubber wrap grips come in both a plain style or with perforations. Perforations, by the way, don't necessarily mean the grip is better in terms of gripping properties. It's basically a cosmetic element, and it's a matter of personal preference as to which style you prefer.

Nonwrap rubber grips. These are natural rubber or synthetic compound grips that do not simulate the wrapped-leather look. Generally, these grips will be "buffed," that is, sanded, for a duller, slightly coarser finish as opposed to most rubber wrap grips. Perhaps the most prominent grip in this category is the Victory grip by Golf Pride, a style that was introduced in the late 1960s and which the company claims is still the most popular grip in golf. It's distinguished by green tread lines and an exclusive hand placement alignment feature, which guides the right-handed player's right thumb and forefinger into position.

Cord grips. Over thirty years ago, Golf Pride began introducing rubber grips into which cordlike material was embedded. The aim here was to create a grip that provided increased holding traction in wet weather. Today, several major companies offer one or more grips that use cord material to some degree.

Cord grips are still considered beneficial in rainy weather and also in areas with high humidity or for golfers whose hands perspire freely. They are generally preferred by better players or professionals who compete frequently and must be ready for all weather conditions. On the downside, a grip such as Golf Pride's Classic Cord model might be considered too abrasive to the hands by weekend amateurs. However, there is a wide variety of cord grips in which the cord element is slightly less abrasive-feeling. There are also a number of "half-cord" models now available, such as Golf Pride's Victory Half Cord. These grips have cord embedded into the underside of the grip, while the top half has no cord and thus provides a softer feel for the thumbs and forefingers.

Air-cushioned grips. These are a relatively new innovation in grips in which "air cushioning" is the predominant feature. The grip is manufactured with tiny pockets of air within the interior walls. These air pockets serve to absorb the shock of impact. Air-cushioned grips generally have a very soft, pliable feel and are popular with golfers who suffer from arthritis and/or those with relatively low hand strength. The Avon Chamois and the Golf Pride Classic II Cushion are good examples of this grip style.

Following is a list of the grips offered by seven major grip manufacturers. This list will help inform you regarding the grips on clubs you may consider buying. It will also serve as a guide for you when the time comes to ensure peak performance with your clubs by outfitting them with a new set of grips. (Grip styles for putters are not listed.)

How Often to Replace Grips—and What Will It Cost?

Many golfers play with the same set of grips on their clubs for years. This is the equivalent to driving your car on bald tires. When your grips are old and slick, whether you realize it or not, you're forced to hold on much more tightly in the swing. This tight gripping leads to all kinds of poor shotmaking.

You may have heard professionals advise that you should replace your grips once a year. This is generally useful advice but it does not go far enough. You should judge how often to replace your grips by how often you play and practice, not by the calendar. Say you live in Florida and play two or three rounds a week year-round (usually in humid conditions). That's something like 120 rounds per year. You should probably replace your grips every six months at least. On the other hand, if you live in the upper Midwest and play once a week for six or seven months out of twelve, about thirty rounds per year, it's likely you can go two seasons before you need new grips. Another factor in how often you need a grip change is the amount of practice time you put in. Finally, it's been noted that synthetic rubber grips tend to last a little bit better than natural rubber compounds, so factor that into the equation also.

Grips are generally not a terribly expensive item. Assuming you have them replaced at a retail golf outlet or pro shop, for rubber and synthetic grips it's reasonable to assume they'll cost between $4 and $6 per club. If you're a do-it-yourselfer, you'll find that you can buy grips for between $1.50 and $3.50 each for various non-leather styles. Cord-embedded grips will be at the higher end of that price range, and natural rubber usually at the lower.

GOLF GRIP SUMMARY

MANUFACTURER	MODEL/MODEL LINE	GRIP STYLE	MATERIAL
Avon	Chamois (Standard, Jumbo in black, charcoal, brown; Women's in black, blue, charcoal)	Nonwrap Rubber	EPDM
	Nexus (Men's Tour and Oversize, Ladies)	Nonwrap Rubber	EPDM
	Tour 2100 Tac	Rubber Wrap/Air Cushion	EPDM
	Duratrax	Rubber Wrap	EPDM
	X-Air	"Woven" Wrap	EPDM
	Thermo	Rubber Wrap	EPDM
Eaton/Golf Pride	Tour Velvet (Men's, Velvet Cord, Velvet Lite, Mid-Size, Women's)	Nonwrap Rubber	Natural Rubber/ EPDM
	Tour Velvet Wrap	Rubber Wrap	Natural Rubber/ EPDM
	Standard Wrap	Rubber Wrap	Natural Rubber
	Player's Wrap	Rubber Wrap	EPDM
	Reverse Wrap	Rubber Wrap	EPDM
	Tour Wrap (Men's, Wrap Cord, Wrap Half Cord, Women's Wrap (in black or blue)	Rubber Wrap	EPDM
	Victory (Men's, Velvet Cord, Half Cord, Jumbo, Women's in 3 colors, Junior)	Nonwrap Rubber	Natural Rubber
	Victory 2000 (Men's and Women's)	Nonwrap Rubber	Natural Rubber
	Classic II Cushion (Men's and Women's)	Air Cushion	EPDM
	Classic Cord	Cord	Natural Rubber
Griptec	Pro Wrap Series (Smooth Wrap, Perforated Wrap, Channel Wrap)	Rubber Wrap	Thermoplastic or EDPM
	700 NP Tour Cord	Cord	Thermoplastic or EPDM
	701 TW Cord Wrap	Cord/Rubber Wrap	Thermoplastic or EPDM
Lamkin	Spiral Wrap (black, tan)	Wrap	Leather
	Sure Tac (black, tan)	Wrap	Leather
	Cushion Core Perma Wrap	Rubber Wrap	EPDM

Lamkin *(cont.)*	Perma Wrap (Standard, Smooth, Cushion-Core, Oversize, Full Cord, Half Cord)	Rubber Wrap	EPDM
	Smooth Cushion Oversize	Rubber Wrap	EPDM
	Traction Wrap	Rubber Wrap	EPDM
	Trac-Line (Standard, Half Cord, Full Cord)	Nonwrap Rubber	EPDM
	Sure-Tac (Standard, Half Cord, Full Cord, Jumbo)	Nonwrap Rubber	EPDM
	True-Tac	Rubber Wrap	EPDM
	V-Trac (Cordless, Full Cord)	Nonwrap Rubber	EPDM
	Diamond Perf	Nonwrap Rubber	EPDM
Mint Grip	Diamond Wrap	Rubber Wrap	EPDM
	Perforated Wrap (Standard, Oversize)	Rubber Wrap	EPDM
	Smooth Wrap	Rubber Wrap	EPDM
Royal Grip	Perf Wrap	Rubber Wrap	EPDM
	Sand Wrap	Rubber Wrap	EPDM
	SandMAXimum	Rubber Wrap	EPDM
	Soft Wrap	Rubber Wrap	EPDM
	Diamond Cord Wrap	Cord/Rubber Wrap	EPDM
	Royal Cord X1	Cord	EPDM
Tacki-Mac	Men's Standard (100% knurled, 3 colors)	Rubber Wrap	Thermoplastic
	Men's Standard (75% knurled, 6 colors)	Rubber Wrap	Thermoplastic
	Men's V	Rubber Wrap	Thermoplastic
	Tour Pro (3 colors)	Rubber Wrap	Thermoplastic
	Standard Smooth Wrap (Standard, Small Cap, Large Bell, Oversize)	Rubber Wrap	Thermoplastic
	Tour Sensation	Nonwrap Rubber	Thermoplastic
	Arthritic (Standard, Oversize for men and women, multiple colors)	Nonwrap Rubber	Thermoplastic
	Ladies Tour Pro (6 colors)	Rubber Wrap	Thermoplastic
	Ladies Standard (5 colors)	Rubber Wrap	Thermoplastic
	Ladies Small Cap (4 colors)	Rubber Wrap	Thermoplastic
	Junior Tour Pro (5 colors)	Rubber Wrap	Thermoplastic

CHAPTER 10

"Peripherals" That Can Help You: Shoes, Gloves, Bags, and Rainwear

You should be armed with ample information to go out into the marketplace and make the best possible selections regarding the clubs and balls you'll play with in the near future. With a little luck, you'll have some funds left in your equipment budget to also upgrade your peripheral golf equipment.

There are four major elements of the golfing peripherals that we'll talk about here: golf shoes, golf gloves, golf bags, and golf rainwear. All have undergone substantial improvements in recent years and offer advantages that will help make your rounds both more comfortable and more enjoyable, and to some degree even help you shoot better scores.

In golf shoes, great strides have been made toward the development of completely waterproof shoes that won't allow a drop of moisture in unless the water gets above your ankles. There is great debate on the subject of traditional golf spikes versus spikeless shoes. Golf gloves are now appearing in increasing numbers in synthetic materials as opposed to traditional all-leather gloves. Golf bag manufacturers have produced a number of new styles that have made bags more user-friendly in terms of carrying comfort, item storage, and protection of your clubs. And there's a tremendous array of golf rainwear that you should know about so you can have a rainsuit handy—you wouldn't want a little shower (much less a big one) to spoil your weekend fun, would you?

This chapter will provide background information on significant developments taking place regarding the various golfing accessories and provide a substantial listing of products available. The lists are not inclusive of every existing manufacturer of shoes, gloves, bags, or golf rainwear, and in some cases the

Florsheim Frogs (left)
Johnston & Murphy Cypress
Limited (right)

manufacturer may have such a long list of models that a complete rundown of each company's products is impractical. In such cases, a representative cross-sample of the line in question is provided. Lastly, in a few cases manufacturers have not provided a specific suggested retail price, so you will occasionally see an estimated rather than a specific price.

Shoe Review

Besides the obvious concerns of overall fit and comfort in a golf shoe, along with style considerations, there are two points regarding shoes that you should be alert to before you go shopping for your next set of spikes:

Degree of Waterproofing

Your golf shoes are going to get wet. This will be a fact of life on most days, not only when you happen to get caught in a shower. If you customarily play your weekend rounds in the early mornings, you'll probably encounter enough dew to seep into a nonwaterproof shoe almost every time you play. If you play on the day after a heavy rain, you'll be treading through plenty of areas of casual water on the course.

If you play a lot of golf, say fifty rounds a year or more, you'll be wise to look for shoes that offer some type of waterproof guarantee.

Fortunately, shoe manufacturers have made fantastic strides in waterproofing their products. This is true even for many of the classic, all-leather models

Etonic Dri-Tech Tour (above left)
Foot-Joy Dry-Joys GX (above right)
Walter Genuin Women's Roma (left)

which you might not normally expect to have top waterproofing properties. In the best of these shoes, the leather upper goes through a multistep tanning process which makes it waterproof, while the leather still maintains its "breathability" properties. Probably more significant, shoes with a waterproof guarantee use one of several waterproof-yet-breathable membranes between the shoe's upper and its lining and a polyurethane lining above the leather outsole and the spike plate to make the completed shoe virtually impervious to water. For example, in Nike's Air Zoom model, which carries a two-year waterproof guarantee, a complete one-piece "bootie" made of Gore-Tex, a material that will be discussed in the rainsuit section, is encased between the outer parts of the shoe and the lining.

Shoes with waterproofing characteristics will generally carry either a one- or a two-year guarantee against water entry. Of course, if you don't play more than once a month, your shoes may stay waterproof for many years. However, if you are the type of golfer who plays a lot, and in competitions so that you have to be ready for all conditions, an investment in one of the two-year-guaranteed waterproof models is a wise one.

Though I can't speak for all models, I can say that I've played in some outrageous downpours with a couple of different brands that carry two-year waterproof guarantees. And I was amazed to find that afterward, my socks were the driest thing on me!

Nike Air Zoom Tour (above left)
Adidas Bernhard Langer II Aditex (above right)
Rockport The Groove (left)

Lighter-Weight Shoes

If you walk your rounds and particularly if you are getting along in years, the weight of your golf shoes should be a consideration. Classic, all-leather shoes with a steel shank and steel spikes provide excellent stability. However, if you are "carrying" four pounds of golf shoes instead of, say, half that much over the six-mile walk that an 18-hole round actually encompasses (because *nobody* walks a course in a perfectly straight line), then you might feel some extra fatigue because of them.

Many top-line models have become much lighter. Reebok, for example, uses a honeycomb-like urethane fiber known as Hexalite as a cushioning agent in the heel and sole of its Attack collection. It also uses a graphite/glass fiber material known as Graphlite for its arch supports. These materials are lighter and much more durable than conventional foam and rubber padding. Many companies now use lightweight EVA rubber outsoles instead of leather. Companies are also offering a number of models with Lite Spikes, in which the traditional steel spike is surrounded by a lightweight plastic shoulder to reduce overall weight. The end result of these efforts is that you will find many models available today that are substantially lighter than you might expect, yet still manage to provide excellent stability while you're walking and swinging.

Alternate—and Care for—Your Shoes

No matter how well made your golf shoes are or how long the waterproof guarantee is, those shoes won't be great for long if you wear the same pair every time you play, then throw them into the trunk of your car to await another day of abuse.

Any golfer who expects to play a moderate amount of golf—including lots of play on consecutive weekend days—should own two pairs of golf shoes, if not more. And you should alternate those two or more pairs; never get in the habit of wearing the same pair two days in a row. You'll get more rounds out of all the shoes you own if they always get some time off between rounds.

If multiple pairs of top-line waterproof shoes stretch your budget, at the least, try to have one pair that is guaranteed waterproof. Then you can plan to use these if rain is expected and for early-morning play. If your second pair is not waterproof-guaranteed, you can plan to use them when the weather conditions are drier.

It's wise to keep shoe trees in all your golf shoes so that they retain their shape despite the stresses they are put under by walking and swinging. Also get in the habit of brushing off the dirt and grass that accumulates around the outsoles after each round. You'll also find that many of the leather uppers used today—particularly white leather uppers—can be cleaned easily with mild soap and water. Caring for today's shoes should be easier than ever.

Mizuno MST II (left)
Adidas Proette Aditex (below left)
Softspikes Extra Traction Cleats (below)

Are Alternative Cleats for You?

The majority of golf shoes today still come with traditional steel spikes. However, there is a strong movement toward the use of various types of shorter cleats made of rubber or polyurethane materials. Among these "alternative cleats" are Tred-Lites, Turfmates, and Softspikes. As an example, a Softspike consists of polyurethane cleats that have twelve 2-millimeter nubs instead of the single, traditional steel spike (see photo on page 330).

Alternative cleats offer two main advantages: (1) They are considered more comfortable to wear than steel spikes, especially when walking in the clubhouse area and on cement or asphalt cart paths; and (2) they are generally considered to cause far less damage to putting greens than do traditional metal spikes. In fact, a number of top private courses in the United States have now banned the use of traditional spikes because they are convinced of this benefit. Publicists for Softspikes claim that as of late 1996, some six hundred courses around the country require golfers to use the nonmetal spikes.

The main criticism of alternative cleats comes from those who believe that they do not provide as much traction as conventional steel spikes in wet conditions, on steep hills, or during the full swing by the player who is active with the feet and legs. Yet, many golfers, including Senior Tour star Ray Floyd, report that they have experienced no problems whatsoever in playing with them.

At between $5 and $9 per set of twenty-four, alternative cleats cost about the same amount as a set of standard steel spikes—although they probably need to be replaced a bit more frequently.

If you're not sure whether alternative cleats are for you, here's a suggestion: Put them in an older pair of shoes for practice sessions. If they feel stable and comfortable there, the next test is in a casual round. If it passes there, then you can consider going to them full-time.

GOLF SHOE PRODUCT LISTINGS

MODEL	TOP FEATURES	COLORS	SUGGESTED RETAIL
Adidas			
Bernhard Langer	Pittard Leather Uppers, P2E integrated insole and outsole disperses spike pressure	White/Green	$180
Bernhard Langer II Aditex	P2E insole technology, 2-year waterproof guarantee, ghilly lacing for lateral stability	White, Brown, Black	$150
Tour Dry	Waterproof and breathable membrane-lined adi-dry system, rubber outsole	White/Black	$95
Proette Aditex	P2E insole technology, lightweight outsole, 2-year waterproof guarantee	White, White/Black	$140
PE Lady Saddle	P2E insole technology, water-repellent leather with sealed seams	White, White/Sand	$85
Ashworth			
15 men's styles	Waterproof leather uppers, waterproof membrane, all leather lining, 2-year waterproof guarantee	Wide variety	$165
Backbay			
Fairfield, Clarendon	100% waterproof leather upper, TPU Graphlon midsole insert	White/Black	$99–$129
Trent, Beacon	Synthetic upper, lightweight crepe outsole, value pricing	White, White/Black, White/Black/Taupe	$50
Bite			
Fogey	Youthful styling, waterproof leather upper, flared rubber outsole w/mudguard	White/Brown, White/Black, White/Forest Green	$90
Stogey	Leather/canvas upper, extra collar/tongue padding	Brown/Cocoa, Khaki/ Forest Green, Black/White	$80
ATV Sandal	Unique sandal for golf featuring All Terrain Bite Spike System	Black/Carmel, Black/Blue	$70

GOLF SHOE PRODUCT LISTINGS

MODEL	TOP FEATURES	COLORS	SUGGESTED RETAIL
Dexter			
LDS Dry Sports	Waterproof leather uppers, padded tongue, washable orthotic footbed, 2-year waterproof guarantee	White, White/Brown, Brown/Black	$100
Dry Bucs	Oil-tanned NuBuc leather uppers, Trisport Light Locking Spike system, waterproof guarantee	Fudge/Brown, Tan/Brown, Fudge, Rust	$90
Etonic			
Ultimate (14 styles)	Pittard's calfskin uppers, Stabilizer spike configuration, Gore-Tex lining, 2-year waterproof guarantee	Wide variety	$260
Dri-Tech Tour	Stabilizer sole combines spikes with rubber turf grips for greater traction, 2-year waterproof guarantee	6 color combinations	$175
Dri-Tech (men's and women's)	Gore-Tex said to be most breathable waterproofing material, 2-year waterproof guarantee	Wide variety	$140
Stabilite Bucs	Rounded last for greater comfort, buc leather uppers, 1-year waterproof guarantee	Brown/Sandstone, Black/Coffee, Brown	$90
Florsheim			
Frogs (12 models)	Waterproof leather, 30-day comfort guarantee, four spikeless models	Wide variety	$120 and up
Foot-Joy			
Classics Dry (8 men's styles)	Waterproof, breathable membrane, waterproof uppers and glove leather linings, 1-year waterproof warranty, Cer-Mec spikes	Wide variety	$250
Classics (31 men's styles, 11 women's)	Waterproof calfskin upper and glove leather lining, Goodyear welt, seam-sealed, huge style and color assortment	Wide variety	$220 men's $200 women's
Dry-Joys GX (5 men's models)	Pittard's waterproof leather upper, IntelliGel thermo-responsive arch insert and tongue, graphite-reinforced TPU outsole	Bomber Taupe/White/Black, Black/White, Brown NuBuc/White, White, Black	$180

GOLF SHOE PRODUCT LISTINGS

MODEL	TOP FEATURES	COLORS	SUGGESTED RETAIL
Foot-Joy (*continued*)			
Dry-Joys (11 men's models, 5 women's)	Dry-Joys waterproof leather system, IntelliGel arch insert, Uni-Flex outsole for flexibility with lateral stability	Wide variety	$150
Aqua-Lites (5 men's models, 3 women's)	Leather upper, breathable membrane, 2-year waterproof guarantee, Lite Spikes, ultralight (app. 13 oz. per shoe)	Wide variety	$99.95
Soft-Joys Sierra (6 men's models, 3 women's)	Waterproof leather upper, interchangeable heel plugs for customized comfort, EVA outsole, Lite Spikes	Wide variety	$93
TCX (4 women's styles)	Waterproof leather upper, molded EVA outsole, Lite Spikes, very light total weight (app. 8.8 oz.)	Black Patent/White, Bronze Metallic/White, Black/Linen, Brown/Linen	$87
Soft-Joys (12 men's models, 3 women's)	Waterproof leather upper, Nylex-covered EVA footbed, Lite Spikes, traditional, athletic, or spikeless styles	Wide variety	$81 traditional $77 athletic $60 spikeless and juniors'
Green-Joys (6 men's models, 3 women's)	PVC upper, EVA outsole, Lite Spikes, junior sizes, economy pricing	Wide variety	$49.95
Walter Genuin			
Oxford	Handcrafted in Italy of finest leathers including lizard and crocodile	Brandy, Black, Burgundy	$738 crocodile $546 lizard
Chester (6 models)	Gore-Tex lining, 100% waterproof, interchangeable with Tred-Lite spikes	Wide variety	$396–$495
Vega (6 women's models)	Four models feature naturally tanned and dyed leather for breathability and woodlike finish	Wide variety	$342–$407

GOLF SHOE PRODUCT LISTINGS

MODEL	TOP FEATURES	COLORS	SUGGESTED RETAIL
Johnston & Murphy			
Islander	Durotech waterproof barrier, Optima cushioning system, saddle style	White/Black, Burgundy/Black	$165
Cypress Limited	Buc saddle style, Trampoline cushioning system	Olive/Tan, Cedar NuBuc/Cedar	$165
Cypress	Dehydro weather-resistant linings, Trampoline cushioning system	5 color combinations	$165–$175
Mizuno			
MST	Comfort collar, flexible polyure-thane outsoles, 2-year waterproof guarantee	5 color combinations	$120
LMST (women's)	Same features as MST	White, White/Black, Burgundy	$105
MST Classic	Synthetic upper, cambrelle lining, lifetime Cer-Mec spikes, 2-year waterproof guarantee	7 color combinations	$105
Soft-Trax	Waterproof leather, rubber outsole with just seven, shorter spikes for green-friendliness	White, White/Black, White/Brown, Black	$120
Zunos Walker	Waterproof leather, casual styling; short spikes can be replaced with "caps" for street wear	Brown, Tan	$105
Nike			
Air Zoom Tour	Zoom Air heel-to-toe cushioning, Gore-Tex lining, Pittard's leather, TPU outsole	White, White/Black, White/Coffee, Black	$150
Air Zoom Tradition	Waterproof leather upper, Zoom Air heel cushioning, rubber outsole, 2-year waterproof guarantee	5 color combinations	$100

GOLF SHOE PRODUCT LISTINGS (continued)

MODEL	TOP FEATURES	COLORS	SUGGESTED RETAIL
Nike (continued)			
Air Access Plus	Leather upper, watershield membrane, Nike Air heel cushion, 1-year waterproof guarantee	5 color combinations	$80
Air Max Apparent	Athletic shoe design, leather upper, lifetime Cer-Mec spikes, 2-year waterproof guarantee	White	$120
Women's Air Classic Plus	Leather upper, Nike Air heel cushion, 1-year waterproof guarantee	White, White/Black, White/Driftwood	$80
Women's Air Classic Pro	Same features as above	White	$80
Reebok			
Attack Collection (3 styles)	Pittard's leather, Gore-Tex lining, Graphlite shank, 2-year waterproof guarantee	7 color combinations	$150–$175
Convertible Collection (Performance, Saratoga XL)	Rubber outsole, convertible spike system including Tred-Lite spikes, 2-year waterproof guarantee	White, White/Black, White/Olive, Brown, Coffee	$125 Performance, $95 Saratoga XL
Permanent Collection	Full leather upper, molded EVA midsole/outsole, permanent ceramic spikes, 1-year waterproof guarantee	White, White/Taupe, White/Burgundy, White/Black	$95
Pump Launch	Athletic shoe styling, waterproof uppers, Lite Spikes	White/Black	$80
Women's Attack Collection	Leather upper, Gore-Tex lining, Graphlite shank, 2-year waterproof guarantee	White, White/Black, White/Taupe, Brown	$130
Women's Comfort Elite Collection (5 styles)	Lightweight leather, molded EVA midsole/outsole, Lite Spikes, 1-year waterproof guarantee	5 color combinations	$50–$80

GOLF SHOE PRODUCT LISTINGS *(continued)*

MODEL	TOP FEATURES	COLORS	SUGGESTED RETAIL
Rockport			
The Groove	Grooved spike plate system with 6 removable plates convertible to steel or rubber plates, Pittard's leather, 2-year waterproof guarantee	White, White/Dirty Buck, White/Brown, White/Black	$250
Golfsport	Full-grain leather uppers, Air Circulator leather footbed, 2-year waterproof guarantee	White/White/Brown, White/Black	$170
Wingtip	TPU outsole, permanent steel spikes, 1-year waterproof guarantee	White, White/Black	$145
Women's Saddle Bal	Leather upper, removable polyure-thane footbed, 1-year waterproof guarantee	5 color combinations	$125
Wilson			
Staff Pro	Leather upper, EVA midsole/outsole, Lite Wate spikes, saddle or wing tip styles	5 color combinations	$99
Staff Prestige	Leather upper, removable cushion insole, TPU outsole, Lite Wate spikes, wing tip style	White	$99
Ultra Spikeless	Leather upper and lining, 1-year waterproof warranty, athletic-cleat-style sole	White, White/Black, White/Taupe	$60
Ultra Performance	Lightweight athletic-style shoe, Lite Wate spikes	White/Gray, White/Navy	$70

Are Gloves Getting "Unreal"?

The majority of golfers at all levels would agree that it's beneficial to your game to wear a golf glove. For right-handed players, the glove is worn on the left hand because the fingers and palm of this hand rest fully on and around the grip. A good glove helps keep your hold on the club secure without forcing your fingers around the grip, restricting the freedom of your swing.

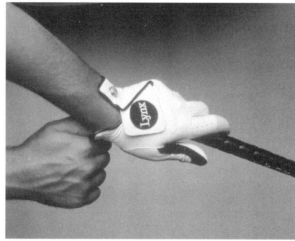

Nike Swoosh (above)
Lynx The Paw (right)

Keep a Couple of Gloves Handy

As with golf shoes, it's wise to have multiple gloves in your bag and to alternate them regularly, particularly if you wear an all-leather glove. If you play a lot of golf on consecutive weekend days and use one glove at a time, you'll wear each one out more quickly than if you give them a chance to dry out fully before their next use. It's always good to have at least three gloves in your bag so that if you happen to get caught in the rain and one glove won't stay dry for the whole round, you have alternates.

After you complete a round, smooth out the leather glove so that it's flat and re-place it in the original packaging or a small sealable plastic bag. Don't leave it out under direct sunlight, as this will make the leather dry out and harden.

Also keep in mind that some leather gloves (as well as most synthetic styles) are actually washable. Follow the instructions given and you should be able to get a cou-ple of extra rounds of good gripping from each glove.

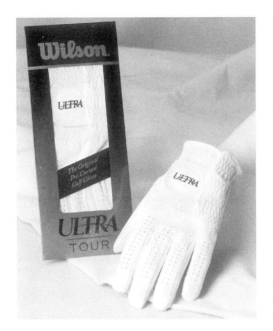

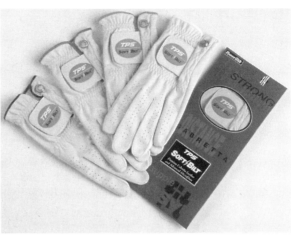

Wilson Ultra Tour (left)
PowerBilt TPS SoftBilt
(above)
Mizuno GraFlex (right)

As you read through the listing of gloves and styles, you'll note that most companies still offer at least one model that's made of real, 100 percent leather. However, a growing number of glove models are made of synthetic fibers. Examples are PowerBilt's TPS Durabilt and Wilson's Ultra Grip. Other companies offer models in which the palm and thumb areas are leather for enhanced feel, but the remainder of the glove is synthetic. Examples: Foot-Joy's Weather-Sof and Etonic's Soft Tech.

Many companies claim that the all-synthetic gloves will perform better than leather in the rain, and even that they provide equal support for the grip in any conditions. This is highly debatable. However, it is undeniable that top-grade, 100 percent cabretta leather gloves are getting expensive. While they can usually be obtained for slightly less in golf retail outlets, some leather gloves sport suggested retail prices exceeding $20. This may be a bit alarming to the golfer who goes through a dozen or more a year. (Keep in mind that some leather gloves have a relatively thicker leather—with these, you may trade off the ultimate in feel for a glove that wears longer.) Meanwhile, most all-synthetic gloves carry a suggested retail in the $10–$12 range, and they will generally wear better than most leather gloves.

An investment in one synthetic glove for a tryout would probably be well worth your while. If the difference in feel is not noticeable to you (and this is a very subjective judgment), that's great. But if you decide that there's nothing that can match the feel of a well-made 100 percent leather glove, well, maybe you can drop a few hints as your birthday and/or Christmas approaches.

For those hardy golfers in colder climes who will not be stopped by temperatures hovering around the freezing mark, you'll also see several winter glove pairs in the listing.

Note: Virtually all gloves listed are available in both men's and women's sizes.

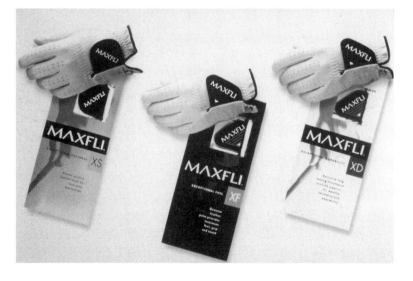

Maxfli XS, XF, XD Series (left)
Grandoe Shock Tech (below)

GOLF GLOVE PRODUCT LISTINGS

MODEL	MATERIAL/FEATURES	COLORS	SUGGESTED RETAIL
Tommy Armour			
Soft Scot II	Cabretta leather with Tritan tanning process	White	$17.50
Royal Scot	Leather palm, synthetic back	White	$10.50
Silver Scot	Full synthetic	White	$9
Daiwa			
Ulti-Mitt	Premium sheepskin cabretta, double stitching, vented fingers	White	$20
Soft-Mitt	Sheepskin cabretta, vented fingers, Daiwa Palm-Fit	White	$15
Pro-Mitt	Economy-priced all-leather glove	White	$12
Etonic			
Soft Tech	Premium washable Abyssinian cabretta at all contact points, combined with breathable, wear-resistant synthetic fiber	White	$16
ST	100% breathable, wear-resistant synthetic fiber	White	$11
Foot-Joy			
Sta-Sof	Extra-soft APL 300 cabretta leather, special tanning process resists water and perspiration, long cuff	Pearl, Black	$19.50
Sta-Sof Alliance	APL 300 cabretta palm, thumb, index finger with DNP synthetic back	Pearl	$16
Sof-Joy	100% cabretta glove at attractive price	Pearl	$12
Weather-Sof	DNP synthetic with cabretta leather thumb and heel area	Pearl	$11.25
Grandoe			
Shock Tech	Deerskin leather with "hollow fiber" structure which acts as air-cushioning layer	White	$19
Flexor	Control Panel on back keeps tight fit; SofFlex cabretta	White, Black	$15

GOLF GLOVE PRODUCT LISTINGS *(continued)*

MODEL	MATERIAL/FEATURES	COLORS	SUGGESTED RETAIL
Conqueror	SofFlex premium cabretta, elasticized Velcro tab closure	White, Black, Red, Navy, Eggplant, Dijon, Wedgewood	$14.50
Player	Sheepskin cabretta, perforated fingers, economy all-leather	White	$11
Survivor	Washable synthetic w/ball marker	White, Black, Red, Navy, Eggplant, Dijon, Wedgewood	$9
H. J. Glove			
Cortex Sponge Cabretta	Thicker soft sponge cabretta compresses for soft feel; flat seam stitching	Pearl White	$15
Gripper Plus	1005 synthetic, flat seam stitching, reinforced palm patch	5 men's colors, 15 women's colors	$8
Super Deluxe Winter Pair	Fleece back, synthetic palm	Black	$18
Kasco			
Eversoft	Hand-cut Ethiopian cabretta leather, 33 total sizes	White, Beige, Black, Pink (women's)	$18
Aqua Soft	100% Indonesian cabretta	White, Beige, Black, Pink (women's)	$14
PSO 350	Value-priced, non-water-treated cabretta	White	$11
DX 600	100% synthetic, snap-on ball marker, 30 total sizes	12 colors	$9.50
All Weather	Suedelike synthetic with leather palm	White, Beige, Light Blue, Navy, Pink (women's)	$8.50
Lynx			
The Paw	100% top-quality cabretta, easy-on diagonal elasticized closure	White, Gray w/assorted trims	$17
Maxfli			
XS	Thin, premium cabretta with Scotchgard protectant	Silver White	$22.50
XF	Combination Pittard's leather palm with synthetic innofiber blend	White	$16

GOLF GLOVE PRODUCT LISTINGS *(continued)*

MODEL	MATERIAL/FEATURES	COLORS	SUGGESTED RETAIL
XD	Synthetic innofiber blend stays tacky when wet, leather thumb and palm patches	White	$16
Mizuno			
GraFlex	Graphite-impregnated leather softens feel, elasticized knuckles, machine washable	Gray	$25
Techno-Flex	16-coil elastic at knuckles, double-stitched thumb resists twisting	White, Black, Blue, Burgundy	$18
Grip Flex	Aqua-tan waterproof leather with synthetic Syntech Lite back	White, Black	$14
Miz	Ladies' model, Ethiopian leather with Lycra-elasticized knuckles	White with various trims	$16
Neumann			
Lite-Tac	All-leather, tackified palm and fingers	White, Beige, Black	$21
Tour Made	Nontackified cabretta, perforated fingers	White, Beige, Black	$20
Combo	Cabretta leather palm, synthetic back	White	$18
Nike			
Swoosh	100% cabretta, seamed palm construction	Light Bone, Black	$22
Player P.A.W.S.	Escaine synthetic nonwoven suede, soft nap, high weather resistance	Light Bone, Black	$14
Greg Norman			
Shark Tooth	Cabretta leather palm, synthetic back, spandex across knuckles, "shark teeth" embroidery	White, Black	$13
PowerBilt			
TPS TourBilt	Premium Ethiopian cabretta sheepskin, machine washable	Pearl White	$20
TPS SoftBilt	Thick Ethiopian sheepskin palm, synthetic back, machine washable	Pearl White	$14
TPS DuraBilt	Full synthetic with wet touch finish	Snow White	$12

GOLF GLOVE PRODUCT LISTINGS (continued)

MODEL	MATERIAL/FEATURES	COLORS	SUGGESTED RETAIL
Ram			
FX Cabretta	Tanning process adds water resistance, terry wristband keeps hands drier	Black, White, Navy, Tan	$18
FX Cabrettex	Full synthetic for durability, water resistance, terry wristband	Black, White, Navy, Tan	$15
FX Game Warmers (pair)	Winter gloves, Cabrettex palm stretch knit back, adjustable sizing strap	Black	$18
Reebok			
Tour Play	100% super-thin Pittard's leather	Not supplied	$19
Medal Play	100% cabretta at midprice level	Not supplied	$14
Marathon Play	Cabretta/synthetic combination, recommended for long practice sessions	Not supplied	$11
All-Weather Play	100% synthetic for durability, wet-weather control	Not supplied	$8.50
Slazenger			
Select Cabretta	Table-cut sheepskin cabretta, Scotchgard protected, flat sewn, double finger vents, double-stitched tab fastener	White	$18.50
All Weather	Water-repellent polyurethane with cabretta leather thumb and heel, washable	White	$12
Wilson			
Ultra Tour	Thin premium Ethiopian cabretta, precured to eliminate bunching	White	$22
Ultra Select	Ethiopian cabretta with Duratan tanning process, slightly thicker for longer wear	White	$20
Ultra Duo	Indonesian cabretta palm, Leather Tech synthetic back	White	$18
Ultra Grip	Leather Tech synthetic, digitized palm for secure gripping	White	$16
Ultra Flex	100% Leather Tech synthetic	White	$14

GOLF GLOVE PRODUCT LISTINGS *(continued)*

MODEL	MATERIAL/FEATURES	COLORS	SUGGESTED RETAIL
Yonex			
Tour	Premium thin Pittard's cabretta, ultimate fit and feel	Gray	$27
Classic and Ladies Classic	All cabretta leather, slightly thicker texture	White, Beige, Black, Gray	$16

Maxfli Women's Golf Bags (above)
Jones Sports Step-Up Single Saddle (left)
Mizuno Omega (below)

Bagging Your Implements

Following is a representative sample from the huge variety of golf bags that are on the market today. Since many companies' bag lines are so extensive, only a representative sampling of the company's total line is shown here.

Along with a description of the various bag features and suggested retail

Taylor Made Tour Staff Bag (left)
Wilson Mountain Pak (below left)
Ping Hoofer (below)

prices, you'll notice that the various bags are classified as either Carry (or Carry/Stand), Carry/Cart, or Cart. These are general classifications that might help you narrow down the type of bag that's best for you. If you walk your rounds and carry your bag most of the time, you will probably want to have a relatively small, lightweight bag that has fewer bells and whistles. The Carry/Cart category lists bags that are suitable to carry but are also fine to put on a cart. Generally, these will be a little larger in top diameter, weigh slightly more, and offer more storage pockets than the pure Carry bags will. Cart bags, meanwhile, are heavier and larger still and in some cases are actually pro-style bags. Most golfers would not venture to haul these around for 18 holes unless they enjoy making steady visits to their chiropractor.

Whatever size and style bag you choose, check to see whether a snap-on rain hood is included. They'll come in quite handy.

With the smaller bags, automatic fold-out stand attachments have become extremely popular. They keep the bag up off the ground so it remains dry and goes through less wear and tear. And you don't have to bend as much to pick it up. There are a number of bags for which the stand attachment is an optional, additional purchase.

Alternate Carrying Styles

If you carry your golf bag a lot, in this age of postural and chiropractic health awareness, you'll be pleased to note that there are alternatives to simply slinging the bag over one shoulder. Two of them are the Izzo Dual Strap and the Bennington Lumbar Caddie bag (see listing).

The Izzo Dual Strap, as its name implies, is a two-piece strap that attaches to the top and bottom rings of your golf bag like a normal strap. If you are carrying the bag on your right side, you insert your right arm and shoulder underneath the upper segment of the strap. Then, as you slide the bag behind you, you slip your left arm underneath the lower strap. Thus, using the Izzo Dual Strap distributes the weight onto both your shoulders rather than just one.

Taking it to another level is the Bennington Lumbar Caddie. After inserting both arms underneath the straps, you take one further step: You clip the lumbar belt around your waist, like a seat belt. This serves to position the bag straight up and down behind your back and, more important, it distributes the weight of the bag onto your hips and legs, where you'll scarcely feel it. Orthopedic experts agree that carrying the bag in this fashion is a great aid to keeping your spine upright and in square alignment. The only drawback is the small effort needed to get "into" the Lumbar Caddie as you head to your next shot.

If you travel a lot, or even a little, surely you'll want to bring your sticks with you and get in an occasional round or two on the road. If this is the case, a one-time investment in a good travel cover is a wise one. Most of the models listed, unlike the basic canvas bag covers of years past, are well padded, particularly around the top end. Thus, you can board your flight with reasonable assurance that your clubs will be delivered to your destination both in one piece and with each shaft still perfectly straight. Generally, the cost of a good travel cover will be at or slightly below the $100 mark.

Sahara Bag Travel Cover (above)
Sun Mountain Orbit (right)

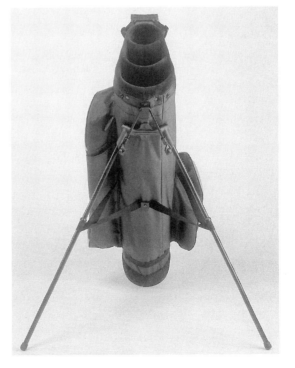

GOLF BAG PRODUCT LISTINGS

MODEL	CLASSIFICATION	FEATURES/BENEFITS	SUGGESTED RETAIL
Bennington			
Lumbar Caddie	Carry/Stand	7½" top, dual straps plus belt attachment transfers weight to hips and legs for optimum posture and comfort	$200
Easy Walker	Carry/Stand	7½" top, full-length dividers w/fur top, full-length side clothing pocket	$140
Deluxe Walker	Carry/Stand	8½" top, waterproof Dynalon material, full-length clothing pocket, hidden valuables pocket, right-side body pad	$200
C.O.O. Midsize	Cart	8½" top, 4-way full-length dividers, front access to all pockets, 2 full-length clothing pockets, 3-can beverage cooler	$240
C.E.O. Oversize	Cart	9½" top, 6-way divided fur top, cellular phone pouch, fur-lined valuables pocket, bottom luggage handler, 3-can cooler	$310
Standard Travel Cover		Fits 9" bag, waterproof Dynalon, padded protector top	$70
Deluxe Travel Cover		Fits 9½" bag, waterproof Dynalon, detachable strap, shoe pocket, padded protector top	$90
Bullet			
Invincible II	Cart	10 pockets, graphite-protected top, ventilated garment pocket, graphite protection top	Not supplied
Golden One	Cart	10 pockets, deluxe shoe pouch, deluxe padded shoulder sling, nylon buckle cover-up	Not supplied
Mini-High Roller Travel Cover		Top end pull handle, built-in wheel base, padded top and bottom, for bags up to 8½" diameter	Not supplied
Burton			
Z-Series	Carry/Cart	8½" top, high-tech lightweight bag, all pockets accessible with bag on cart	$100
Destin	Cart	9" top, traditional styling, 6-way top with graphite protection	$175

GOLF BAG PRODUCT LISTINGS *(continued)*

MODEL	CLASSIFICATION	FEATURES/BENEFITS	SUGGESTED RETAIL
Burton (*continued*)			
Voyager	Cart	9" top, stonewashed nylon, 7 pockets, coal-chute side pockets, graphite protection	$210
Explorer	Cart	Roomy model (9½" top), flap side pockets, 2-tiered ball pocket	$249
Pinehurst	Cart	Big 10" top, traditional styling, all vinyl, triple-zippered ball pocket	$375
Standard Bag Cover		Fits 9" bag, detachable carrying sling, foam-backed nylon, 6 colors	$70
Deluxe Bag Cover		Designed for 9½" or larger bags, rectangular design, interior shoe pocket, 6 colors	$98
Daiwa			
Protege	Carry	Handy small bag w/6½" top, saddle-type side pockets, 7 colorful patterns	$115 solids, $125 patterns
Expedition II	Cart	8½" top, 100% nylon exterior, 6-way top divider, 5 solid colors	$140
Classic/Ladies Classic	Cart	9" padded fur-lined top, multicompartment ball pocket, hidden umbrella well, 6-way divider, trunk handle	$230
Douglas			
D-1	Carry	"Triangular" shape, 4 club dividers, umbrella sleeve, angled pockets for easy access, optional stand	$99–$109, optional stand $20
Gemini			
Stand	Carry/Stand	Lightweight, 4-way dividers, rain hood, large ball pocket	$120
Carriage	Cart	8½" top, polyduck w/vinyl trim, 6-way dividers, trunk handle, padded top	$149
Vulcan Cart	Cart	8½" top, multicolored padded nylon, all pockets face out	$179
Jupiter Plus	Cart	9" top, padded polyduck, 6-way full-length dividers, 10 compartments, trunk handle	$219
Gregory Paul			
Little Guy	Carry	Traditional carry, 7½" top, fleece 3-way dividers, vinyl trim rain hood	$110

GOLF BAG PRODUCT LISTINGS *(continued)*

MODEL	CLASSIFICATION	FEATURES/BENEFITS	SUGGESTED RETAIL
Gregory Paul (*continued*)			
Classic Stand	Carry/Stand	8½" top, 3-way fleece-lined dividers, lightweight nylon twill	$129
Double Saddle	Carry	8" top, 2 long side garment pockets	$112
Spirit	Carry/Cart	8½" top, 3-way full-length dividers, top valuables pocket, travel/rain hood	$135
Classic	Cart	9" top, traditional styling w/vinyl or leather trim, 6-way full-length dividers	$160
Izzo			
Delight II	Carry	Ultralight bag at 1 pound total weight, fits 14 clubs	$78
Acclaim II	Carry/Stand	Graphite shaft protection, rain hood, fits well on carts	$190
Cruiser	Carry/Stand	8½" top, symmetrical back pad for comfort, lightweight, graphite shaft protection	$190
Izzo Dual Strap		Dual strap improves carrying balance, fits almost every carry bag, 4 sizes	$29
Jones Sports			
Packer	Carry	3 sizes (6½", 7¾", 9" tops), polyduck/antron/nylon, full shaft saver top on all	$65, $82, $98
Lightweight Series	Carry	7¾" top, shaft saver top, double side saddles	$100
Step-Up Single Saddle	Carry/Stand	7¾" top, bilevel bottom keeps grips separated, shaft saver top	$115
Super Deluxe	Cart	9½" fur-lined top, dual saddle pockets, double ball pockets, trunk grip	$145
Travel Covers		6 models (3 medium, 3 large), 4 padded models, 2 with shoe pockets	$50-$80
Lynx			
Lynx Stand	Carry/Stand	8½" top, lightweight nylon, 5 pockets, wide shoulder strap, full-length dividers	$141
Lynx Cart	Cart	9" top, 6-way full-length dividers, 9 pockets	$208
Lynx Staff	Cart	11" and 9" top diameters, double lock-stitched nylon, 5-point harness sling, travel hood	$300, $400

GOLF BAG PRODUCT LISTINGS *(continued)*

MODEL	CLASSIFICATION	FEATURES/BENEFITS	SUGGESTED RETAIL
Maxfli			
Stand Bag	Carry/Stand	8" top, removable stand, 4-way full-length dividers, shoe pockets, rain hood	$75
Women's	Cart	8" top, stylish tapestry print, fur-lined cuff, matching clutch bag and head covers, bottom assist handle	$89
Staff	Cart	8", 9", 11" sizes, fur-lined top, self-healing zippers, hidden umbrella well	$169, $225, $399
Miller			
Light P	Carry/Stand	8½" top, twill fabric, 4-way elliptical top, travel hood	Not supplied
JX	Cart	8½" top, "pelican" spill-proof ball pocket, travel hood, umbrella well	Not supplied
Light EX	Carry/Cart	High-tech 9" top airliner, double ball pocket, padded lightweight nylon, travel hood, valuables bag	Not supplied
Extra	Cart	9½" top, unique split pocket for convenient apparel storage, fashion colors	Not supplied
Ladies NTLX	Cart	Foam-padded laundered nylon, roomy vanity pocket, "pelican" spill-proof ball pocket, 9" top	Not supplied
WBC Travel Cover		Foam-padded top, detachable shoulder strap, roomy vanity pocket, "pelican" spill-proof ball pocket, 9" top	Not supplied
DBC Travel Cover		Same as WBC except does not include travel wheels	Not supplied
Mizuno			
Ultra Stand	Carry/Stand	Lightweight, 6-way padded full-length dividers, 8 pockets including valuables pocket, rain hood	$140
Sierra	Cart	9" top, polyduck, western saddle style trim, 5 pockets, 6-way padded full-length dividers	$120
Omega	Cart	High-tech bag including cellular phone pocket, 4-can beverage holder, valuables pocket	$150

GOLF BAG PRODUCT LISTINGS *(continued)*

MODEL	CLASSIFICATION	FEATURES/BENEFITS	SUGGESTED RETAIL
Ping			
New Moon	Carry	Ultralight carry bag for leisurely rounds, holds 14 clubs	$50
L8+	Carry	Carry bag w/optional stand and soft cover for graphite protection	$87–$132
Hoofer	Carry/Stand	"Hoof"-shaped bottom design makes club insertion easier, water-repellent fabric, 2 clothing pockets	$160
T 9.5	Cart	Classic vinyl bag w/9½" top, soft cover club divider, dual ball pockets, reinforced handles	$195
Pro Group/Hot-Z			
Mesa	Carry	3-way full-length club dividers, dual-entry apparel/shoe pocket, rain/travel hood	$85
Safari		Lightweight padded nylon, padded Durasuede sling, 3-way full-length dividers, rain hood	$127
Sahara			
9820 Travel Cover		Zippered opening, 12" x 9" front pocket with Velcro closure, 2 handles, partial padding with full padding optional	$90
Scott			
Deluxe Padded Travel Cover		Heavily padded top section, leather ID window	$90
Ultimate Roller Travel Cover		Fully padded top, rigid back panel, precision wheels, top handle, shoe-accessory pocket	$120
Sun Mountain			
Orbit	Carry/Stand	Pillow top graphite protection, 10" diameter top, 6 pockets	$145
Summit S	Carry/Stand	Pillow top graphite protection, roller bottom stand mechanism, 6 pockets	$150
Meridian	Carry/Cart	Laminated fabric construction, lift assist strap, 6 pockets	$150
Caravan	Cart	Lift assist strap, 4-point strap attachment, 7 pockets	$238
Travel Light II Travel Cover		2-way heavy-duty zipper, interior storage pockets	$53

GOLF BAG PRODUCT LISTINGS *(continued)*

MODEL	CLASSIFICATION	FEATURES/BENEFITS	SUGGESTED RETAIL
Taylor Made			
Pacesetter	Carry	Lightweight polyester fabric (4 lbs. total), 4-way full-length dividers, 6 pockets, rain hood	$125
Grandstand	Carry/Stand	Ultrasuede shaft protection, 6 pockets, dual strap optional	$140
Staff	Cart	10" top, 6-way full-length dividers, 3-point harness, extra-large clothing pocket, hip pad	$400
Top Flite			
Convertible Stand	Carry/Stand	Removable full-length clothing pocket, removable stand mechanism, 5 pockets including glove pocket, rain hood	$160
Expedition	Carry/Cart	Poly-tech padded material, 9 pockets including triple ball pocket, water bottle, rain hood	$150
Cart Tech	Cart	High-tech bag with 6 outward-facing pockets, full-length divider, separate putter compartment, men's/women's sizes and colors	$140
Tour Lite	Cart	10 pockets for all clothing/accessory storage needs	$180
Wilson			
Mountain Pak	Carry	Easy-access clothing pocket, 8" top with 6-way divider, 8 pockets including water bottle pocket, single or double strap, with/without stand	$140-$180
Techno-Smart	Carry	Lightweight ripstop nylon, 8 pockets including beverage pocket, single or double strap, with/without stand	$140-$190
Valet	Cart	8½" top, velour graphite protection, 6-way top, 12 pockets, patented rain hood	$210
Cart Smart Plus	Cart	Super-tech look w/all 7 pockets facing outward, 420D nylon, multicolors, combo rain hood/shoe pouch	$210

Shoot Scores When It Pours

There are not many weekend amateurs who can honestly say that they go to the golf course well prepared for rain. Weekend players are notorious for their optimism with regard to rain passing them by. Their famous last words are, "There's a break in the sky, right over there!" Never mind that that "break" is quickly blowing *away* from you, and there's nothing but storm clouds overhead.

Every golfer who plays more than 20 times a year ought to own a complete rainsuit. If you have selected a golf bag with adequate storage pockets, and particularly if you usually play golf in a cart, the rainsuit should always be in your bag. If you have a small, light carry bag and you don't want a rainsuit stuffed into it at all times, well, okay. But at the very least you should check the weather reports and take that rainsuit with you whenever there's a moderate chance of precipitation coming your way.

A rainsuit will not only improve your degree of comfort, it will also improve your score. The wetter you are, the more frustrated you'll get. This will cause you to miss more shots and get even more frustrated as your score balloons. It's a vicious circle. The amateur who's well prepared for wet-weather play has a big edge on his or her unprepared opponents.

You'll see a wide range of types of rainsuits in the listing that follows (along with a wide variety of styles for both men and women). The technology in rain-

Sport-Haley Ladies' Whitecap, Men's Rapids

Forrester's Elite Gore-Tex Jacket

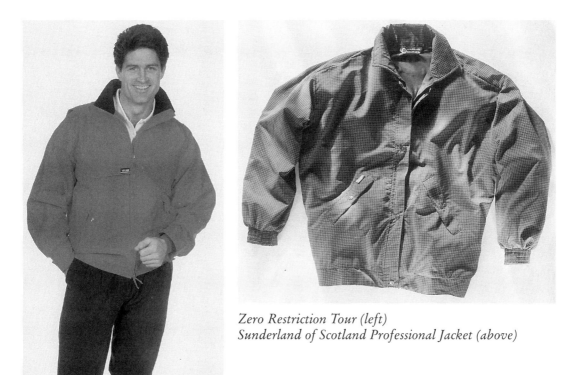

Zero Restriction Tour (left)
Sunderland of Scotland Professional Jacket (above)

suits today is remarkable. The most trusted material used in waterproof rainwear is Gore-Tex, a windproof, waterproof, "breathable" membrane that is laminated to the textile to make it a "Gore-Tex fabric." Manufacturers who use Gore-Tex fabric must enter into a licensing agreement with Gore-Tex that assures that product design and the sealing processes for the garments are of the highest standard, so that the garment remains both waterproof and comfortably breathable through extended use.

Many of the rainsuits listed are fashioned from Gore-Tex. The suggested retail prices of these rainsuits tend to be high—maybe even higher than for that new dress suit you bought for your daughter's wedding!

If a suit made from Gore-Tex is simply beyond what you can afford, there are other alternatives. Most of these rainsuits will offer a fabric that has been coated with a waterproofing material. They may also work acceptably for you, as long as you're aware that their waterproofness (without any periodic treating of the material) is not likely to last as long as Gore-Tex fabric. One of the better examples of such an economy rainsuit is Sun Mountain's Cirrus model, which carries a one-year waterproof guarantee and a suggested retail of $110.

Sun Ice Greenwich (left)
Mizuno All Weather Rainsuit (above)

GOLF RAINWEAR PRODUCT LISTINGS

MODEL	FEATURES/BENEFITS	COLORS	SUGGESTED RETAIL
Ashworth			
Rotofil	Half-zip pullover, 100% microfiber w/Cool Max printed mesh lining, zip-close pants pockets, lower leg zip and snap closure	Navy, Red Pepper jacket; Navy pants	$290
Ultrex	Half-zip seamed pullover, nylon microfiber w/Ultrex coating, Cool Max jacket lining, nylon taffeta pants lining	Eclipse, Evergreen, Oyster	$300
Duckster			
Gore-Tex	Ultrasoft microfiber shell, Gore-Tex lining, no-leak pockets, 2-way zipper, gathered elastic waistband, back pockets	Peerless Green, Navy	Not supplied
Solid Weathertek	Weathertek fabric is waterproof and breathable, inner storm flap, sealed seams, concealed leg zippers	Navy, Black, Forest	Not supplied
Duffer Rainsuit	Lightweight nylon, elasticized waistband and cuffs, snap-up storm flap, side-opening pocket access	Navy, Black, Hunter	Not supplied
Forrester's			
Elite Gore-Tex	Treated shell to repel water/stains, Gore-Tex liner, action-back vents, leg and fly zips, hip pocket, matching Gore-Tex hat	Coal, Hunter, Indigo	Approx. $400
Ladies' Elite	Microfiber shell fabric, Gore-Tex outer cuffs, knit inner cuffs, seam-sealed Gore-Tex liner, Gore-Tex hat	Purple or Earth splash print jacket; Black, Purple pants	Approx. $385
Rain and Wind Breaker	Teflon HT finish, full mesh lining, back vents, matching hat	Evergreen, Black, Burgundy	Approx. $150
Ladies Rain and Wind Breaker	Supplex nylon, Teflon HT finish, full mesh lining, matching hat	Periwinkle, Emerald, Iris	Approx. $150
LaMode			
Waterproof Rainsuit	Microfiber fabric with microporous coating for protection/breathability, sealed seams	Navy/Tartan	$185
MacGregor			
6000 Microfibre	Lightweight Gore-Tex plaid lining, full-cut, shoulder pleats, pants w/4-pleat front, matching Gore-Tex hat	Sandstone, Navy	$480
3500	Waterproof Tactel, cottonlike finish, taffeta/ nylon mesh lined, leg zippers w/storm flaps	Navy w/assorted trims	$176

GOLF RAINWEAR PRODUCT LISTINGS (continued)

MODEL	FEATURES/BENEFITS	COLORS	SUGGESTED RETAIL
MacGregor (continued)			
3800 (Women's)	Tactel nylon, taffeta/nylon mesh lined, underarm eyelets, elastic waist w/drawstring	Navy w/assorted trims	$176
Mizuno			
Classic All Weather	ASG (Action Super Golf) microfilament nylon, Scotchgard treated, heat-sealed seams	Navy, Spruce	$240
Munsingwear			
Penguin	Water-resistant polyurethane, concealed hood, jacket folds to pocket size	Navy, Yellow, Pinehurst, Red, Black	$95
Nike			
Storm F.I.T.	100% polyester microfiber half-zip pullover shell, polyester mesh liner, seam-sealed, relaxed-fit elastic-waist pants w/20" side zippers	Navy, Light Bone jacket, Navy pants	$320
Greg Norman			
GMS 6603/6804	100% Tactel nylon, thermoplastic seam-sealed, saitos lining	Black, Royal jacket, Black pants	$350
Sport-Haley			
Rapids	100% Aquatech nylon w/Gore-Tex liner, stand-up collar, nonrestrictive sleeves, fully seam-sealed, adjustable pants hem	Navy/Black, Camel/Black	$390
Riptide	100% Aquatech waterproof microfiber, coating retains 80% integrity after 20 washings	Black, Indigo, Mushroom	$212
Current	Waterproof Micronyl nylon, fully seam-sealed, "short within pant" construction for guaranteed seat protection	Bordeaux, Black, Hunter	$132
Women's Whitecap	Microsoft microfiber, fully seam-sealed, longer-length jacket, nonrestrictive sleeves	Green/Black or Olive/Black jacket, Black pants	$234
Women's Waterfall	Lightly brushed microsoft microfiber, bomber-style jacket, nylon taffeta pants liner	Claret, Black	$224
Sun Ice			
Masters	Savannah outer fabric, Gore-Tex LTD liner, fully seam-sealed	Black plaid/Black, Navy plaid/Navy	$390
St. Andrews	Gore-Tex nylon mesh lining, waterproof, fully seam-sealed	Black, Navy, Linen, Evergreen, Red	$340

GOLF RAINWEAR PRODUCT LISTINGS (continued)

MODEL	FEATURES/BENEFITS	COLORS	SUGGESTED RETAIL
Medinah	Soft waterproof shell, nylon mesh lining, fully seam-sealed	Black/Loden/Linen, Navy/Evergreen, Bluestone/Black/Linen, Pulp Yellow/Black	$215
Greenwich	Soft waterproof shell, nylon mesh lining, fully seam-sealed	Linen/Black, Navy/Burgundy/Black, Bluestone/Black, Evergreen/Navy	$190
Newberry	Trilustre shell, nylon mesh lining, waterproof, seam-sealed, value-priced	Navy/Evergreen, Evergreen/Navy, Black/Bluestone, Bluestone/Black	$130
Sun Mountain			
Tempest	Waterproof Burlington microfiber shell, maximum breathability, generous cut, suspended lining, seam-sealed, 5-year waterproof guarantee	Alder/Hunter, Ocean/Black, Hunter/Burgundy, Navy/Burgundy, Black/Burgundy	$365
Cumulus (Men's and Women's)	Softest "H2Off" fabric, quiet, breathable, 3-year waterproof guarantee	Navy, Garnet, Black, Spruce, Tan	$210
Altos (Men's and Women's)	Coated microfiber fabric, sealed seams, taffeta lining, vented construction, 2-year waterproof guarantee	Navy, Wine, Black, Clay, Tan	$190
Cirrus (Men's and Women's)	Economy-priced, soft fabric, extra seat lining, 1-year waterproof guarantee	Hunter, Navy, Claret, Black	$110
Zero Restriction			
Tour	Heavier weight for year-round use, expansion pleats, telescopic cuffs, Gore-Tex shell w/Cool Max lining, adjustable hem pants, rear pocket	Navy, Forest, Tan, Red, Black	$520
Tour Lite	Slightly lighter for 3-season wear, Gore-Tex shell, Airflow Supreme stretch lining, expansion back pleats, elastic or adjustable snap waistband	Navy, Forest, Black	$446
Ladies Tour Lite	Same features as Tour Lite with women's cut and fit (pants are Tour Weight)	Navy, Red, Forest, Black	$494

Directory of Golf Equipment Manufacturers

The following is an alphabetical list of all manufacturers of golf equipment whose products are listed or mentioned in this book. Included are company name, mailing address, regular and (if available) toll-free telephone numbers, and type of equipment that is listed herein. You can use this contact list as a source for ordering or obtaining information on both current products and products that the companies will be offering in the future.

This list does not include all manufacturers of the given types of golf equipment that are on the marketplace.

Adams   1215 Executive Dr. E., Richardson, TX 75081. (214) 644-2353, (800) 622-0609. Drivers, fairway woods, irons, wedges, putters

Adidas   541 NE 20 St., Suite 207, Portland, OR 97232. (503) 230-2920, (800) 289-2724. Golf shoes

A. J. Tech   2590 Pioneer St., Vista, CA 92083. (619) 599-8090. Golf shafts

Aldila   15822 Bernardo Center Dr., San Diego, CA 92127. (619) 592-0404, (800) 854-2786. Golf shafts

Alien Sport   2085 Landings Dr., Mountain View, CA 94043. (415) 961-0505, (800) 989-GOLF. Wedges, putters

Apollo   1025 Criss Circle, Elk Grove Village, IL 60007. (708) 956-0330, (800) 233-2590. Golf shafts

Tommy Armour   8350 N. Lehigh Ave., Morton Grove, IL 60053. (847) 966-6300, (800) 723-4653. Drivers, fairway woods, irons, wedges, putters, gloves

Ashworth	2791 Loker Ave. W., Carlsbad, CA 92008. (619) 438-6610, (800) 800-8443. Golf shoes, rainwear
Avon Grips	508 W. Seventh St., Cadillac, MI 49601. (616) 779-4390, (800) 334-7477. Golf grips
Backbay	International Golf Footwear, 20 Trafalgar Sq., Nashua, NH 03063. (603) 595-8040, (800) 771-9000. Golf shoes
Bennington	2500 White Rd., Irvine, CA 92714. (714) 955-0390, (800) 624-2580. Golf bags
Black Ice	285 Venture St., San Marcos, CA 92069. (619) 752-7990, (800) 404-9990. Drivers, fairway woods, irons, wedges, putters
Bridgestone	15320 Industrial Park Blvd. NE, Covington, GA 30209, (770) 787-7400, (800) 358-6319. Drivers, fairway woods, irons, wedges, putters, balls
Bullet	2803 S. Yale St., Santa Ana, CA 92704. (714) 966-0310, (800) 842-3781. Drivers, fairway woods, irons, putters, balls, bags
Burton	2700 25 Ave. SE, Jasper, AL 35501. (205) 221-3630, (800) 848-7115. Golf bags
Callaway	2285 Rutherford Rd., Carlsbad, CA 92008. (619) 931-1771, (800) 228-2767. Drivers, fairway woods, irons, wedges, putters
Carbite	6370 Nancy Ridge Dr., Suite 110, San Diego, CA 92121. (619) 625-0065, (800) 272-4325. Irons, wedges, putters
Cayman	1120 W. Broad Ave., Suite B-3, Albany, GA 31706. (912) 883-5017, (800) 344-0220. Golf balls
Cleveland	5630 Cerritos Ave., Cypress, CA 90630. (714) 821-4200, (800) 999-6263. Drivers, fairway woods, irons, wedges, putters
Cobra	1812 Aston Ave., Carlsbad, CA 92008. (619) 929-0377, (800) 223-3537. Drivers, fairway woods, irons, wedges, putters

Confidence	75-150 Sheryl Ave., Suite B, Palm Desert, CA 92211. (800) 346-0098. Drivers, fairway woods, irons
Ray Cook	1396 Poinsettia Ave., Vista, CA 92083. (619) 599-8000, (800) 531-7252. Irons, wedges, putters
Otey Crisman	2803 S. Yale St., Santa Ana, CA 92704. (800) 842-3781. Wedges, putters
Daiwa	7421 Chapman Ave., Garden Grove, CA 92641. (714) 895-6689, (800) 736-GOLF. Drivers, fairway woods, irons, wedges, putters, bags, gloves
Dexter	1230 Washington St., West Newton, MA 02165. (617) 332-4300. Golf shoes
Douglas	1801 North Central Park Ave., Chicago, IL 60647. (800) 621-0084. Golf bags
Duckster	P.O. Box 15307, Suite 200, Northgate II, Chattanooga, TN 37415. (423) 875-4506, (800) 261-9411. Golf rainwear
Dunlop	P.O. Box 3050, Greenville, SC 29607. (864) 241-2200. Drivers, fairway woods, irons, wedges, putters, balls
Dynacraft	71 Maholm St., Newark, OH 43058. (614) 344-1191, (800) 321-4833. Club components, assembled clubs
Eaton/Golf Pride	Hwy. 401 North Bypass, Laurinburg, NC 28352. (910) 276-6901. Golf grips
Etonic	147 Centre St., Brockton, MA 02402. (508) 583-9100, (800) 638-6642. Golf shoes, gloves
Florsheim	120 South Canal St., Chicago, IL 60606. (800) 265-7876. Golf shoes
FM Precision	535 Migeon Ave., Torrington, CT 06790. (860) 489-9254, (800) 227-3327. Golf shafts
Foot-Joy	333 Bridge St., Fairhaven, MA 02719. (508) 979-2000, (800) 225-8500. Golf shoes, gloves

Forrester's	1875 SE Belmont St., Portland, OR 97214. (503) 230-9480, (800) 556-4653. Golf rainwear
Gemini	5335 Village Market, Wesley Chapel, FL 33543. (813) 973-4652. Golf bags
Walter Genuin	6703 Levelland Dr., Suite A, Dallas, TX 75252. (214) 248-2366, (800) 531-2218. Golf shoes
Goldwin	2460 Impala Dr., Carlsbad, CA 92008. (619) 930-0077, (800) 609-4653. Drivers, fairway woods, irons, wedges, putters
Golfsmith International	11000 N. IH-35, Austin, TX 78753. (512) 837-4810, (800) 349-3392. Club components, assembled clubs
The GolfWorks	4820 Jacksontown Rd., Newark, Ohio 43055. (800) 848-8358. Club components, assembled clubs
Bobby Grace	12200 28 St. N., St. Petersburg, FL 33716. (813) 573-1945, (800) 4-MALLET. Putters
Grafalloy	1020 N. Marshall Ave., El Cajon, CA 92020, (619) 562-1020, (800) 727-3241. Golf shafts
Grandoe	74 Bleecker St., Gloversville, NY 12078. (518) 725-8641. Golf gloves
Gregory Paul	89-91 Lake Ave., Tuckahoe, NY 10707. (914) 779-0589, (800) 727-0070. Golf bags
Griptec	1681 McGaw Ave., Irvine, CA 92714. (714) 252-8500, (800) 853-4747. Golf grips
H. J. Glove	31364 Via Colinas, Suite 105, Westlake Village, CA 91362. (818) 889-2223, (800) 426-3509. Golf gloves
Ben Hogan	8000 Villa Park Dr., Richmond, VA 23228. (804) 262-3000, (800) 88-HOGAN. Drivers, fairway woods, irons, wedges, putters, balls
Izzo Stix	5800 Franklin St., Suite 103, Denver, CO 80216. (303) 292-2441. Drivers, irons, wedges

Izzo Systems	12364 W. Alameda Pkwy., Unit M, Lakewood, CO 80228. (303) 988-2886, (800) 284-1220. Golf bags
Javelin Blue	220 Sunrise Ave., Palm Beach, FL 33480. (561) 832-2445, (800) 492-2445. Drivers, fairway woods, irons
Johnston & Murphy	1415 Murfreesboro Rd., Suite 460, Nashville, TN 37217. (615) 367-8101, (800) 443-7414. Golf shoes
Jones Sports	17230 NE Sacramento St., Portland, OR 97230. (503) 255-1410, (800) 547-8447. Golf bags
Kasco	5238 Royal Woods Pkwy., Suite 140, Tucker, GA 30084. (770) 496-0977, (800) 431-2560. Golf gloves
Kunnan	9606 Kearny Villa Rd., San Diego, CA 92126. (619) 271-8599, (800) 399-8599. Drivers, fairway woods, irons, putters
Lamkin	6530 Gateway Park Dr., San Diego, CA 92173. (619) 661-7090, (800) 642-7755. Golf grips
LaMode	13301 S. Main St., Los Angeles, CA 90061. (310) 327-5188, (800) 678-5246. Golf rainwear
Lynx	16017 E. Valley Blvd., City of Industry, CA 91749. (818) 961-0222, (800) 233-5969. Drivers, fairway woods, irons, wedges, putters, bags, gloves
MacGregor	1601 S. Slappey Blvd., Albany, GA 31701. (912) 434-7000, (800) 841-4358. Drivers, fairway woods, irons, wedges, putters, balls, rainwear
Maruman	5870-B Oakbrook Pkwy., Norcross, GA 30093. (770) 446-2655, (800) 533-2716. Drivers, fairway woods, irons, wedges, putters
Maxfli	728 N. Pleasantburg Dr., Greenville, SC 29607. (864) 241-2200, (800) 768-4727. Drivers, fairway woods, irons, wedges, putters, balls, bags, gloves
Merit	4001 Cobb International Blvd., Kennesaw, GA 30152. (770) 427-0550. Drivers, fairway woods, irons, wedges, putters

Miller

5790 Shelby Dr., Memphis, TN 38141. (901) 362-3000, (800) 489-2247. Golf bags

Mint Grip

3959 Teal Ct., Benicia, CA 94510. (707) 746-7314, (800) 524-1241. Golf grips

Mitsushiba

210 W. Baywood Ave., Orange, CA 92665. (714) 282-0137, (800) 722-4061. Drivers, fairway woods, irons, wedges, putters

Mizuno

5125 Peachtree Industrial Blvd., Norcross, GA 30092. (770) 840-4747, (800) 333-7888. Drivers, fairway woods, irons, wedges, putters, shoes, bags, gloves

Munsingwear

8000 W. 78 St., Minneapolis, MN 55439. (612) 943-5000, (800) 336-5002. Golf rainwear

Neumann

610 S. Jefferson, Cookeville, TN 38501. (615) 526-2109, (800) 251-6857. Golf gloves

Nicklaus

7830 Byron Dr., West Palm Beach, FL 33404. (561) 881-7981, (800) 322-1872. Drivers, fairway woods, irons, wedges, putters

Nike

One Bowerman Dr., Beaverton, OR 97005. (503) 671-6453, (800) 922-6453. Golf shoes, gloves, rainwear

Greg Norman

42 Thomas Patten Dr., Stoughton, MA 02368. (617) 341-5000, (800) TEE-OFF-1. Golf gloves, rainwear

Odyssey

1945 Camino Vida Roble, Suite J, Carlsbad, CA 92008. (619) 431-9966, (800) 487-5664. Wedges, putters

Ping/Karsten Mfg.

2201 W. Desert Cove, Phoenix, AZ 85029. (602) 870-5000, (800) 528-0650. Drivers, fairway woods, irons, wedges, putters, balls, bags

Gary Player

3930 RCA Blvd., Suite 3001, Palm Beach Gardens, FL 33410. (561) 624-0300, (800) 4-PLAYER. Drivers, irons, wedges

Players	12254 Iavelli Way, Poway, CA 92064. (619) 486-2043, (800) 922-7529. Drivers, fairway woods, irons, wedges, putters, balls
PowerBilt	P.O. Box 35700, Louisville, KY 40232. (502) 585-5226, (800) 848-7693. Drivers, fairway woods, irons, wedges, putters, gloves
ProGroup	6201 Mountain View Rd., Ooltewah, TN 37363. (423) 238-5890, (800) 735-6300. Golf bags
Pro Select	835 Church Ct., Elmhurst, IL 60126. (708) 530-1424, (800) 224-6532. Drivers, fairway woods, irons, putters
Rainbow	22500 S. Vermont Ave., Torrance, CA 90502. (310) 328-8418, (800) 328-8418. Drivers, fairway woods, irons, wedges, putters
Ram	2020 Indian Boundary Dr., Melrose Park, IL 60160. (708) 681-5800, (800) 833-4653. Drivers, fairway woods, irons, wedges, putters, gloves
Ram Tour	238 Industrial Circle, Pontotoc, MS 38863. (601) 489-2244, (800) 647-8122. Golf balls
Rawlings	20301 Nordhoff, Chatsworth, CA 91311. (818) 349-3164, (800) 443-8222. Drivers, fairway woods, irons, putters
Reebok	42 Thomas Patten Dr., Randolph, MA 02368. (617) 341-5000, (800) TEE-OFF-1. Golf shoes, gloves
Rockport	220 Donald J. Lynch Blvd., Marlboro, MA 01752. (508) 485-2090, (800) 762-6030. Golf shoes
Royal Grip	444 W. Geneva, Tempe, AZ 85282. (602) 829-9000, (800) 828-3439. Golf grips
RTS	22122 20 Ave. SE, Suite 148, Bothell, WA 98021. (206) 402-6400, (800) 638-5573. Drivers, fairway woods, irons
Sahara	7965 Artcraft Rd., El Paso, TX 79932. (915) 833-1145, (800) 669-LOGO. Golf bag travel covers

Scott	631 S. 20 St., Omaha, NE 68102. (402) 341-1492, (800) 341-1492. Golf bag travel covers
Slazenger	10 Slazenger Dr., Greenville, SC 29605. (864) 422-0200, (800) 766-2615. Drivers, fairway woods, irons, wedges, balls, gloves
Kenneth Smith	12931 W. 71 St., Shawnee, KS 66216. (913) 631-5100, (800) 234-8968. Drivers, fairway woods, irons, wedges, putters
Snake Eyes	13000 Sawgrass Village Circle, Suite 30, Ponte Vedra Beach, FL 32082. (904) 273-8772, (800) 270-8772. Drivers, fairway woods, irons, wedges, putters
Softspikes	1901 Research Blvd., Suite 350, Rockville, MD 20850. (301) 738-7756, (800) 638-0075. Nonmetal golf spikes
Sport-Haley	4600 E. 48 Ave., Denver, CO 80216. (303) 320-8800, (800) 627-9211. Golf rainwear
STX	1500 Bush St., Baltimore, MD 21230. (410) 837-2022, (800) 255-6003. Putters
Sun Ice	2150 Post Rd., Fairfield, CT 06430. (203) 256-5656, (800) SUN-ICE6. Golf rainwear
Sun Mountain	301 N. First, Missoula, MT 59802. (406) 728-9224, (800) 227-9224. Golf bags, rainwear
Sunderland of Scotland	20844 Plummer St., Chatsworth, CA 91311. (818) 988-0006; (800) 999-6599. Golf rainwear
Tacki-Mac	3300 W. Desert Inn Rd., Las Vegas, NV 89102. (702) 252-4799, (800) 634-1062. Golf grips
Taylor Made	2271 Cosmos Ct., Carlsbad, CA 92009. (619) 931-1991, (800) 456-8633. Drivers, fairway woods, irons, wedges, putters, bags
Teardrop	32 Bow Circle, Bldg. 1, Hilton Head Island, SC 29928. (803) 686-4995, (800) 829-7888. Wedges, putters

Titleist	333 Bridge St., Fairhaven, MA 02719. (508) 979-2000, (800) 225-8500. Drivers, fairway woods, irons, wedges, putters, balls
Top Flite	425 Meadow St., Chicopee, MA 01021. (413) 536-1200, (800) 225-6601. Drivers, fairway woods, irons, wedges, putters, balls, bags
True Temper	8275 Tournament Dr., Suite 200, Memphis, TN 38125. (901) 746-2000, (800) 537-5000. Golf shafts
Unifiber	3855 Ruffin Rd., San Diego, CA 92123. (619) 576-8080, (800) 742-2860. Golf shafts
UST	14950 FAA Blvd., Fort Worth, TX 76155. (817) 267-2219, (800) 621-6728. Golf shafts
Vulcan	525 Tyler Rd., St. Charles, IL 60174. (630) 584-3636, (800) 842-1836. Drivers, fairway woods, irons, wedges
Wilson	8700 W. Bryn Mawr, Chicago, IL 60631. (312) 714-6600, (800) 622-0444. Drivers, fairway woods, irons, wedges, putters, balls, gloves, bags, shoes
Wood Brothers	200A N. Houston Ave., Humble, TX 77338. (713) 446-0445, (800) 800-8424. Drivers, fairway woods, irons, wedges, putters
Yonex	3520 Challenger St., Torrance, CA 90503. (310) 542-8111, (800) 44-YONEX. Drivers, fairway woods, irons, wedges, putters, gloves
Zero Restriction	224 First Ave., Red Lion, PA 17356. (717) 244-3385, (800) 367-0669. Golf rainwear
Zevo	1040 Joshua Way, Vista, CA 92083. (909) 699-1771. Drivers, fairway woods, irons, wedges